THE SHAPING OF ENVIRONMENTAL POLICY IN FRANCE

Joseph Szarka

Berghahn Books
New York • Oxford

First published in 2002 by **Berghahn Books**

www.BerghahnBooks.com

©2002 Joseph Szarka

Library of Congress Cataloging-in-Publication Data
Szarka, Joseph
   The shaping of environmental policy in France/Joseph Szarka.
      p. cm. -- (Contemporary France : v. 6)
   Includes bibliographical references and index.
   ISBN 1-57181-999-1 (cl. : alk. paper). -- ISBN 1-57181-495-7 (pbk. :
   alk. paper)
      1. Environmental Policy -- France -- History   I. Title.   III. Contem-
porary France; v. 6.
GE190.F8 S93 2001
365.7'056'0944--dc21   2001043995

THE SHAPING OF ENVIRONMENTAL POLICY IN FRANCE

Contemporary France
General Editor: Jolyon Howorth, University of Bath

CONTENTS

LIST OF TABLES

LIST OF ABBREVIATIONS

ACCA	Associations communales de chasse agréées
ACF	Advocacy coalition framework
ADEME	Agence de l'environnement et de la maîtrise de l'énergie
ANDRA	Agence nationale pour la gestion des déchets radioactifs
ANRED	Agence nationale pour la récupération et l'élimination des déchets
BSE	Bovine spongiform encephalopathy
CAP	Common Agricultural Policy
CELRL	Conservatoire de l'espace littoral et des rivages lacustres
CFC	Chlorofluorocarbon
CFDD	Commission française du développement durable
CGP	Commissariat général du plan
CNIR	Conseil national inter-régional (des *Verts*)
CNVA	Conseil national de la vie associative
CODER	Comités de développement économique régional
CPNT	Chasse, Pêche, Nature, Tradition
CRII-RAD	Commission de recherche et d'information indépendante sur la radioactivité
CSP	Conseil supérieur de la pêche
DATAR	Délégation à l'aménagement du territoire et à l'action régionale
DDAF	Directions départementales de l'agriculture et de la forêt
DDE	Directions départementales de l'équipement
DIREN	Directions régionales de l'environnement
DRIRE	Directions régionales de l'industrie, de la recherche et de l'environnement

EC	European Community
ECJ	European Court of Justice
EDF	Electricité de France
EEC	European Economic Community
EM	Environment Ministry
ERE	Entente radicale et écologiste
EU	European Union
FGMN	Fonds de gestion des milieux naturels
FNE	France Nature Environnement
FNSEA	Fédération nationale des syndicats d'exploitants agricoles
FOE	Friends of the Earth
FRAPNA	Fédération Rhône-Alpes de protection de la nature
GE	Génération Ecologie
ICLEI	International Council for Local Environmental Initiatives
IFEN	Institut français de l'environnement
INERIS	Institut national de la recherche sur l'environnement industriel et les risques
INSEE	Institut national de la statistique et des études économiques
LA21	Local Agenda 21
LOADDT	Loi d'orientation pour l'aménagement et le développement durable du territoire
MATE	Ministère de l'aménagement du territoire et de l'environnement
MEI	Mouvement écologiste indépendant
MEP	Member of the European Parliament
NGO	Non-governmental organisation
NIMBY	Not in my back yard
NT	National Trust
OECD	Organisation for Economic Cooperation and Development
ONC	Office national de la chasse
ONF	Office national des forêts
ORSEC	(Plan d') organisation des secours
PCF	Parti communiste français
PER	Plan d'exposition aux risques
PNR	Parcs naturels régionaux
POS	Plan d'occupation des sols
PPP	'Polluter pays' principle

PPR	Plans de prévention des risques naturels prévisibles
PR	Proportional representation
PS	Parti socialiste
RPR	Rassemblement pour la République
SEA	Single European Act
SEPANSO	(Fédération des) sociétés pour l'étude, la protection et l'aménagement de la nature dans le sud-ouest
SGCI	Secrétariat général du comité interministériel
SPPPI	Secrétariat permanent pour la prévention des pollutions industrielles
TGAP	Taxe générale sur les activités polluantes
TGV	Train à grande vitesse
UDF	Union pour la démocratie française
WCED	World Commission on Environment and Development
WTO	World Trade Organisation
WWF	World Wide Fund for Nature
ZA	Zone d'alerte
ZERMOS	Zones exposées aux risques de mouvements du sol et du sous-sol
ZNIEFF	Zone naturelle d'intérêt écologique, faunistique et floristique
ZPS	Zone de protection spéciale

PREFACE

apart from significant and positive cuts in ozone-depleting substances, progress in reducing other pressures on the state of the environment has remained largely insufficient.

European Environment Agency (1999: 7)

real progress has been made, but the general view among the public and policy makers is that progress has been considerably slower than envisaged or hoped[1]

IFEN, 1998a: 10

Recent reports on the state of the environment at national and international levels make disconcerting reading. Considerable gains have been made in terms of reduced pollution and increased energy efficiency. Yet performance gains delivered by technological progress have been eroded by absolute increases in demand for energy and materials arising from economic growth. Does this mean that environmental policy has 'failed'? Rather than jump to this conclusion, one premise of this book is that environmental policy making is subject to conflicting pressures. On the one hand, world demographic trends and social inequalities push for an agenda of economic expansion. On the other hand, environmental problems arising both at input stages (resources are neither limitless nor free) and output stages

---

[1] 'Les progrès sont donc réels mais le sentiment général, dans la population comme chez les responsables, est qu'ils sont sensiblement plus lents que ce qui était prévu ou souhaité.'

(pollution and degradation undermine quality of life objectives) militate for multidimensional policy objectives. Because science and technology have not solved these problems, political solutions are required to effect social compromises which ideally would be effective, efficient and equitable.

The existence today of highly developed environmental policies indicates that the need to act is not in contention, but that the scale of intervention clearly remains problematic. Comparative studies have shown that the nature, scope and efficacy of policy are influenced by political traditions and institutional designs.[2] Yet the literature is uneven in terms of coverage, with considerable attention devoted to the USA, the UK and Germany but far less to other nations. As regards France, a growing number of publications has been published in the French language, yet few of these provide discussions of environmental policy making which are comprehensive and theoretically informed.[3] In the English language, relatively little has been published on environmental policy in France, with the only book-length survey available to date being the environmental performance review published by the OECD (1997).[4] The present book is intended to help fill these gaps.

In an age of transboundary environmental problems, the focus on the nation-state may surprise. Though not the sole actors faced by new challenges, individual nations remain central protagonists. Policy initiatives require impetus and commitment at the national level, regardless of whether their sponsors be governments, lobbies, non-governmental organisations (NGOs) or public opinion, or whether the arena for discussion is domestic, European or international. Thus Brenton (1994: 8) formed the view that 'the key players in international environmental matters have remained the national governments'. This is not to imply that central governments remain all-powerful, only that they constitute a key locus of policy development and implementation. Further, national histories condition both the manners of making policy and its content. In discussing the British case, Lowe and Ward (1998: 4) proposed that 'each national polity has a particular set of social, economic and institutional issues that shapes the national

---

[2] Examples include Vogel (1986), Dalal-Clayton et al. (1996), and Héritier, Knill and Mingers (1996).

[3] Major exceptions are Lascoumes (1994) and Barraqué and Theys (1998).

[4] However, the following short studies in English provide useful introductions to the topic: Buller (1998) and Larrue and Chabason (1998).

interest and policy positions and gives rise to distinctive national policy styles'. In relation to Spain and Germany, Aguilar Fernández (1994: 39) noted 'the resilience of national institutional designs in the process of European unification'. Likewise in France, the configuration of the polity and the habits of policy making elites have impacted on the style, content and effectiveness of environmental policy.

To develop these points, the main aims of this book are to explore a representative set of environmental issues which have come to the fore in France, analyse policy responses to them, explain the diverse factors that have shaped policy and evaluate outcomes. Further, because of the cross-cutting nature of environmental issues and their extensive politicisation in Western democracies, the present study will explore some of the wider processes of political change in France. Consequently, in discussing French environmental policy, this book is as much about the French polity as about the environment. It is hoped that this approach will be of value both to audiences concerned with international comparisons of the handling of environmental issues, and to those interested in the organisation of political life in France.

The first part of this book considers the range of social, political and institutional factors that have shaped environmental policy. Chapter 1 is concerned with cognitive and conceptual issues. It reviews how popular notions of the 'environment' are the result of social constructions which favour holistic apprehensions, whereas the constraints of political processes have required a disaggregation of the environment into a series of policy sectors. The chapter outlines the theoretical models for making sense of the policy process to be used in this book, as well as its major research questions and propositions. Chapter 2 examines the impact of French civil society on policy framing, with particular attention to the green movement, environmental organisations and changes in public opinion. The search for political solutions is developed in Chapter 3, which considers the part played by green parties in the French polity in their bid to influence environmental and socioeconomic policy making. In Chapter 4, elite behaviour in the shaping of environmental policy is explored through a review of three dimensions of institutional capacity building, namely the political, the administrative and the territorial. In Chapter 5, the influence of European integration on national environmental policy is examined.

The book's second part presents a series of policy case studies.

Chapter 6 discusses the 'natural environment', particularly nature conservation, the hunt lobby and defence against natural catastrophes. Chapter 7 focuses on the 'industrial environment', analysing the regulatory framework for pollution control, the prevention of technological hazards and innovations in policy instruments, particularly the use of environmental taxation. The study of the 'human environment' in Chapter 8 is concerned with policy development in relation to water, waste and air. Chapter 9 opens out the analysis to consider whether France is moving towards a model of sustainable development, an ambitious goal implying greater integration of environmental and social aims into economic development. The final chapter summarises the distinctive features of the French approach to environmental policy and tries to identify lessons for the future.

Although this book aims to provide comprehensive analysis of French environmental policy, exhaustive treatment has proved impossible. Regrettably, this has meant that issues as important as noise, the 'national heritage' (the preservation of buildings, monuments etc.) or transport policy have been omitted, partly for reasons of space, and partly to maintain coherence in the analytical approach. No doubt other omissions and shortcomings will be identified, for which I accept full responsibility. At the same time, I remain heavily indebted to a range of individuals and organisations. Interviews with officials in the French Environment Ministry and its field services gave me insights into the burdens shouldered by practitioners. Discussions with fellow researchers enriched the analysis. Particular thanks go to Bernard Barraqué and Pierre Lascoumes, who pointed out aspects of the French approach which I was in danger of overlooking, and to Ingolfur Bluhdorn for commenting on earlier drafts. The final stages of writing benefited from an EUSSIRF grant to use the facilities of the European University Institute, Florence. As I cannot name everyone who has helped me in my work, I simply offer this book's existence as a testimony to the help of others, and hope that it will be of interest and value to a wide range of readers.

Part I

Shaping Factors

1

THEORETICAL PERSPECTIVES ON ENVIRONMENTAL POLICY ANALYSIS

Introduction

The 'environment' is a generally used term, but its range of usage can lead to lack of clarity and misunderstandings. Accordingly, the aim of this chapter is to outline the cognitive and conceptual frameworks which will enable analysis of the environment and of environmental policy. An initial section outlines the subject matter of the inquiry by considering the social construction of the environment, namely the ongoing societal negotiation of meaning and values through which issues are constituted, communicated and accorded legitimacy. It will be argued that the prevalent, though often unacknowledged, tendency is to view the environment in holistic terms. Policy makers, however, cannot deal with the environment as whole, but must target their interventions at its components. Thus the second section examines the political deconstruction of the environment, by which is understood the disaggregation of environmental demand into discrete segments amenable to influence by policy makers. At the same time, a degree of coherence or 'integration' must be maintained with other policy domains. Environmental policy making thereby becomes a transversal, multidimensional activity involving a large number of contexts, actors, instruments and processes. Capturing this complexity in analytical terms is no easy matter. The third section develops the conceptual tools to respond to this challenge by reviewing theories of policy analysis applicable to the environment and setting out the research questions that later chapters seek to answer.

The Social Construction of the Environment

The range of issues covered by the notion of the 'environment' is disparate to the point of the bewildering. They include conservation of wildlife and the countryside, preservation of biodiversity and ecosystems, allocation of natural resources to ensure economic growth and development, the management of natural and technological risks, as well as the enhancement of the built environment and the improvement of the quality of life. Worries have been expressed internationally over the destruction of rain forests (with loss of habitats and extinction of species); acid rain, depletion of the ozone layer and global climate change. More localised issues include problems with waste disposal, especially of nuclear materials; major accidents such as Bhopal (1984) and Chernobyl (1986), and oil tanker spills such as the Exxon Valdez (1989 in Canada), the Sea Empress (1996 in Wales) and the Erika (1999 in France); threats to food and water from the toxic residues of industrial pollution and pesticide use, BSE ('mad cow disease') and concerns about genetically modified crops.

Though the material similarities between these issues are slight, they share the same mode of conceptualisation. Their meaning is to be found not on the side of the object or phenomenon, but on the side of the subject or human participant. Thus Yearley (1991: 52) observed that 'the social problems perspective . . . leads us to ask how it is that environmental issues have come to be seen as an objective social problem'. A general response to this question is that meanings, values and intentions emerge by a process of societal engagement. More specifically, Liberatore (1995: 59) proposed that 'environmental problems are not given *per se* but are socially constructed and the way this construction process develops is influenced by the prevailing cultural, economic and political conditions in different social contexts'. On this view the 'environment', rather than existing 'out there' as an entity independent of human involvement, is the product of knowledge and understanding of various sorts: scientific, technical and technological, but also political, philosophical and moral.

If the social construction of the environment is a sense-making operation, it also encompasses an ordering and a prioritising of concerns. The identification of sets of environmental preferences among social groups yields classifications in terms of their different orientations. Thus Dalton (1993) distinguished between 'conservationism', constituting a first wave of wildlife preservation and nature protection societies set up in developed countries towards the end of the nineteenth century, and a 'new environmental wave' in the 1960s and 1970s, which spawned organisations such as Friends of the Earth, Greenpeace and Robin Wood. Rucht (1989: 64) offered a three-fold typology of environmental concern: *conservationism* referred to nature conservation, *environmentalism* involved 'a pragmatic attitude to the preservation or improvement of the human environment', whilst *ecologism* implied 'a holistic vision of a decentralised, democratic, and egalitarian society existing in harmony with nature'. Clearly, each position contained its own policy agenda.

To the extent that these classifications indicate underlying cleavages in attitudes to the environment, they can be considered helpful. However, it would be inappropriate to view the societal divisions they set out as rigid and unchanging. On the contrary, the growth in environmental concern in the 1980s and 1990s was accompanied by a blurring of hierarchies of priority and increased overlap between categories of opinion, making practical distinctions between 'environmentalism' and 'ecologism' increasingly insecure. The tendency to view environmental issues as interconnecting led to conceptualisations of the environment in holistic terms. Ironically however, holism does not form a whole but comes in particular varieties, as Table 1.1 indicates.

Holistic constructions of the environment have their origins in the biological study of the interactions among animal and vegetal life-forms, and their dependencies on non-living surroundings. Observation of these interdependencies gave rise to the notion of 'ecosystem', defined by Tanley as 'any unit that includes all of the organisms in a given area interacting with the environment' (quoted in Cunningham, 1998: 312). For biologists the 'given area' usually has delimited, local dimensions. However, the concept is sometimes extended to embrace planet Earth, as if the world formed a single system. Two versions of this construction are indicated in Table 1.1. 'Biosphere 1' relates to climate change, a process known to exist since the origins of our planet, but whose current course has been influenced by industrial civilisation, with the

Table 1.1 Holistic constructions of the environment

Social construction	Themes	Principal discourse varieties
natural ecology	ecosystems genetic diversity	scientific, biological
biosphere 1	climate change greenhouse effect acid rain etc.	scientific, interdisciplinary
biosphere 2	Gaïa the living planet interconnectedness of all species	evolutionary spiritual ethic
political ecology	political processes and institutions	political
	social structures North/South relations	egalitarian
sustainable development	environmentally sound development social progress intergenerational equity	economic political egalitarian

massive release of carbon dioxide and other gases resulting in an enhanced greenhouse effect. The planet as a whole is understood to be affected, though the precise repercussions are expected to vary by region. 'Biosphere 2' refers to the 'Gaïa hypothesis' put forward by Lovelock (1988), for whom the planet's animate and inanimate components form a system which has been self-regulating (in relation to parameters such as surface temperature, atmospheric composition etc.) throughout Earth's evolution. Lovelock based his 'Gaïa hypothesis' on scientific observation and deduction, but its intellectual ambition has so far ruled out empirical verification. In the 'biosphere 2' construction, the stress on the interconnectedness of species opens the door to ethical, normative stances, such as those found among animal rights activists. 'Deep ecology' provides the widest extension of holistic, ecosystems thinking, again reinterpreted through a moral perspective. This school of thought proposes that human existence depends on natural ecosystems developed over the millennia: harm done to nature is harm done to ourselves, since to undermine the natural order is to destroy the human life realm. It therefore proposes replacing an anthropocentric (or human-centred) orientation, with an ecocentric one.

The ideology of political ecology is a complex amalgam of scientific, environmental and social themes. This type of ecosystems thinking covers not only a range of interrelationships within the physical world but embraces economic and social problems attributed to the materialistic exploitation of natural resources. Radical changes are advocated within the economy and the polity to bring about an egalitarian, non-exploitative society living in harmony with nature. With sustainable development, a holistic conceptual frame is again in evidence in the ambitious linkage of socioeconomic development with environmental safeguards. Its stress on intergenerational equity introduces an ethical dimension which blends themes from 'deep ecology' and 'political ecology'.

Close study of the direction of influence between these schools of thought cannot be attempted here. The key point is that due to their separate and intertwined existence, the idea that the 'environment' constituted a *single* referent has become a widespread, if usually unstated, assumption in Western opinion. Holistic constructions of the environment do, however, pose problems. From a philosophical perspective, it can be asked whether a unitary entity termed 'the environment' can be said to exist at all, given the plurality of phenomena and concerns that the term covers. From a policy perspective, it can be asked whether holistic constructions are capable of giving empirical purchase on specific environmental issues.

The Political Deconstruction of the Environment

The term 'deconstruction' is used to cover two areas of meaning. The first is the idea of empirical disaggregation. Whereas various ecologisms propose a holistic vision of the environment, policy making is usually sectorised. Policy makers must have a reason to act, and are galvanised by specific problems displaying social or economic urgency. The second is the idea of analytical dissection. The policy maker's task includes the mobilisation of inputs (what resources, allocated to whom and to what purposes) and the assessment of outputs (what outcomes, with what effectiveness and for whom). In turn the policy analyst, in modelling policy processes, contributes to the segmentation of the objects of policy intervention (namely, the substantive issues at stake) and of its means (stages, actors etc.). The process by which environmental policy making parcels out its object will be explored by identification of key cognitive frames and the policy arenas that accompany them.

Segmenting the environment

Policy decisions in the everyday world typically arbitrate between human and non-human interests, with the former usually given priority. Moreover, human interests are multiform, and conflicts arise between social groups over the allocation of amenity and resources. Even the self-same individuals can express varying preferences according to situation: for example, pedestrians like traffic-free zones, but feel inconvenienced by them as motorists, holiday-makers enjoy travel abroad but are resentful of tourists at home. Because holism provides few pointers for interrelating socioeconomic concerns with specific environmental agendas and according priorities to each, segmented conceptualisations persist (see Table 1.2).

Although environmental concerns are multifarious, in Table 1.2 they have been regrouped into four main policy arenas: nature conservation, resource management, environmental protection, and quality of life. Nature conservation includes the preservation and regeneration of species close to extinction (and latterly of biodiversity in general), the maintenance of aesthetically pleasing landscapes, the setting aside of nature reserves. This approach is variously anthropocentric or ecocentric in its orientation. However, the remaining approaches are markedly anthropocentric. The resource management perspective targets economic growth and development. Whilst in the 1970s, a time of major price hikes for oil and raw materials, the prime concern was with the *depletion* of resources and the 'limits to growth' (Meadows et al., 1972), in the 1990s aggravated climate change due to the *use* of fossil fuels was the major worry. 'Environmental protection' has become a replacement term for pollution control and repair of environmental damage. The 'quality of life' approach is concerned with the welfare

Table 1.2 Segmented constructions of the environment

Social construction	Themes	Principal discourse varieties
nature conservation	protection of flora and fauna protection of the countryside, mountains, rivers and seas	naturalist aesthetic ethic
natural resources	raw materials mining, agriculture energy overexploitation 'sources and sinks'	economic industrial/ instrumentalist
environmental protection	pollution control – air, water, soil hazards, noise	technological/ technical/ normative
quality of life	health	medical humanitarian
	built environment: amenities	social
	'national heritage': monuments, landscapes	cultural

of human beings. It stresses objective factors such as environmental conditions supportive of good health, but includes a subjective dimension in its concern with intangible experiences such as personal fulfilment and happiness. Thus Scheuch (1994: 81) offered the insight that 'the notion of "quality of life" is characteristically an expression of cultural doubt at a moment of relative material well-being in a social system'.

The latter observation provides a reminder of the ambivalence and conflicting pressures existing within society to which policy makers must respond. Each segment of environmental concern allows the development of particular discourses, stresses relatively distinct value systems and leads to specific policy prescriptions. In consequence, demand for environmental action is not a uniform, homogenous aspiration. Segments of environmental demand are unequal in size: the preference for 'clean air, clean water' is unanimous, whereas nature conservation often generates conflicts over amenity or livelihood. Even in the absence of overt competition between different constructions of the environment, one dimension can assume dominance. Certain segments lend themselves more easily to operationalisation within policy frameworks than others: thus water and energy policies have long histories, whereas vehicle congestion and emissions pose comparatively recent challenges. Finally, the distribution of power and resources inevitably impacts on the scope, ambitions and conduct of environmental policy. In brief, (de)constructions of the environment are important because they both frame segments of environmental demand and propel distinct policy agendas.

French views of the environment

So far the focus has been on constructions of the environment applicable to a wide range of contexts. But nation-specific traits also exist. With regard to France, the generic constructions already discussed are modulated by particular geographical and social characteristics.

France covers a vast territory, some 550,000 square kilometres, of which 56 percent is farm land and 28 percent covered by woodlands (INSEE, 1995: 20). France had a predominantly rural population up to the Second World War. The major rural exodus thereafter profoundly altered French society, but family connections with the countryside often remained strong, rural traditions have retained their place and agriculture is still accorded great political priority. These factors have given a particular spin to a key category of French environmental concern, illustrated in the following speech by Jacques Chirac, French President from 1995, formerly a Minister of Agriculture and MP for a rural constituency (Corrèze):

> At a time when concerns over the environment and the quality of life are prioritised, who can deny the irreplaceable role played by agriculture in conserving our surroundings? The enhancement of the countryside, the protection of our landscapes, our flora and fauna, are likewise the result of the labour of our farmers who put ecology into practice on a daily basis, in perhaps too discrete a manner. The wine grower, the stockbreeder, the forester, the market gardener do not only produce goods: they are the guardians of values

intimately bound up with a rural locality and constitute a civilisation, in the strong sense of the term.[1]

The quotation contains in cameo several of the shaping influences of French views on the environment. The physical location is the countryside, and the stewardship activities cited are farming and forestry. Both activities are presented in an entirely positive light as essential in economic and environmental terms, giving a twofold legitimacy to the agricultural lobby, which retains major political influence in France. In presenting nature solely as a provider for human needs, the philosophical backdrop is resolutely anthropocentric. In this view, the conservation of nature and the maintenance of agriculture are considered synonymous activities, to be undertaken by the same actors. Moreover both arenas are associated with apparently unquestionable rural values and traditions. This construction of the environment in terms of 'nature' subordinated to farming, forestry and hunting will be called the 'managed rurality perspective'.

The French outlook contrasts with British visions of the countryside (where landscaped vistas, stately homes and the gentrification of village life are largely divorced from agricultural concerns), and with German anguish over *Waldsterben* (forest dieback), namely the destruction of a 'natural heritage' by acid rain. Moreover, it differs markedly from a vision of nature conservation in which wildlife and habitats have value in themselves. Indeed the North American concern with 'wilderness' is viewed with suspicion in France, where the idea of excluding people from nature protection zones arouses passionate resistance. Conversely, the appropriation of nature by hunting is considered by its proponents to be an inalienable republican right. The political consequences of these cultural predispositions will be developed in Chapter 6.

The second major construction of the environment prevalent in France will be termed the 'resource management approach'. The

---

[1] 'Alors que les préoccupations en matière d'environnement et de qualité de la vie sont devenues des priorités, qui peut nier le rôle irremplaçable que joue l'agriculture dans la préservation du cadre de vie? La mise en valeur de notre espace rural, la sauvegarde de nos paysages, de notre flore, de notre faune, c'est encore le résultat du labeur de nos paysans, qui pratiquent l'écologie du quotidien avec, peut-être, beaucoup trop de discrétion. Le vigneron, l'éleveur, l'arboriculteur, le maraîcher ne sont pas seulement des producteurs de marchandises: ce sont les dépositaires de valeurs intimement liées à un terroir et qui constituent, au sens fort du terme, une civilisation.' Quoted in Alphandéry, Bitoun and Dupont (1991: 13–14).

1970s economic crisis marked French environmental policy in major ways. The newly created Environment Ministry immediately found itself confronted with the need to reconcile economic and environmental objectives. The declaration by Environment Minister Poujade (1975: 233) that 'France has refused to pit economic development against the environment, endeavouring to reorientate growth, not stop it'[2] became the enduring credo of subsequent administrations. In response to the energy crisis, a government decision to expand nuclear-power generation was taken without parliamentary debate and tacitly accepted by the French public, despite mass rallies by political ecologists (discussed in Chapter 2). The 'resource management approach' was developed along two tracks. In relation to the industrial environment, the authorities phased in a proactive stance on the regulation of pollution from the mid-1970s. Policy makers also became attentive to limiting technological hazards. Chapter 7 will show that technocratic elites thereby dampened the political salience of these policy arenas, whilst buttressing the competitive position of French industry. In relation to the human environment – by which is understood policy towards water, waste and air – technological and engineering solutions prevailed, as will be seen in Chapter 8. Moreover, health issues were to the fore, with only belated attention to the quality of water and air as the support of a wide range of life-forms. In summary, the 'resource management approach', like the 'managed rurality perspective' accorded primacy to human interests, but gave limited consideration to the dependency of human and non-human life-forms on the biosphere.

Over the 1980s and 1990s the rise in salience of issues such as holes in the ozone layer, acid rain and especially climate change revealed that environmental problems had changed in scale. Most importantly, the new need was to put the environment at the centre of environmental policy – in other words, to go from an anthropocentric to an ecocentric orientation. This involves a major cognitive shift, prior to policy renewal even being envisaged. The pace of readjustment has been slow. In the French case, the skew in constructions of the environment has led to considerable bias and polarisation. Review of the environmental consequences of intensive agriculture has been resisted by the farming lobby,

---

[2] 'La France (. . .) s'est refusée à opposer le développement économique et l'environnement, s'efforçant d'infléchir la croissance, non de l'arrêter.'

which remains imbued with a static vision of 'managed rurality'. Likewise even relatively small enhancements in the protection of wild species has attracted the ire of the hunting lobby. On the political stage, the resulting conflicts have translated into a caricatural opposition between the provinces and Paris (and Brussels), between 'rural traditionalists' and 'green extremists'. The 'resource management approach' has not aroused the same level of conflict, partly because of the different mix of socio-economic actors involved, partly because of the 'softly-softly' strategy of the authorities. In consequence, French environmental policy has a paradoxical character. Some arenas are marked by controversy and a highly charged political climate. Others are the ring-fenced preserve of specialists and special interests. Here too the dynamics of constructing and deconstructing what count as environmental issues form a hidden dimension of agenda-setting and policy formulation.

Modelling the Environmental Policy Process

Given the range of issues embedded within the term 'the environment' and the complexity of policy responses to them, no single theory or explanatory model can capture their various dimensions. In consequence, the method adopted in the present analysis is to outline complementary theoretical frameworks which, in combination, allow the identification and explanation of the sociopolitical processes at work in the field of environmental policy making.

The advocacy coalition framework

As a considerable body of literature indicates, understanding the development of policy content requires investigation of the manners in which policy actors behave and interrelate. The 'advocacy coalition framework' (ACF), as set out by Sabatier (1986) and Sabatier and Jenkins-Smith (1993), provides a useful model of these processes. The ACF goes beyond a descriptive model of policy processes by identifying the causal factors determining policy development, and locating their origins as either internal to a dominant advocacy coalition or external to it. It provides a rounded model by building on previously existing policy research methodologies. Thus the 'top-down' perspective typically stressed the legal structuring of the implementation process: starting with a policy decision contained in legislation, it explored the extent to which stated objectives were achieved. Conversely, a 'bottom-up' perspective aimed to understand the behaviour of a range of actors at the operational level, since it posited that their interaction modifies policy objectives by adjusting the latter to their own ends, thereby blurring the boundaries between formulation and implementation. The ACF aimed to synthesise 'top-down' and 'bottom-up' approaches. The policy subsystem is proposed as the unit of analysis, which for Sabatier (1992: 34) included 'bureaucrats, legislative personnel, interest group leaders, researchers and specialist reporters within a substantive policy area'. This composite approach to the policy subsystem distinguished it from traditional institutional approaches dedicated to one type of actor (such as legislatures, administrative agencies, interest groups or a single level of government) or a limited combination thereof, such as 'iron triangles' (the symbiotic relationship between the executive, an administrative agency and a leading pressure group).

Further, Sabatier identified two types of contexts which acted upon policy subsystems. He called the first 'relatively stable parameters', namely the core attributes of the problem area, a given distribution of resources, underlying cultural values and social structures, as well as its 'constitutional rules' governing behaviour. (For present purposes, these will be termed the 'rules of interaction' to avoid confusion with France's written constitution.) The second was termed 'dynamic system events', namely changes in socioeconomic conditions and technology, in public opinion, in systemic governing coalitions, and impacts from other policy domains. Though the policy subsystem is shaped by these broad parameters, its members retain scope to interact and produce outputs within a series of policy cycles embracing formulation, implementation, evaluation, through to reformulation, second-phase implementation and so forth. Sabatier (1993) insisted that the time-frame must be the long-term – periods longer than a decade – so allowing for an accumulation of incremental impacts, as well as the incorporation of policy analysis and actor learning. His ascription of rival coalitions within a policy subsystem is distinctive. The ACF proposes that actors can be aggregated into a small number of advocacy coalitions (usually two to four) on the basis of concerted action over time and a shared set of 'normative and causal beliefs' which 'glues' them together. One such coalition will be dominant at any given time, using substantive policy information in an advocacy fashion.

The model has attracted considerable interest, and detailed critiques can be found in Greenaway, Smith and Street (1992: 39–46) and Bergeron, Surel and Valluy (1998). For the present analysis, the main question is whether the ACF can be adapted to the contexts of French environmental policy making. On the positive side, the concept of a 'policy subsystem' is of a piece with the sectorisation of policy noted above. In addition, the exogenous factors impacting on policy sectors – 'relatively stable parameters' and 'dynamic system events' – are conceived in sufficiently generic terms to apply to different national contexts. However, the identification, composition and workings of 'advocacy coalitions' present problems. The stress on common beliefs as the 'glue' holding coalitions together is awkward in any context. Why stress beliefs, rather than interests? Indeed Sabatier and Jenkins-Smith (1993: 223–5) found themselves in disagreement over this point, the former stressing beliefs, the latter interests. In the French case, a stress on core beliefs risks registering commonplaces since policy actors invariably motivate their preferences by recourse to 'Republican values' or the malleable concept of the 'public interest'. Most importantly, the concept of advocacy coalitions is easier to apply to the pluralist context of the USA than to France, where the range of actors in a particular subsystem is usually circumscribed, and their interaction characterised by polarisation (namely a distillation into two rival camps). The workings of advocacy coalitions also pose difficulties. In stressing a congruence of values, the ACF suggests that coalition members line up in the same direction, but is laconic on the type of relations that pertain among then. Do they discuss and agree on policy preferences? Are some coalition members dependent on others? How easy is it to enter or exit a coalition? All of these factors relate to the degree of 'coupling' between policy actors and are likely to have a bearing on policy change.

Policy networks analysis

By identifying types of 'coupling' between actors, policy networks analysis contributes towards refining our understanding of the dynamics of policy subsystems. The classification developed by Rhodes (1990) and Rhodes and Marsh (1995) proposed five types of network, ranged along a continuum in terms of their level of integration and degree of closure. At the 'closed' pole were 'policy communities', defined by Rhodes (1990: 304–5) as 'networks characterised by stability of relationships, continuity of a highly restrictive membership, vertical independence based on shared service delivery responsibilities, and insulation from other networks and invariably to the general public . . . They are highly integrated. Policy communities are based on the major functional interests of government – for example, education, fire'.[3] At the 'open' pole were 'issue networks', characterised by a 'large number of participants and their limited degree of interdependence'. Intervening groupings were constituted by 'professional networks', 'intergovernmental networks' and 'producer networks'.

Although the policy networks approach has been taxed with a lack of theoretical parsimony and an in-built descriptive bias, its comprehensive formulation affords several advantages. Firstly, the reason for considering networks at all is because it is 'the networks that actually make policy' (Jordan, 1990: 476). Similarly Richardson (1996: 36) urged that, in relation to both national and European policy processes, 'focusing on networks of stakeholders may therefore help us to analyse the detailed process by which policy ideas are translated into specific policy proposals'. Secondly, investigation in terms of different types of network allows engagement with the complexity of the modern polity, since no one characterisation holds for all policy subsystems. Thirdly, as pointed out by Hassenteufel (1995: 93), the notion of a continuum of network types allows a reformulation of the opposition between pluralist and corporatist approaches. Rather than adopt a macro-level perspective which considers pluralism and corporatism as mutually exclusive, meso-level analysis (that is, at the sectoral level) allows the hypothesis that different types of network, some closer to the pole of corporatism, others closer to the pole of pluralism, can be at work within a polity. A fourth advantage is that networks analysis not only encourages a sharper differentiation of systems of interest intermediation, but also offers a framework for discussion of *transitions* in such systems, for example from closed policy communities to wider policy networks. Fifthly, Rhodes's policy network definitions use

---

[3] Likewise Jordan and Richardson (1983: 609) used the term to denote 'those individuals and groups (be they public or private) who regularly interact in a given policy area'.

behavioural features for the aggregation of policy actors, and these are more amenable to identification than are the shared belief-systems proposed by Sabatier. In the present analysis, these characterisations of policy subsystems will be used to provide a map of the policy terrain, and navigational aids to direct the analysis across it. However, the destination will be constituted by the explanation of policy change.

French perspectives on policy analysis

Turning to the application of these theories to the French context, it should first be noted that Sabatier's ACF has received relatively little attention in France, whilst the Rhodes formulation has attracted some hostile reactions.[4] Although a wide-ranging review of public policy analysis in France cannot be undertaken here,[5] some key contributions do display congruent features with these approaches.

Thus Mény (1989a) used the 'policy community' model to identify two complementary aspects of French policy subsystems. On the one hand, he noted that technocratic elites, usually recruited from the most prestigious educational institutions (such as the *Ecole Nationale d'Administration, Ecole Polytechnique* and the *grands corps* linked to those institutions), exercised considerable influence on policy through their presence at strategic points of government and the civil service. On the other, Mény (1989a: 390) pointed to the 'institutionalisation of interest groups', namely the legitimisation and co-optation into policy making of those groups considered responsible and representative by government, and the exclusion of those not so deemed. This division between 'insiders' and 'outsiders' was justified by officialdom on the basis of the slippery notion of *l'intérêt général* (the public interest).

The model proposed by Muller (1992) took the 'policy community' analysis a step further by stressing three interlinked components in French public policy modes during much of the postwar period: the central role of the state, the marginal importance of local government and a system of interest representation based on *corporatisme à la française* ('French-style corporatism'). Muller and Saez (1985: 135–6) identified the key features of this

---

[4] For examples, see Le Galès and Thatcher (1995).
[5] But for a useful overview, see Smith (1999).

form of neocorporatism as: (1) the sectoral representation of social interests, monopolised by a single organisation; (2) a close relationship between that organisation and a specialised segment of the administration; and (3) a tendency towards the exclusion of other social actors, and of other arms of government, resulting in the lack of an arena for comprehensive, multipartite negotiations. This model's recourse to statist and neocorporatist components calls for detailed comment.

The term 'corporatism' is recognised as problematic since it covers a vast range of sociopolitical arrangements, running from the trade guilds of the medieval era, through the fascist regimes of the early twentieth century, and up to the neocorporatist influence discerned in liberal democracies of the late twentieth century. Aiming to clarify the pertinence of this sprawling concept for the recent period, Schmitter (1970: 93) proposed that 'corporatism can be defined as a system of interest representation in which the constituent units are organised into a limited number of singular, compulsory, non-competitive, hierarchically ordered and functionally differentiated categories, recognised or licensed (if not created) by the state and granted a deliberate representational monopoly within their respective categories in exchange for observing certain controls on their selection of leaders and articulation of demands and supports'. In contrast to pluralist visions of the polity, characterised by a multiplicity of actors engaging in lively competition to influence public policy formulation, latter-day corporatism is a mode of interest intermediation in which private-interest groups, operating on a basis of concentration, monopolisation and social closure, actively participate in both policy formulation and implementation.

The conceptual and empirical richness of the term has provoked a debate on the 'varieties of corporatism'.[6] Consideration of two major strands of the debate will allow clarification of how the present analysis proposes to apply a neocorporatist model. Firstly, the term 'macro-corporatism' has come to refer to a tripartite system of economic interest representation, in which the 'social partners' (state representatives, the peak employers' organisation and leading trade unions) conduct national-level negotiations on regulation of the labour market (employment, incomes policy, working conditions etc.). Exploring the model of 'macro-corporatism' in the French context, Goetschy (1987: 177) considered that France

---

[6] Cf. Williamson (1985), Cawson (1986: 68–83) and Wiarda (1997: 71–93).

offered an 'awkward example' due to the internal conflicts of trade unions and their lack of authority over workers, whilst Cox and Hayward (1983) concluded that it was simply inapplicable.

Secondly, in the variety known as 'meso-corporatism' interests are aggregated not at the national level, or on the basis of social class, but in terms of sector (such as industrial branch), with interest-group representatives and state officials engaging in bipartite policy discussions.[7] If there is relatively little support in the literature for France as an example of macro-corporatism, a significant measure of consensus can be found attesting to the existence of meso-corporatism. Thus Jobert (1988: 11–12) stressed that corporatism in France was confined to the meso level. Meso-corporatism and *corporatisme à la française* as defined by Muller and Saez (1985) are functionally indistinguishable. For Muller (1990), its archetype was constituted by agriculture, since an interest group – the FNSEA (the hegemonic French farmers' union) – staked ownership over a sector and for long enjoyed an exclusive relationship with the associated organ of state, the Agriculture Ministry. Likewise Keeler (1981: 186–7) noted that 'the FNSEA has provided the state with all of the essential services of a corporatist client: it has served as a fixed channel of communication, as a bargaining agent that aggregates and moderates agricultural demands and mobilises sectoral support for policies that it participates in formulating, and as a supplementary bureaucracy that assists in policy implementation'. However, sectoral corporatism in France is not limited to agriculture. Other policy fields cited by Muller (1990) included energy and aeronautics. With regard to French environmental policy, Brénac (1985, 1988) and Gerbaux (1988) were the first to develop extended analyses within a neocorporatist framework.

Meso-corporatism – involving the mapping of a policy domain, the emergence of organised private interests who negotiate and implement policy, and the conjoined development of politico-administrative capacity – can be identified in key environmental sectors in France, namely nature protection and the hunt lobby, industrial pollution control, and water management. This analysis is developed in Chapters 6, 7 and 8. However the proposition will not be made that neocorporatist relationships explain French environmental policy as a whole (and even less the gamut of

---

[7] For discussion, see Cawson (1986: 106–18).

policy in other domains). Rather, the meso-corporatist model will be used to elucidate early patterns of interaction between public administration and socioeconomic actors in specific sectors, identify recent problems associated with exiting from these societal arrangements and help assess the environmental consequences incurred. In addition, the compartmentalised nature of meso-corporatist policy subsystems accords with the notion of 'policy communities'. Indeed, Rhodes and Marsh (1995: 35) proposed that the corporatist model of interest mediation is most usefully conceptualised as a species of policy network, rather than as a standalone case. Further, the exit from neocorporatism can be modelled more clearly by mapping it as a movement along the policy networks continuum from the 'closed' towards the 'open' pole.

Where the French literature departs markedly from American and British discussions is in its 'statist' perspective. This divergence undoubtedly has its origins in objective differences in the historical trajectories of the nations in question, with the unitary and centralised French state standing in sharp contrast to the federal American state or the composite state of the United Kingdom. Nevertheless, it is worth probing the received idea of the French state as an imposing and hyperactive policy actor. Hayward (1982: 112) emphasised the existence of a 'dual policy style' in France, understood as 'the distinction between heroic and hum-drum decision making'. 'Heroic' decision making involved 'a capacity for policy initiative, a potential for far-sighted planning and a propensity to impose its will' (Hayward, 1982: 116). In French, the state's capacity for autonomous action is termed *volontarisme*; examples include the creation of the nuclear electricity generating sector, high-speed trains, aeronautics (Concorde, Airbus) and satellite launches (Ariane). Yet in many domains the reality of the policy process tended to the 'humdrum', but was merely dressed up in 'heroic' language. The gap between an entrepreneurial and grandiloquent political rhetoric and mundane policy incrementalism points up the *trompe-l'oeil* character of the French state during the Fifth Republic. This disjunction is particularly marked in environmental policy, and will be treated in detail in Chapter 4.

The appearance of a strong state was reinforced by the relationship between its political and administrative components. Considered in political terms, France displays a centralisation of decision making in Paris, a concentration of power in the hands of the executive, and limited 'checks and balances' between the different branches of government. Considered in terms of the administration, the definitions and size of the public sector have contributed to an inflated view of the state's powers. Whereas in the British context, the 'civil service' is a restricted category covering the employees of central public institutions (excluding, for example, the military and the judiciary), in the French context, the apparently equivalent term – *la fonction publique* – is far wider in scope. Not only does it include the teaching profession and the police force, but when, for example, a number of banks and industrial firms were nationalised in 1981 to create the largest public sector in Western Europe, their employees suddenly discovered that they too could be considered as *fonctionnaires*. Moreover, the field services of 'spending' ministries, such as Health, Agriculture etc., are numerically strong at the departmental level and exercise considerable authority at the policy implementation stage. Thus the *extent* of the French public sector coupled with the *extensiveness* of the term *fonction publique* ensure that the French administration is larger than in other European nations. These features contribute to the omnipresence of *l'Etat* – which, significantly enough, the French write with a capital letter.

The policy role of state functionaries is legitimised by republican discourse which stresses the public interest over private preferences. Thus Rouban (1990: 525) could maintain that in policy communities 'the administration keeps the upper hand'.[8] In French political rhetoric, the corollary of the state as prime policy actor is the deprecation of 'lobbies' as unrepresentative and illegitimate. In addition, a discourse which legitimised state primacy created prejudice against policy networks analysis, since this latter approach implies a key role for private actors when, in the 'official' view, their very presence in policy making was suspicious or illicit. These various features contributed to the legend of a powerful central state characterised by its top-down and exclusionary practices, whose positive attraction was its (supposed) capacity to implement policy but whose negative consequence was the creation of ambivalence among the French. Whilst vigorous state action alienates dissenting citizens, the possibility of seizing the levers of state galvanises political opposition. On this view, the state becomes a receptacle of power which can be conquered by political organisations to attain their own ends – a view

---

[8] 'l'administration garde un poids préponderant'.

to which green parties have largely subscribed, as will be seen in Chapter 3. Yet on closer examination, the apparent unity of the state as a politico-administrative entity transpires to be a façade. Successive stages of fragmentation are introduced by institutional division into legislature, executive and judiciary (each jealous of the prerogatives of the other); by the compartmentalisation of government into ministries (vying with each other for resources); by the transfer of operational responsibilities to quasi-autonomous agencies and field services (often acting in isolation or rivalry); and by the complex distribution of competencies between national, subnational and supranational authorities (often acting in competition), with Europeanisation and decentralisation since the 1980s exacerbating these tensions. Thus the notion of the state as a unitary actor and solitary policy maker has become progressively untenable. The segmentation of policy domains into ever greater areas of specialism, the rise in complexity of associated formulation and implementation processes, and the increase in the number of actors militate for recognition of policy networks. Overall, however, a certain complementarity emerges between the models outlined. Whilst the statist perspective on French political life recognises important structural features of the polity, policy subsystem perspectives allow inspection of the conduct of organised interests in their interactions with officialdom.

Research questions

The foregoing discussion raises a series of research questions. An initial set is descriptive. Who are the major policy actors and in what ways do they direct environmental policy? How has policy been formulated and implemented? A second set concentrates on explanation and evaluation of the substantive content of policy. What changes in environmental policies can be discerned over the long term, and have they improved effectiveness? What are the causes of policy renewal? And what are the impediments to innovation? A third set relates to social and political processes. What are the political conditions which make more affirmative environmental policy possible? Who benefits from policy renewal or inertia? How have systems of interest representation evolved?

Thus the analysis will be primarily concerned with determining the nature of policy development and explaining its causes. Significantly Sabatier, Mény, Muller, Rhodes and Marsh all argued that major causes of change arise externally. For Sabatier (1993: 36) 'external system events' are a major catalyst. The causes of the transformation of French policy communities given by Mény (1989a) were also exogenous, specifically the transfer of decision making prerogatives to European institutions, international pressures (such as market liberalisation) and the tendency of groups excluded from policy formulation to sabotage implementation. Muller (1992) likewise pointed to the influence of the EC and the spread of market norms, whilst stressing in the French context the importance of decentralisation and the rise of local government from the 1980s as a catalyst of change. Rhodes and Marsh (1995: 59) gave four sources of exogenous change: developments in markets, in ideology, in scientific knowledge, and in institutions (such as the EU). Powerful as these causal factors are, Rhodes and Marsh (1995: 60) warned against considering externally induced change as a *deus ex machina*. Refining the analysis, Hassenteufel (1995: 103–5) posited that the *pressure for change* could come from outside a policy network, whilst the *content of change* was decided internally; his list of internal change factors included the weakening or strengthening of existing actors, the emergence of new ones, modification of member strategies or of the content of exchanges between them, and changes in coalition structures- an approach reminiscent of Sabatier's ACF.

These considerations have led to three main hypotheses. The first and most fundamental one relates to political exchange: if policy is conditional on an underlying bargain reached within a dominant advocacy coalition, then policy renewal will depend on a change in the dominant coalition (or in its composition) and on striking a new deal. Secondly, following Sabatier and Jenkins-Smith (1993: 221–2), it is hypothesised that policy innovation requires the conjunction of major perturbations external to the subsystem *and* skilful exploitation of new opportunities by previously dominated actors. The third hypothesis is that advocates of significant environmental policy renewal can succeed only if they rewrite the 'rules of interaction' in such a way that they engineer a reallocation of resources commensurate to their objectives. The resources in question can be tangible (for example, capital in its various forms) or intangible (for example, electoral support, political influence). Thus study of the shaping of policy relates as much to process as to product: it aims to specify an arena bringing together an assortment of actors, identify a repertoire of actions, deduce the 'rules' governing behaviour, and show the differential consequences for policy arising from changes in actors, actions and 'rules'.

Because of its challenges to the political status quo, the environmental problematic provides a different route to investigation of the polity. Research into environmental policy streams provides insights into the functioning of national political systems because the transversal nature of environmental issues creates new demands (in terms of institutional capacity and societal coordination) and highlights social and economic conflicts (related to priority setting, resource allocation etc.). This produces a two-way research agenda: study of environmental policy illustrates the capacity and limits of a national polity, whilst study of a national polity reveals the opportunities and constraints for environmental policy making.

Summary

The term 'environment' will be used not to designate a unitary entity with an independent existence, but to refer to a variety of overarching social constructions. These articulate the complex interlocks between 'nature' or the 'biosphere', a set of social and ethical concerns, a body of economic and political preferences, and a scientific or technological order. Thereby they offer competing visions for the well-being of humans and the planet. Because of these cross-cutting characteristics, environmental policy has considerable importance in its own right, as well as revealing the dynamics of wider political and social processes, precisely because successful policy making requires the integration of diverse life realms and aspirations. At the same time, practical constraints result in the marked tendency to sectorisation of environmental issues, which in turn frames and shapes policies in terms of content and effectiveness. Theoretical and analytical approaches to environmental policy therefore need to be sufficiently flexible and comprehensive to correlate the range of policy actors with the challenges they face, and to relate substantive reforms to changes in their patterns of interaction. A shorthand formulation of the main research questions of this text is: 'What shape are French environmental policies in?' Answering this question will involve both investigation of the causal sequences that produce specific policy configurations and assessment of actual outcomes.

2

PUBLIC OPINION, THE GREEN MOVEMENT AND ENVIRONMENTAL GROUPS IN FRANCE

Introduction

From the 1960s, anxiety over the environment has increased as a result of spectacular accidents and accumulative pollution, leading to changes in public opinion, mass mobilisation and the growth of pressure groups. The model proposed by Sabatier (1986) suggested that 'external system events' could significantly impact on policy subsystems, with one category being changes in public opinion. Thus this chapter considers whether societal expressions of environmental concern have been sufficiently strong and effective to shape environmental policy.

Following on from the arguments of Chapter 1, this concern will be treated not as a homogenous mass, but as a series of segments of demand, each of which expresses particular constructions of the environment, and articulates its own issues, values and priorities. Indeed, the coherence and unity of environmental views have regularly been questioned in the literature. Thus Witherspoon (1996: 56) judged that 'the notion that there is a single "true" opinion towards the environment is simply not fruitful'. Dalton (1993: 60–1) argued that conservationists pursued 'consensual social goals within the existing socio-economic structure', whilst political ecologists presented 'a more basic critique of the values of the prevailing social order of advanced industrial democracies'. Norris (1997) identified three dimensions: 'old green' (by which was understood protection of the local country-side and wildlife, as well as opposition to the encroachments of housing, roads and industry); 'new green' (environmentalist preferences as expressed by Friends of the Earth for example), and anti-nuclearism. Thus three broad categories of opinion recur: conservationist/conservative, environmentalist/reformist, and ecologist/radical. Whilst these divisions are not presented as watertight, they are useful for tracing changes in attitudes.

Can these orientations be found in France? And to what extent have they contributed to the societal shaping of environmental policy? To consider these questions, this chapter's first section analyses the structure and expression of public opinion towards the environment as revealed by poll data. It explores the uptake of environmental issues, surveys general levels of mobilisation and offers a preliminary assessment of the influence of public opinion on environmental policy-making. The second section focuses on the characteristics and impact of the green social movement in France. In particular, it analyses the defeat of anti-nuclearism in the late 1970s and investigates its wider consequences. The third section considers the organised expression of the green movement formed by the main environmental groups. It outlines their out-looks, membership and resources, reviews their relations to public authorities and assesses their ability to influence policy.

Public opinion and the environment

Can citizen pressure influence the course of policy making? For it to constitute a driver of environmental policy, two sets of conditions must be fulfilled. On the input side, pressure must exist, have means of articulation, and be expressed with sufficient force. On the output side, the institutional characteristics of the polity and the attitudes of key policy actors must be sufficiently respon-sive to translate public preferences into policy. Discussion of the output side is held over for later chapters; only the input side will be considered here.

Signs of citizen pressure are discernible in opinion poll data. Witherspoon (1994: 107) claimed that a 'pro-environment' attitude has become so widespread that it constituted a 'secular religion'. Based on their European survey, Ashford and Halman (1994: 78) concluded that 'concern about the environment and about human rights is almost universal', with over 90 percent of respondents polled in 1990 expressing concern. From a longitudinal analysis of Eurobarometer data, Hofrichter and Reif (1990) formed similar conclusions. Although saliency declined throughout Europe between 1976 and 1978, the importance attributed to environmental issues grew steadily in most countries between 1978 and 1989. The timing of this change was a little later in France and Belgium, where the decline continued during 1978–83, but with salience increasing thereafter. Ténière-Buchot (1985) argued that these variations followed the economic cycle, with concern waning in times of economic crisis and high unemployment.

In France, four phases of public reaction to the environment were identified by Dobré (1995: 11–12). In the early 1960s, the French were largely unconcerned with environmental issues. After 1968, an 'ecological sensibility' emerged in which criticism of consumer society was twinned with a concern for nature conservation, pollution and the quality of life. In the 1970s, nuclear energy monopolised attention, but faded in importance in the early 1980s, bar a peak of anxiety after the 1986 Chernobyl explosion. At the end of the 1980s, public concern reached heightened levels particularly with regard to air and water pollution, waste and global warming. Eurobarometer data showed that this increased concern was particularly marked in France: between 1988 and 1992, French respondents considering the environment to be an 'urgent and immediate issue' increased by 21 percent, as compared to +15 percent of the British and +4 percent of the German cohorts (Dobré, 1995: 27). Swings in the salience of environmental issues continued in the 1990s as the country traversed recession. These findings lend support to the 'issue attention cycle' posited by Downs (1972) in which environmental concerns wax and wane whilst retaining a high level of popularity overall. However, ascertaining the causes of shifts in public opinion is problematic. Are peaks of concern generated by the 'objective' state of the environment? Or are they generated by media discourse, electoral campaigns and the actions of policy elites? Parameters for analysis include not just the intensity of public concern, but also its content, articulation and structure.

What then is the public concerned about? A recurrent theme found in the data is a diffuse and nagging anxiety over a general entity termed the 'environment'. In a major international survey, Dunlap, Gallup and Gallup (1993) found that the quality of the global environment was rated as 'very' or 'fairly' bad by a majority of respondents in twenty-one countries – often massively so

(80+ percent). However, only in Poland, Russia and South Korea did a majority complain that their local environment was 'fairly' or 'very' bad, with the majority elsewhere considering it to be 'good'. The most extreme case was Denmark where only 12 percent of respondents held a poor opinion of their local environment, but 92 percent thought the world environment was in bad shape. This finding points up a consistent pattern: the further afield one went from everyday experience, the more respondents reacted negatively in large numbers. Yet whereas individuals can form a direct assessment of the scale and causes of environmental degradation in their everyday surroundings, global developments are communicated indirectly – by the media, educational systems and political campaigns. Where environmental risks are perceived as threatening in vague and distant terms, the result is impotence rather than activism. Observably, anguish over a catch-all construction of the 'environment' is not an immediate spur to policy innovation. At this level, polls do not translate directly into policies.

Whilst acting as a vehicle to express public concern, polls fail to be compelling as policy catalysts because of an underlying ambiguity over whether the environment is treated as a *valence* issue or as a series of *positional* issues.[1] The difference is that whereas a positional issue provokes 'pro' and 'con' stances, a valence issue does not. The 'environment' in its generality constitutes a valence issue, given that there is no constituency openly in favour of a polluted environment. A 'soft consensus' exists on the need for as healthy and risk-free an environment as possible. However, individual environmental problems do translate into positional issues. Nuclear power generates clear 'for' or 'against' positions. Similarly, transport policy is sometimes simplified into a public transport versus private car trade-off. Once such positions are identified, the 'soft consensus' breaks up as individual and collective interests emerge and enter into conflict. Indeed, the existence of multiple constructions of the environment makes the development of a series of positional issues possible. However, it is striking that the most usual type of opinion poll treats the environment from the perspective of a valence issue, as will be seen from Table 2.1.

Although minor year-on-year variations in priorities can be

---

[1] For discussion, see Stokes (1992).

Table 2.1 Public concern over the environment in France

In your view, what should be the two main priorities of the State in relation to environmental protection?

	1993 %	1994 %	1996 %
Reducing air pollution	46	46	54
Reducing water pollution	43	42	38
Treatment of industrial waste	35	33	30
Hazard prevention in the nuclear industry	18	19	20
Conserving flora and fauna	21	17	18
Developing environmentally friendly technology	15	16	16
Conserving landscapes	12	14	13
Reducing noise	10	13	11

Note: The % columns aggregate respondents' first and second choices.
Source: IFEN (1996a: 1)

discerned in Table 2.1, the data have remained relatively stable over time. What is of more interest here is the structure and orientation of the poll itself. First and foremost, the concerns identified are all valence issues; the desirability of clean water, clean air, proper disposal of waste etc. meets with universal approval. Respondents are *not* asked to position their views in relation to the causes of problems *nor* to specific modes of solving them. Thus air pollution is not treated as resulting from the activities of specific categories of actor, among whom responsibility can be distributed in proportion to harm done, with policy options delineated in relation to categories of cause. On the contrary, respondents are merely invited to *prioritise* one issue over another. This process of hierarchical ordering might be construed as a public consultation over the allocation of a limited pool of resources. But if that were the case, an invitation to attribute only middling priority to 'hazard prevention in the nuclear industry' would not be a sensible option.

In reality, this type of poll sets up a *competition* between broadly equivalent issues. As a result, the need to respond to each and all is obscured. Moreover, in any list of priorities something must come bottom: jumping to the conclusion that the last item has no importance is understandable, but mistaken. The competition is even more intense in polls which invite the expression of priorities in relation to different categories of issues, such as the environment versus unemployment. On inspection, both the environment and unemployment are valence issues. In other words, it is rare to hear individuals express preference for a highly polluted environment or for a high level of unemployment. Societal consensus goes in the opposite direction in each case. However, setting the environment *against* employment creates the appearance of a position issue, and encourages the view that there must be a trade-off between the two, that one must be sacrificed to the other. The pernicious consequence of the pollster's strategy is that whole categories of environmental concern are downgraded from the outset.

Closer inspection of opinion polls reveals further reasons for taking up a critical distance. Bourdieu (1993: 148) pointed out that not every respondent has a prior opinion on the questions asked, that not all opinions are equivalent (so their aggregation produces meaningless artefacts), and that a standardised battery of questions involves a closed selection and framing of priorities. These reservations can be developed along several dimensions. Firstly, polls treat the population as an undifferentiated whole from which emerges a majority view, whereas in reality considerable segmentation occurs. Such cleavages have political importance in terms of agenda setting, and where particular communities suffer disproportionately and unjustly. Secondly, the usefulness of opinion poll data is constrained by methodological problems. Not only does the phraseology of the pollsters introduce bias, but the use of single-issue questions obscures relationships to other domains of the respondent's life situation. Ideological divergences and social conflicts and are skated over. Consequently polls can be transformed into an instrument to replicate the received ideas of the day. Thirdly, respondents' knowledge of issues may be insecure. In a 1990 French poll, 71 percent of respondents admitted to not knowing the causes of pollution, though by 1993 their numbers fell to 44 percent (Dobré, 1995: 41). Fourthly, opinions are not stable. When large swings occur, their causes do not emerge from the polls per se. Thus Scheuch (1994: 93–5) noted that satisfaction with the state of the environment nearly halved in a span of six years (from 40 percent in 1978 to 22 percent in 1984), a change that he attributed not to real conditions but agenda-setting by the media. Yet to prove this point requires further research. The danger is an infinite regress of polls on polls. Fifthly, actual behaviour is rarely explored. Dunlap and Van Liere (1977: 17) noted that 'the link between attitudes and behaviour is often rather tenuous'. There can be a gap between rehearsing the views of the day and actual levels of 'offering willingness', that is the propensity of respondents to take pro-environmental action. From their pan-European survey, Ester, Halman and Seuren (1993: 166) concluded that 'environmental concern is quite prevalent among Europeans . . . but environmentally conscious behaviour is the exception rather than the rule'.

These objections are not so damning as to render opinion polls useless. Data can be probed for internal consistency and representativeness, and compared to other sources such as voting trends, membership of citizens' groups, size of public demonstrations, etc. Supplementary analysis of the characteristics and values of particular social subgroups, such as that undertaken by Peixoto (1993), avoids the trap of overgeneralisation (though it entails the problem of the construction of group typologies). However, the problems are serious enough to require caution in the interpretation of poll data. In consequence, even focused and credible expressions of concern, such as the preference for 'clean air, clean water', do not translate easily into policy. The call that 'something must be done' can be loud and compelling, but leaves unanswered the questions of what exactly is to be done, by whom and who will pay.

Yet if the ex ante value of polls for policy makers is limited, ex post uses need to be flagged up. The first of these is policy feedback, namely a means of communication between citizens and political elites to ascertain whether initiatives are moving in an acceptable direction. The second is policy legitimisation: apparent public support vindicates government against critics in opposition. Nevertheless, French authorities have been cautious in their recourse to direct consultation: referenda are rare, and none has been on an environmental issue. Overall, polls in France have *not* been used as a environmental policy making instrument but act as a 'barometer' for policy makers, providing information on the 'climate' of their decision-making, but offering little content. Thus the conclusions drawn from this discussion of the intensity, articulation and structure of French opinion on environmental issues are that public preferences are sufficiently focused and persistent to merit the policy maker's attention, but that the links between public opinion and actual policy are loose. Direct impacts of civil society on policy making, if they exist, must be sought elsewhere.

The green social movement

The 'green movement' refers to the range of social actors who promote environmental agendas and employ conventional and unconventional means to further them. It is a variegated and broad-based phenomenon whose concerns encompass conservationism, environmentalism, political ecology and anti-nuclear protest, but which also has affiliations to regionalism, pacifism, civil rights, feminism and Third World concern.[2] Like other 'new social movements' of the late 1960s,[3] it has been composed of large numbers of small groups, characterised by fluid organisation and intergroup rivalries. Above all, it has been typified by the eclecticism of its ideas, and by its limited integration of a diverse range of philosophical sources.[4] Although 'old green' ideas have a history of over a century, 'new green' strands of anti-nuclear protest and political ecology exhibited continuity with the May 1968 movement. Common themes noted by Chafer (1985: 9) included hostility to remote political power structures, rejection of 'productivism',[5] and criticism of consumer society. Because these factors were held responsible for degradation of the environment and dehumanisation of society, political ecologists developed a broad political project which combined environmental care with social reform. Continuity with May 1968 is also found in action repertoire. Anti-nuclearism, the most prominent component of the green movement in the 1970s, was marked by recourse to unconventional events, mass demonstrations and confrontation with public authorities.

---

[2] For histories of the French green movement, see Vadrot (1978), Sainteny (1992), and Bennahmias and Roche (1992).

[3] Space precludes discussion of new social movements per se. Definitions and theoretical grounding can be found in Habermas (1981), Cohen (1984, 1985), Eder (1985), Touraine (1985) and Melucci (1991). Comparative studies include Dalton and Kuechler (1990), Kriesi et al. (1995), Jenkins and Klandermans (1995), and Marks and McAdam (1996). For studies of France, see Cerny (1982), Spanou (1991), Duyvendak (1994), and Waters (1998).

[4] A rich literature has developed on the ideas of French ecologism, notably: Journès (1979, 1982), Prendiville and Chafer (1990), Waechter (1990), Alphandéry, Bitoun and Dupont (1992), Boy (1992), Hastings (1994), Foing, (1994), Simonnet (1994), Jacob (1995), Whiteside (1995) and Prendiville (1997).

[5] Namely the tendency of industrial society to produce and consume ever more goods and services.

The anti-nuclear movement

French anti-nuclearism contested the use of nuclear energy for *civil* purposes,[6] unlike Britain where the Campaign for Nuclear Disarmament rejected *military* uses.[7] A wave of protests was sparked by the decision of the Messmer government in March 1974 to greatly increase electricity production by nuclear power in response to the oil crisis. The decision provoked fears of environmental and health risks, dissatisfaction over the lack of democratic consultation, as well as a questioning of the financial costs. From being a marginal phenomenon, the anti-nuclear movement swelled in intensity between 1971 and 1977, drawing together between 20,000 and 60,000 protesters (Rucht, 1994: 144).

In a first phase of demonstrations at sites of proposed nuclear power stations, anti-nuclear campaigners linked with regionalists to defend local prerogatives (Heijden, Koopmans and Guigni, 1992). As the movement gathered in strength over 1975–6, the government's response grew more repressive. Violent clashes between riot police and demonstrators in the July 1977 protest at the fast-breeder reactor of Creys-Malville led to a number of injuries and one death. Traumatised, the pacifist component of the movement backed away from mass demonstrations. In an unfavourable climate characterised by economic crisis and increasing unemployment, this retrenchment sapped the movement of its vitality.

Support from erstwhile political allies proved short-lived. The Socialist Party was critical of nuclear power in the 1970s, and sought to woo the ecology vote by the promise of a referendum on civil nuclear energy. On election to the presidency in 1981, Mitterrand announced the cancellation of a new nuclear power station at Plogoff, but the proposed referendum was never held. The Socialists in office continued the energy policy of their predecessors, whilst scaling back the nuclear construction programme for pragmatic reasons, once the excess capacity of *Electricité de France* (EDF) became apparent. In the early 1980s protests were few, given that large-scale demonstrations had proved ineffective.

---

[6] Detailed histories can be found in Garraud (1979), Rüdig (1990), Prendiville (1994: 11–18), and Rucht (1994).

[7] To the extent that mobilisation against nuclear weapons remained muted, French ecologists hardly broke with the national consensus on defence policy. For discussion, see Howorth (1984) and Chafer (1984, 1985).

Not even the nuclear accidents at Three Mile Island in 1979 and at Chernobyl in 1986 could revive anti-nuclearism as a mass movement, although sporadic opposition continued into the 1990s.[8] The reality was that 'the movement has lost the battle over nuclear power' (Rucht, 1994: 150). The defeat had knock-on effects for the wider green movement in France. These will be developed firstly in relation to public policy and secondly in relation to the movement itself.

The Jacobin state . . .

The example of civil nuclear energy constitutes an extreme case of 'Jacobin' (or centralised) environmental policy. The decision to push France from a position of incidental reliance on nuclear energy to dependency (8.5 percent of electricity production in 1972, 75 percent by 1989) was made by an elite policy caucus, without electoral mandate or parliamentary debate. Yet the executive's *capacity* to implement the 'Jacobin model' in energy policy was contingent on a rare combination of factors. Firstly, in French political culture, a strong state has often been invested with the mission to act in the national interest. Secondly, General de Gaulle's stress in the 1960s on enhancing national security by reliance on France's independent nuclear strike capability encouraged a bunker mentality which was subsequently transferred from military to civil uses of nuclear energy. Thirdly, the state commanded considerable resources. Although oil price hikes heralded a period of economic crisis, in 1973 France was still benefiting from a long wave of postwar economic expansion. Massive public investments in infrastructure remained a proposition that was both feasible and ideologically acceptable. Feasible, because the public deficit and state debt had not yet exploded under the effect of unemployment and social security payments. Ideologically acceptable, due to the planning tradition of the postwar period. Fourthly, a technocratic elite argued its case on the basis of its own competencies. Although major challenges lay ahead as each generation of reactor – gas-graphite, light-water and fast-breeder – developed problems, much of the scientific and technological know-how was already in place and vested in the

---

[8] For example, in June 1997, demonstrations were held at Carnet, Brittany, against the building of a 'European pressurised water reactor', considered to be the first in the next generation of nuclear power stations.

powerful *Corps des Mines*. Moreover, existing institutions could be harnessed to the new tasks. The *Commissariat à l'énergie atomique*, which had presided over military nuclear energy since 1945, oversaw the new phase of civil development, in conjunction with the nationalised monopoly EDF (sometimes described as a 'state within the state', due to its vast resources and prerogatives). Fifthly, the industrial potential existed, with major companies in the sector being supported by public investment. The mid-1970s saw the apogee of French industrial policy, with its stress on selective intervention and close cooperation between the state and a small number of 'national champions', spurred on by subsidies.[9] Sixthly, the policy outcomes were finite and targeted, namely the building and operation of some fifty-nine nuclear reactors. Finally, whilst the arguments over security and long-term costs related to decommissioning and nuclear waste storage were lost on many, nuclear-derived electricity was presented as essential and cheap for all.

In summary, the top-down 'Jacobin model' found perhaps its most concentrated expression in nuclear power. The main characteristics of the energy policy community were: (a) hyper-centralisation of political, economic and technological resources, (b) close cooperation between a small number of highly specialised public and private actors and (c) measurable policy outcomes. It is worth stressing on the input side, the presence of considerable political will and on the output side the existence of (some) benefits for all. Taken on its own terms – namely, the objective of increasing national independence in energy sourcing over the medium term – the policy was a success.

Whether the programme can be considered a success over the long term is, however, a different matter. Since the 1970s, the scope and content of the criticism of the French nuclear programme has changed. From being largely a political issue, nuclear power has become an economic issue. Because of inattention to cost-benefit analysis, the French state commissioned an excessive number of nuclear reactors, leading to overcapacity and major indebtedness for EDF. The hidden costs of the programme are emerging now that the earliest reactors are reaching the end of their working life; their decommissioning is revealing immense logistical complications and costs. Whilst engineers are likely to move up the learning curve

---

[9] For further details, see Szarka (1992: 42–59).

in terms of the management of decommissioning processes, the total costs will accelerate once the majority of plants constructed in the 1970s and early 1980s reach retirement age, probably around 2020–30. Further, the issues of nuclear waste are attracting increased concern, since materials will remain harmful to many future generations. No satisfactory long-term solutions have been found for the nuclear waste produced within the electricity production cycle. Moreover, decommissioning – involving the disposal of contaminated buildings, soil and other materials – will increase current volumes of waste many times over. Meanwhile the industry's solution to the disposal of plutonium by burning it as a fuel known as 'mox' has brought further problems because of the greater instability of this material as compared to conventional uranium, which leads to increased hazards and costs. In addition, wider recourse to the 'mox' cycle in French power stations creates the risk that terrorists will have easier access to weapons-grade plutonium.

The operating environment of energy utilities was transformed in the 1990s. Deregulation, privatisation and internationalisation have transformed the market place. Despite its rearguard action against EU energy directives, EDF can no longer maintain its monopoly within France, but must open national markets to domestic and foreign suppliers. The centralised, monolithic structures that characterised EDF are being undermined by decentralised, small-scale producers. Alternative sources of energy are becoming available: combined heat and power plants, for example. The costs of fossil fuels as compared to nuclear sources of electricity have dropped, notably with the 'rush to gas'. Technological progress is giving greater credibility to renewable sources of energy, and to energy efficiency programmes. EDF's traditional policy of inciting greater levels of electricity consumption within France (in order to run nuclear power stations at optimal capacity) is out of step with the current need to husband resources and conserve energy. In an era characterised by concerns over climate change, EDF's claim that nuclear power is 'clean' (since it produces few greenhouse gases) is not credible given the serious problems caused by nuclear waste. Taken together, these trends have reinforced the green movement's arguments against nuclear power, though in ways and at junctures that the greens had not anticipated.[10]

---

[10] For further details and discussion, see Jasper (1990), Hecht (1998), and Rivasi and Crié (1998).

Finally, the Jacobin policy community that characterised the nuclear energy industry did *not* become the archetype of French environmental policy making. In this pure form it was the 'heroic' exception, not the 'humdrum' rule, since it owed its rise to specific technological, social and political contexts.

... *versus a weak and defensive civil society?*

Prendiville (1994: 111) argued that an underlying cause of the marginalisation of the French green movement was that 'civil society is weak and cannot constitute the lever against the State the environmentalists would wish for'. This adequately encapsulated the 'us and them' mentality of the ecologists during the 1970s in their espousal of a militant strategy. But was it French civil society that was weak, or just the green movement?

Research on a range of social movements in Europe allows contextualisation of the French case. Ashford and Halman (1994: 79–80) concluded that 'among Europeans, the French are the most likely to become involved in actions of an extreme sort, and France has the highest proportion of respondents who have actually taken part in demonstrations and have occupied buildings or factories'. However, the readiness to take non-conventional actions to achieve political ends has been largely limited to the economic and social domains. In the mid-1990s, France saw major demonstrations against social security reforms, lorry-drivers' road blocks, farmers' protests, as well as occupations of public buildings by the unemployed, and of churches by illegal immigrants. All of these examples resulted in government (and sometimes private sector) concessions to the protesters, and dent the case for a 'weak' civil society in France. This raises the question of why France saw few environmental demonstrations in the 1980s and 1990s.

In their cross-national comparison of new social movements, Fuchs and Rucht (1994) noted a *decrease* in 'mobilisation potential' or 'active support' in France and Italy over the 1980s in relation to political ecology and anti-nuclearism. In all five countries surveyed (France, the Netherlands, West Germany, Italy and Britain), 'the ecology movement had the largest and the anti-nuclear power movement the smallest potential' (Fuchs and Rucht 1994: 96). In addition, anti-nuclearism had the most opponents. The French case was particularly clear cut in that active support for anti-nuclearism was low, whereas opposition among the public was high – unlike other countries where opinion was either favourable or evenly split.

Thus the social context and configuration of the French green movement were untypical, and this exceptionalism proved a recipe for failure. The minority status of French anti-nuclear protesters in public opinion made it easy for the state to quell their voice. Yet because anti-nuclearism in the 1970s had formed 'the spearhead of the ecology movement' (Touraine et al., 1983: 4), its blunting led to wider demobilisation among greens. Heijden, Koopmans and Guigni (1992) found that the French environmental movement declined from around 1980. Because political ecology acquired a reputation for being an extremist and defeated cause, a paradoxical reaction set in among the French public. Although (as discussed above) environmental concerns increased in salience in the mid and late 1980s, mobilisation was limited. Consequently, changes of strategy were required within the green movement to develop its legitimacy and increase its influence.

Environmental Groups

In the 1980s the stress fell once again on non-governmental organisations (NGOs), whose activities took in a greater array of environmental issues than the highly specific anti-nuclear movement had done. In certain respects, this refocusing represented a return to environmentalism, and was accompanied by a shift in action repertoire from the 'unconventional' to the 'conventional'. Rather than colliding with the public authorities, environmental groups adopted a strategy of working with them or applying pressure. But what was the scope for moving from 'outsider' to 'insider' status within policy subsystems? To consider this question, the leading environmental NGOs in France will be reviewed, firstly in order to identify their philosophy, activities and size of membership, and secondly to investigate their ability to act as intermediary bodies between the public and the authorities, and thereby influence the policy process.

The main groups

France Nature Environnement
Formerly known as the *Fédération française des sociétés de protection de la nature*, the largest environmental group is *France Nature*

Environnement (FNE). It offers an umbrella to a vast range of national organisations such as the *Ligue française de protection des oiseaux*, the *Société nationale de protection de la nature*, the *Rassemblement des opposants à la chasse*, regional groups such as FRAPNA and SEPANSO, and numerous local affiliates.[11] Given its original emphasis on nature conservation, FNE is broadly comparable with the British National Trust (NT), with the crucial difference that it is not a significant property owner and enjoys fewer resources. A survey by IFEN (1996b: 98) of member *associations* noted that rural groups tended to be more naturalist, whilst environmentalist tendencies are stronger in the industrialised regions of Ile de France and Provence-Alpes-Côte d'Azur.

Thus as its current name suggests, *France Nature Environnement* has spread beyond nature conservation to embrace a wide range of environmental concerns, but it has always distanced itself from political ecology. Its willingness to engage in the political sphere has been limited to conventional means, such as membership of official committees. It thereby conforms to the model proposed by Rohrschneider (1991: 255): 'nature conservationists engage in political activities that do not challenge the authority of political institutions . . . [they] prefer conventional interest group modes of participation such as lobbying'. Yet in the 1990s the ability of FNE to apply political pressure was impeded by its loose, decentralised structures, and by financial and leadership crises. As FNE (1998) acknowledged, it was barely represented in Brussels and had too little involvement in international fora. Nevertheless it remains the largest environmental organisation in France, with considerable expertise in nature conservation.

WWF

Originally known as the World Wildlife Fund, the group changed its name in 1991 to the World Wide Fund for Nature. Its primary aim is nature protection, in particular to prevent the extinction of endangered animals. The appeal of such threatened species as the panda (found on the WWF's logo), the tiger and the elephant allow it to sell a wide range of consumer products in order to fund its activities. It is a highly international organisation and well established in Brussels. In addition, WWF maintains a 'commercial

---

[11] Barthélémy (1994: 91) calculated that FNE brings together upwards of 140 national and regional associations and over a 1000 local ones.

partnership' with firms, from whom it receives a third of its funding (Cans, 1994). Being heavily involved in educational programmes to increase environmental awareness, it attracts large numbers of children and young people. It has largely avoided overt political stances, and has eschewed political ecology.

Amis de la Terre

Whilst in the UK Friends of the Earth (FOE) built its reputation on 'green consumer' issues (famous campaign targets included non-returnable Schweppes bottles and chlorofluorocarbon spray cans), the French branch was unable to touch the public imagination in the same way, but has concentrated on political activism. Founded in 1971, it constituted an 'an important component of the French anti-nuclear energy movement' (Rucht, 1989: 81). Its members have included prominent political ecologists such as Brice Lalonde (politician), René Dumont (agronomist) and André Gorz (political theorist). In its early years, the group preferred electoral campaigns to lobbying, with Dumont and Lalonde standing as presidential candidates (in 1974 and 1981 respectively). Its radical politicisation, its inability to recover from the defeat of anti-nuclearism and its limited success in developing new environmental campaigns have conferred an ambiguous status on *Amis de la Terre* as being not just an environmental group but not quite an ecology party. The small French branch is buttressed by the international presence of FOE, including a permanent office in Brussels for EU lobbying.

Greenpeace

Greenpeace has done more than any other organisation to propound the mystique of the 'green warrior'. Its marine heroics have successfully attracted international media coverage. As an environmental group, it is known for its campaigns against seal culling, whaling and the fur trade, and against toxic wastes (such as the Brent Spar protest). As a pacifist organisation, it campaigns against military and civil uses of nuclear energy.

The group has repeatedly taken France as the target of high-profile campaigns, arousing the hostility of the authorities. Being unique in ruffling the national consensus on the nuclear deterrent, Greenpeace is sometimes considered 'anti-French'.[12] In 1985,

---

[12] The commentaries by Picaper and Dornier (1995) and Vermont (1997) are in this vein.

French secret service agents bombed the Greenpeace ship *Rainbow Warrior* whilst in dock in New Zealand, killing one crew member. Though condemned by governments and NGOs around the world, the attack produced little adverse impact within France.[13] During the nuclear tests initiated by President Chirac in 1995, the authorities moderated their bellicose stance to Greenpeace: the aim was to win the media war rather than eliminate the opposition.[14]

Despite maintaining a high profile in the media, Greenpeace has not prospered in France in recruitment terms (see below). Like *Amis de la Terre*, it suffered from the defeat of anti-nuclearism. Further, its strategies can only appeal to radicals but its hierarchical organisational culture runs counter to the preference for decentralisation found among French political ecologists. Consequently, the French branch is the poor relation within Greenpeace International.

The green diaspora

To enable cross-national comparisons, membership figures for the main environmental groups are provided in Tables 2.2 and 2.3. These data are presented as indicative rather than precise, since they are problematic for several reasons. Organisations do not share identical conceptions of membership; they may or may not keep accurate internal records, or be willing to disclose them. Permanent membership may, in any case, be an overstringent criterion, given a trend to more flexible and spontaneous participation. In addition, the typology remains approximate. The rubric 'conservation' aggregates a number of groups, but does not include all possible candidates, given that ownership of the federating term is itself contested. (Claims made by hunters to being conservationists are often rejected by naturalists.) Comparisons are lopsided when there are no closely equivalent organisations across nations, as is the case with the British National Trust, which alone has a membership of over two million. Nevertheless the data serve the purpose of indicating broad orders of magnitude.

Table 2.2 reveals considerable unevenness in the appeal of environmental groups across different European countries.

---

[13] Detailed coverage of the 'Greenpeace affair' can be found in Bornstein (1988).

[14] For details, see Derville (1997). Elliot (1997) provided a useful retrospective on French nuclear tests in the Pacific.

Table 2.2 Membership of main environmental groups

	France	Germany	Netherlands	Switzerland	UK
Year	1995	1995	1995	1995	1990
Conservation	850,000	155,000	725,000	100,000	3,236,000
WWF	170,500	337,500	690,000	558,000	247,000
Greenpeace	35,000	507,000	586,000	130,000	372,000
FOE	5,000	220,000	35,000	–	110,000

Source: Heijden (1997: 39), except UK: Department of the Environment (1992: 233)

Table 2.3 Changes in total membership of main environmental groups

	France	Germany	Netherlands	Switzerland
1980	508,000	62,500	421,000	218,000
1985	860,000	273,000	440,000	227,000
1989	860,000	879,000	1,060,000	258,000
1991	921,000	855,000	1,764,000	258,000
1995	1,060,500	1,219,000	2,036,000	788,000

Source: Heijden (1997: 39)

Nature organisations attract a larger number of members than 'second wave' environmental organisations (Greenpeace, FOE). This phenomenon is especially marked in France, where militant groups critical of existing institutions have enjoyed little popularity: support has gone to 'old' rather than 'new' green groups. Table 2.3 indicates that membership growth was significant over the period 1980–95, confirming the increased salience of environmental issues.

However, the range of environmental groups extends considerably beyond the 'big four'. To give a few more prominent examples, the *Conféderation syndicale du cadre de vie* specialises in the urban environment and housing conditions, the *Association française pour la protection des eaux* and *Eaux et rivières de Bretagne* lobby for improved water quality, CRII-RAD provides independent assessments of radioactivity levels in the interests of public health and safety. Thus a broader survey of groups reveals the full range of segments of environmental demand outlined in Chapter 1, which the 'big four' alone do not represent. Further, the CNVA (1992: 12) reported that in the period 1975 to 1990 some 12,800 new environmental groups and 17,300 hunting and fishing groups were set up (though no figures were collected for disappearances). According to IFEN (1996b: 97–8), five to six thousand environmental groups can be considered as active, with some 3 percent of the French population as members. On this estimate, the total membership of environmental *associations* is approximately 1.7 million. But is this spread sufficient to support the assessment made by Duclos and Smadja (1985) that groups 'are significant in the strengthening of intermediate structures in French society' or does French environmentalism remain weak, as some commentators have proposed?[15]

Environmental groups in the policy process

The preceding survey has indicated the fragmentation of the green movement, with 'old green' groups numerically stronger than 'new green' ones. Although environmentalism and ecologism have edged together over time, a fault-line persisted between many nature conservationists and political ecologists. This affected group tactics and interrelationships. Rucht (1989: 86) commented that environmental group networks in France during the 1980s, were 'highly polarised . . . have only weak ties and rarely join together for common actions and campaigns'. Whilst ideological cleavages softened over time, segmentation of environmental groups was maintained by other factors. To survive long term, groups need to preserve their identity and present clear issue appeal. Yet environmental demand is heavily conditioned by short-term, local requirements: mobilisation is frequently triggered by proposals for new roads, location of waste facilities etc.

Issue specialisation, limited size and suspected 'not in my back yard' mentalities constrain the ability of environmental groups to influence policy, by leaving them open to the charge of being unrepresentative. French politicians have often considered *associations* as

[15] For example, Bornstein (1988: 112) wrote: 'the French ecology movement has always remained small compared to its counterparts elsewhere in Europe'. From their cross-national survey, Heijden, Koopmans and Guigni (1992: 21) concluded that 'France clearly has the weakest environmental movement'.

unwanted rivals with no mandate.[16] The French establishment has likewise displayed bias against intermediary groups. The appeal to the *intérêt général* provides the authorities with a powerful rationale for selective deafness to special pleading. In principle, only the state is able to discern the collective good, whilst interest groups are held in suspicion as self-serving. In practice, the executive accommodates long-established producer groups (e.g. the agricultural lobby, the car lobby), whilst displaying ambivalence to civil society *associations*, whether it be in the domain of the environment, consumer protection or citizens' rights.

Due to this ambivalence, the participation of environmental groups has been channelled by officialdom following top-down 'rules of interaction'. The 1976 Nature Act and its 1977 implementing decree established validating procedures which confer official status on recognised groups. Known as the *agrément* ('consent'), this process selects and rewards those associations considered to be competent, credible and capable of acting in the public interest. In 1991 there were 1,434 *associations agréées* in the environmental sector (IFEN, 1996b: 99).[17] As indicated by Mény (1986, 1989b), these procedures constitute a form of state legitimisation of interest groups. A number of advantages accrue to recognised *associations*. Access to issue networks is facilitated. Environmental groups have representatives on national consultative bodies such as the *Conseil national de la protection de la nature*, *Conseil national de la chasse et de la faune sauvage*, *Conseil supérieur de la pêche*, *Commission supérieure des sites*, *Conseil d'information sur l'énergie nucléaire*, *Conseil supérieur des installations classées*, *Comité national de l'eau* and the *Conseil national du bruit*. The major official forum for environmental issues is the *Haut comité de l'environnement*, which was reformed in 1976 and 1982 to ensure wider representation and includes twenty representatives of environmental groups; it is consulted on all major matters of environmental policy. Groups are also represented on committees at local/regional levels. Though often found wanting in practice, the 1983 *loi Bouchardeau* on public inquiries into major construction projects allowed associations to put forward counter-proposals to the inquiry inspector. Recognised groups also have the right to defend

---

[16] See Palard (1981: 221–2).

[17] Perceived laxity in the attribution of the *agrément* lead to its revision in the 1995 *loi Barnier* (Blatrix, 1997). However, Greenpeace France did not receive the *agrément*, and outside the whaling issue, was not invited into official consultation procedures (Chartier, 1997: 27–8).

community interests before the courts. Finally, the *agrément* can lead to the allocation of public subsidies. FNE has been the environmental organisation to receive most aid, accounting for 1.2 billion francs from a total income of 6 billion (Debièvre, 1993). However, the legitimisation process also institutionalises *associations* and conditions their development path. 'Insider' status improves the standing of the groups concerned and encourages professionalisation, but limits independence. As Hayward (1984: 98) pointed out: 'why some groups are selected for privileged 'insider' status depends . . . upon their willingness to act as (junior) partners'. The FNE, which has representatives on a range of committees at national and subnational levels, constitutes a case in point. Because of its dependence on subsidies, its statutes can only be changed by ministerial agreement (Chibret, 1991: 729). Since *associations* provide ideas, expertise and commitment, they help compensate for lack of resources of the Environment Ministry. Indeed, Lascoumes (1994: 193) considered that in the 1980s, environmental groups formed the Environment Ministry's 'actual field services'.[18] The disadvantage is that they transform from pressure group into 'pressured group' (Hayward, 1984), resulting in a complex web of dependence and interdependence between *associations* and state organs.[19]

In revisiting the insider/outsider model of interest group mediation, Maloney, Jordan and McLaughlin (1994) stressed the differences between consultation, negotiation and bargaining. Consultation with public authorities represented only a limited form of inclusion in the policy process, with no guarantee of influence on outcomes. Groups involved in negotiation and bargaining could influence policy, but this higher level of access implied having resources to exchange, and a willingness to exchange them. In addition, public policy making is often marked by bureaucratic incrementalism. However, groups which propound radical change, who have few resources (whether financial, specialist knowledge or public support) or whose identity would be compromised by perceived 'collaboration' remained outsiders. In consequence, the fact of being an insider or outsider depended not just on ascription of status by central authorities, but also on the characteristics and strategy of the groups concerned. Radical ecology groups constitute a case in point, since their marginality to the

[18] 'les véritables services extérieurs'.
[19] For further examples, see Spanou (1991: 188–225).

policy process is the result not just of exclusion by the French state, but arises due to a lack of resources to exchange and their reluctance to enter into 'bargainable incrementalism'. Indeed the costs of involvement in issue networks for even the large mainstream groups are considerable. The FNE (1998) complained of the weaknesses of its position: its representatives operated on an unpaid basis, made considerable commitments of their time, but their recommendations were rarely followed, leading to frustration and funding shortages. Moreover, the consultation committees of the French government listed above serve an advisory function but do not have decision making powers (Spanou, 1991: 161). Dominated by the authorities, undermined by lack of resources and members, the influence of French environmental groups on the policy process has been modest.

Conclusions

The particular segmentation of environmental demand in France is the product of the structuring of public opinion, the configuration of the national green movement, and the positioning and strategic interplay of NGOs. The radicalisation of environmental concern in the 1970s – via anti-nuclearism and its attack on the state – led to major setbacks for the green movement once its 'spearhead' was broken. This outcome conditioned the development path of the movement in the early 1980s, temporarily depressing public environmental interest to lower levels than in neighbouring countries. The aftermath of anti-nuclear defeat reinforced the fragmentation of French environmental groups, with ecology groups put into near quarantine. In consequence, environmental concern in France has displayed an uneven configuration in terms of (a) the weighting accorded to specific segments of demand and (b) their variation in intensity over time. It is this lumpiness and diffusion – rather than indifference – which has characterised French public attitudes to environmental issues and dampened the direct impact of civil society on the conduct of public policy.

Opinion polls reflect the mood of the public, but have provided relatively few signals for policy, which requires declarations of means and ends. The exception is the preoccupation with pollution control, where state agencies have been expected to respond proactively. However, the French green movement cannot point to a major victory over the public authorities, nor is any national policy switch attributable to the activities of environmental groups. But as *associations* swelled in numbers, some were co-opted by the executive into consultation procedures. Mainstream groups characterised by an 'old green' outlook fitted relatively easily into a system of state sponsorship and policy incrementalism, but rarely mobilised the resources to significantly alter policy. The major 'losers' were the political ecology groups, whose anti-nuclearism remained unpopular. Once both unconventional action and pressure group activity revealed their limits, a new strategy became necessary for ecologists. As these 'new greens' were intensely political, a feasible extension of their strategy was to enter electoral contests, win access to government and change policy from within. Rather than use a 'lever against the State', the political ecologists would seek to operate the levers of state.

3

GREEN PARTIES IN THE FRENCH POLITICAL SYSTEM

Introduction

Because green parties have played a significant role in increasing the political salience of the environment, this chapter explores their impact. The entry of French greens into the party system proved a logical development. It offered hope for the politically minded radicals who suffered from the defeat of the anti-nuclear protest movement, the limited size and legitimacy of environmental groups and their restricted lobbying potential. Conservatives too came to realise that the favourable climate of public opinion towards the environment represented an under-mobilised resource. For radicals, mainstream politics offered the means to effect significant change by rewriting the 'rules of interaction'. For conservatives, more limited and defensive objectives were desirable. The challenge for all was to engineer a change in the 'systemic governing coalition' (Sabatier, 1986) capable of attaining their priorities.

The evolving green political spectrum raises conceptual and terminological issues. The term 'greens' is frequently used to designate left-wing radicals. However, this usage runs the risk of glossing over a number of distinct positions. 'Political ecologists' do indeed recommend radical social and political change. Yet the ranks of the greens also include reformists or 'environmentalists' who seek incremental improvements in environmental performance. The latter have sometimes aligned themselves with the left, and sometimes avoided any political positioning at all. In addition, right-wing currents exist which have reworked environmental concerns within a restrictive ideological framework, notably by stressing conservation of the countryside and rural traditions such as hunting.

To provide a wide-ranging survey, this chapter will analyse the French parties which express these contrasting strands of environmental thought, and consider their impact on the polity. The first section discusses their aims and distinctive features, and situates their development in the context of party system change in France. A second section analyses and explains their electoral strategies and performance during the 1980s and 1990s, whilst a third section examines the specific question of why political ecologists have experienced difficulty in converting electoral capital into policy capability.

Environmentalism and the French Party System

In the rapidly changing social, economic and electoral context of the recent period, the French party system has evolved considerably. In the 1970s, the so-called *quadrille bipolaire* developed in which the *Rassemblement pour la République* (RPR) and the *Union pour la démocratie française* (UDF) drew together on the right, whilst the *Parti socialiste* (PS) and the *Parti communiste français* (PCF) put forward a common platform of the left, leading to a PS–PCF coalition government over 1981–4. During the 1980s, links between erstwhile allies slackened due to policy disagreements and internal dissensions. At the same time, social change and the disillusionment of voters with the performance in office of both left and right led to the loosening of traditional loyalties based on class and ideology. The main parties of government – the PS, PCF, RPR, UDF – suffered a significant decline in popularity. In the parliamentary elections of 1981, 1986, 1988, 1993 and 1997, the incumbents were in each case ousted. Further, the share of first-round votes going to the four major parties fell from 95 percent in 1981 to 63 percent in 1997. In consequence, polarisation in terms of twinned blocks gave way to a multi-party system in the 1990s.[1]

---

[1] For analysis of recent developments in the French party system, see Szarka (1999) and Hainsworth (1999).

These developments created opportunities for a range of new entrants. As discussed in Chapter 2, the origins of French political ecology lie in the 'new social movements' of the late 1960s, particularly environmentalism, anti-nuclearism and pacifism, but also regionalism, feminism and civil rights movements. However, hunt lobbyists and some nature conservationists felt they had no common cause with these movements. Heterogeneity of aims resulted in disagreements and disorganisation even among political ecologists. Early electoral participation was on an ad hoc basis, with *les Amis de la Terre* putting forward several candidates in 1973, whilst ephemeral groupings such as *Ecologie 78* and *SOS-Environnement* appeared in the 1978 parliamentary elections.[2] Structured parties, however, did not emerge until the 1980s, with the rise in salience of the environment, the decline of the main parties and an increased willingness among greens to compete in elections. Within these general trends, highly specific political outlooks and electoral trajectories exist, and these will now be explored in detail.

Les Verts

The *Verts, confédération écologiste – parti écologiste* was established in January 1984 and has become the leading political ecology party. Its desire was to 'break the mould' (Hainsworth, 1990) of French politics and create a radically new kind of party politics. As its full title indicates, it federated a number of politically orientated ecology associations that had existed for over a decade.[3] The process of creating a national federation was fraught, due to a strong desire by activists for local autonomy, and because of the opposition of many sympathisers to the green movement's institutionalisation within mainstream politics. Traditionalists and naturalists considered that party political activity was irrelevant to scientific ecology, whilst radicals harboured reservations about representative democracy due to their 'left-libertarian' orientation.[4] The emphasis on grass-roots democracy was accompanied

[2] Analysis of the early years can be found in Bridgford (1978), Gurin (1979), Boy (1981), Parkin (1989: 89–110) and Jenson (1989).

[3] For fuller histories of the *Verts*, see Sainteny (1992: 11–25) and Prendiville (1994: 35–47).

[4] As noted by Kitschelt (1993: 95) 'the common denominator of the Green phenomenon is the quest for a new 'paradigm' of democratic political action'. Kitschelt (1990) developed the notion of 'left-libertarianism'

by fear of recuperation by the political system and, in the initial years, by a reluctance to compete for power.[5]

The organisation and culture of the *Verts* has been marked by the party's libertarian values and social movement history. The stress on bottom-up decision making and on written procedures gives the party a complicated structure. For the *Conseil national inter-régional* (CNIR), 75 percent of representatives are elected by regional associations, and 25 percent directly by the national assembly. In turn, the CNIR elects an executive body (the *collège exécutif*). In principle, the *Verts* do not have a party leader, but four spokespersons of equal rank (although one of them proves predominant in practice), with the prerogatives of the central caucus being circumscribed by grass-roots democracy. As the *Verts* are opposed to the institutionalisation of power, the professionalisation of leading politicians has been resisted. With its strong base and weak centre, the complex organisation of the *Verts* has hampered the party's effectiveness.

Its electoral programmes have stressed the underlying problems of contemporary society. Environmental degradation is considered not as a by-product of deficient technology, but as the consequence of the dysfunctional nature of 'productivism', of the dash for growth and of the global market economy. The *Verts* have sought solutions not in technical measures but in broad-based political renewal. Since 1986, the party's platform has reiterated the halting of the French nuclear electricity programme, the need to switch to rail, and the importance of work-sharing. It has rallied to the theses of sustainable development, stressing altruistic North-South relations. It is particularly critical of the concentration of power in the hands of elites, proposing greater democratisation, proportional representation and regionalisation. The party's European stance has been in a state of flux. During the 1992 referendum, the leadership and membership were split on the Maastricht treaty (Rüdig, 1996: 268). The party embraces the values of 'cultural liberalism' (Grunberg and Schweisguth, 1990), including greater civil rights for women, homosexuals, ethnic minorities, and legalisation of soft drugs. A desire to radically

---

[5] A 1978 tract by the *Mouvement écologique* stated that: 'Les écologistes sont sceptiques et critiques à l'égard du pouvoir politique. Ils ne croient pas au pouvoir. Ils ne pensent pas qu'il soit possible de changer la société et encore moins de changer la vie "du haut du pouvoir". Rien de fondamental ne se règle par le pouvoir' (quoted in Journès, 1982: 51–2).

change 'the rules of interaction' at all levels has been a leitmotif of the *Verts*. Their 1995 presidential candidate – Dominique Voynet (1995) – campaigned for a Sixth Republic in France, a new constitution for Europe and a reformed World Trade Organisation (WTO). Yet despite their ambitions, for many years the *Verts* avoided party alliances and stressed political non-alignment, practising advocacy *without* coalition (discussed below). Whether radical ecologists have the support and the capacity to effect major change will be a central issue in this chapter.

Génération Ecologie

The creation of *Génération Ecologie* (GE) in 1990 by Brice Lalonde provided voters with a reformist variant of political ecology. Competition between GE and the *Verts* constituted an instance of the division of ecologists between 'realists' and 'fundamentalists' seen in a number of countries.[6] The difference between these two orientations for Prendiville (1992: 450) was that: 'they [the *Verts*] wish to politicise ecology by creating a social movement before taking power. Lalonde has an ostensibly different ambition in that he prefers to ecologise politics by participating in the governmental process as soon as possible'. Lalonde's political career illustrates this preference: after involvement in the 1968 demonstrations, he became a militant in the new Left during the 1970s, head of French Friends of the Earth, presidential candidate in 1981, a leader of the *Entente radicale et écologiste* (ERE) in the 1984 European elections, and Environment Minister in the Rocard government (1988–91).

Whilst its political programme had similarities to the *Verts*, GE acquired a reputation for moderation and readiness to share power. Both parties stressed global environmental strategies, worksharing and a deepening of democracy, but GE accepted French nuclear power and was favourable to the Maastricht Treaty. Lalonde had criticised as unrealistic the refusal of political alliances by fellow ecologists as early as the 1978 parliamentary elections.[7] His tactical pragmatism was illustrated by his presence in the left-wing Rocard government and by his willingness to conduct a study on international 'ecological dumping' for the right-wing

---

[6] For detailed comparisons, see Hoffmann-Martinot (1991) and Doherty (1992).
[7] See Journès (1982: 61–4).

Balludur government in 1993. In 1991, Lalonde supported military intervention to end Iraq's occupation of Kuwait – unlike the *Verts*. Indeed, the latter disliked him for his opportunism, willingness to compromise and electoralism. In putting up rival lists to the *Verts* in the 1984 and 1994 European elections, Lalonde in each case split the ecology vote and prevented the election of any candidates (discussed below).

GE was dominated by the personality of Lalonde and interpreted as a vehicle for his ambitions. In contrast to the *Verts*, the party was characterised by its strong centre and weak base, although its members repeatedly called for more democratic procedures. Sainteny (1998a) noted that in its early heyday, GE could recruit established politicians since the charisma of its leader and the benefits of his holding office translated into electoral gains and political remuneration through appointment to the chairs of public sector organisations. But, confronted by a collapse in the party's votes and frustrated by a leader who was declining in influence and leaning to the right, in 1994–5 prominent personalities such as Noël Mamère and Yves Piétrasanta left GE, first to found their own parties, and later to join the *Verts*. What remained of GE shifted from being a centre-left party in 1990–3 to one of the centre right in 1995, when Lalonde supported Chirac in the presidential elections (leading to yet more resignations). By the 1997 parliamentary elections, the lack of voters, the haemorrhage of its activists and the sidelining of Lalonde led to the virtual disappearance of GE.

Nouveaux Ecologistes

This small and short-lived party provides an example of the political opportunism manifested by right-wingers seeking to exploit the electoral popularity of environmental issues. It came to prominence in the 1993 parliamentary elections when it fielded some 500 candidates on a platform of opposition to cruelty against animals, especially vivisection. The party's organiser – Bernard Manovelli – had led a chequered political career, having been linked to various far-right movements. Holliday (1994: 73) suggested that Manovelli had founded the party 'chiefly to take advantage of the new law on state funding of political parties'. Public funding was estimated to be worth 10 million francs per year for parliament's five-year term (*Le Monde*, 25.3.1993: 8). Subsequently the *Verts* took Manovelli to court for electoral irregularities. Despite its misleading name, the

Nouveaux Ecologistes demonstrated how short-term political capital could be made from 'traditional' environmental positions. Although the party soon folded, the animal rights agenda has been popularised by the foundation set up by Brigitte Bardot, who has shown sympathies for the far-right *Front National*.

Chasse, Pêche, Nature, Tradition

Led first by André Goustat and since 1998 by Jean Saint-Josse, *Chasse, Pêche, Nature, Tradition* (CPNT) is largely an emanation of the hunt lobby. It is hostile to European nature directives, and seeks to loosen the regulatory framework related to hunting. However, the hunt lobby's recourse to the ballot box has necessitated an extension of its issue appeal. In its 1989 campaign, CPNT claimed that 'hunters and anglers are the main defenders of the environment'.[8] In the 1990s it repositioned itself as a bastion of French rural traditions in a context where farmers and rural residents felt alienated by national and European policies. The gradual increase in its vote (discussed below) indicates that tapping into a construction of the environment as 'managed rurality' (see Chapter 1) remains popular, particularly in the agricultural and hunting communities of southwest France. CPNT seeks to further its agenda by putting pressure on the parties of the mainstream right, whilst violently opposing the *Verts*. This strategy demonstrates the extent to which environmental issues have lent themselves to polarisation along the left-right axis.

In summary, the spread of green parties has reproduced at the political level the segmentation of environmental demand noted in previous chapters. Animosity has deepened between environmental reactionaries, such as CPNT, and political ecologists. Within the latter, a split manifested between radical and reformist preferences. Reformist environmentalism, as embodied by *Génération Ecologie*, responded by and large to quality of life issues and environmental protection, whilst radical ecology (with the *Verts*) proposed fundamental socioeconomic change. As a result of these differences, conflict between these various orientations became endemic, as will be seen by analysis of electoral politics.

---

[8] 'Chasseurs et pêcheurs sont les premiers défenseurs de 1'environnement' (quoted in Alphandéry, Bitoun and Dupont, 1991: 31).

Performance in the Electoral System

A myth of recent years is that the French polity is impervious to new politics: hence green parties are supposedly doomed to failure. In this mould, Prendiville (1994: 110) claimed that 'the political system in France is relatively closed which means that any discourse which is not sufficiently integrated into it has little chance of being heard by the general public'. Similarly, O'Neill (1997: 190) stated that 'the Fifth Republic confronts minor, let alone new, parties with formidable obstacles . . . this classic adversarial system provides only a minimal role for minor parties such as the Greens'. However, these interpretations merit closer investigation. Firstly, if a 'classic' adversarial system functioning to exclude small parties exists anywhere, it exists not in France but in Britain, with its majoritarian voting system contested by two parties of government. Secondly, whilst the French party system is undoubtedly adversarial and tends to the bipolar, it is also a multi-party system in which new parties regularly appear and prosper. The rise of the *Front National* has been one of the most visible examples. Thirdly, it is important to distinguish within the political system three related but distinct arena – electoral mechanisms, the party system and coalition government. Degrees of success or failure of small parties arise from their strategies across all three arena, rather than from the supposedly 'inevitable' effects of any one.

Electoral mechanisms have a complex impact on party performance. Variability in outcomes is influenced by the nature of the election and the voting system applying. Six types of election exist in France: municipal, departmental, regional, parliamentary, presidential and European. Municipal, regional and European elections are conducted under proportional representation (PR). Presidential, parliamentary and departmental elections are conducted under two-ballot majority voting systems. PR can favour small parties, whereas 'first past the post' systems marginalise them. At the same time, the French two-ballot system provides its own openings. Voters in the first round can express their real choice with little fear of a wasted vote, so allowing new entrants to acquire toeholds which in time can be extended. The second round allows for three-way contests, but is usually a run-off between two mainstream candidates, encouraging electors to exercise a tactical vote (*vote utile*). At this stage, the party system, and relations within it, becomes paramount: voters assess politicians on proximity to their own ideological allegiances and policy positions, and regularly switch their vote either to support a cognate candidate or block the path of an unacceptable one. This structural feature encourages alliances between parties, offering a premium to compromise in an otherwise highly conflictual system.

In consequence, the French political system offers many points of access with barriers to entry of varying heights. The combination of a fluid party system, hybrid electoral system and frequent recourse to coalition government produces a mercurial 'free market' for votes and favours in which parties and politicians can made quick returns, but in which political capital can be squandered or snatched away. The decline of the four main parties has led to electoral instability and forced them to look beyond their 'traditional' alliances (namely that of the PS and PCF on the left, and the RPR and UDF on the right). This has opened greater opportunities for new entrants than their voting percentages might suggest. However, the peculiar feature of recent years has been that few new entrants were both acceptable as allies and willing to form alliances. After a period of courting the *Front National*, the main parties of the right placed it in political quarantine in the late 1990s. Meanwhile, in the late 1980s, the policy of the *Verts* was to refuse alliances. Thus the underlying problem for new parties is not the supposed impermeability of a monolithic political system, but the complexity of a heterogeneous one. With a choice of greasy poles to climb, the requirements are for numerous candidates and militants, versatility of political skills, extensive logistic and financial support, and consistency of endeavour. At a secondary level, these requirements push for institutionalisation and professionalisation of parties, and alliance building. Despite an initially low level of adaptation to these requirements, French greens have attained a measure of success, by learning to exploit second-order elections and form electoral alliances.

Second-order elections

The term 'second-order elections' refers to contests held at local, regional and European levels. These do not impact on the national legislature and executive. Because less is at stake, French voters are more relaxed about 'experimenting' with new entrants.

In European elections, voters rarely mobilise for or against European policies, but tend to register a protest vote against incumbent parties at member-state level or express nationalist preferences (Portelli, 1994; Buffotot and Hanley, 1995). This provides an invaluable opportunity for small parties, particularly in those countries (including France) where European elections are contested under PR. The first breakthrough for the *Verts* came in 1989, when they polled over 10 percent of the vote and returned nine MEPs. Ten years later, the outcome was almost identical (see Table 3.1). The key determinant of these outcomes was the fact that only one key ecology party contested the elections.[9] By contrast, in both 1984 and 1994 political ecologists were divided between two lists, the Lalonde groupings (ERE, GE) on the one hand, and the *Verts* on the other. Because of the split vote in those years, it proved impossible for either party to cross the 5 percent threshold and win seats in the European parliament.

CPNT, champion of the hunt lobby and of 'managed rurality', gradually improved its performance. In 1989, it fought on an anti-Brussels ticket, questioning the necessity of pan-European nature protection legislation, and receiving 4.1 percent of votes. In 1994, its vote slipped marginally to 3.95 percent, due to the large number of rivals also on an anti-European slate. In 1999, the parlous state of the mainstream right and renewed mobilisation (catalysed by restrictions on hunting and widespread discontent in rural France) allowed CPNT to emerge with 6.77 percent of votes. It won seats for the first time, and returned six MEPs.

Four main lessons emerge from European elections. Firstly, new parties can acquire credibility and develop political competence.

Table 3.1. Results of political ecologists in European elections

Year	Party/Lists	Votes cast	% of total vote	Seats
1979	Various	888,134	4.4	0
1984	ERE	654,444	3.3	0
	Verts	680,086	3.4	0
1989	Verts	1,919,797	10.6	9
1994	GE	391,905	2.01	0
	Verts	575,247	2.95	0
1999	Verts	1,701,713	9.71	9

[9] In 1999, Waechter's *Mouvement écologiste indépendant* (MEI) scraped 1.53 percent of the vote. The MEI had seceded from the *Verts* in 1994 after the abandonment of the non-alignment strategy.

Secondly, the electoral polls of French ecologists, which have oscillated up and down by around a million votes, lend support to the thesis of an 'issue-attention cycle' (Downs, 1972), in which public interest in the environment periodically increases and decreases. Thirdly, parties can easily squander their capital. If no French MEP was elected on an ecology list in 1984 or 1994, the collapse was due solely to infighting and the inability to agree on the common list that was essential given the nature of the election and the size of electorate. Fourthly, a united 'environmental' vote is now an impossibility. Not only did disagreements between 'realists' and 'fundamentalists' impede alliances among political ecologists, but their lack of a common cause with the rural conservatism of CPNT ruled out a 'grand coalition'. Indeed, due to their opposing views on hunting, CPNT and the *Verts* have become implacable enemies, particularly at local levels.

The first elections to regional councils under universal suffrage took place in 1986, subsequent to the decentralisation reforms of 1982–3. Being less constrained by the political status quo and fought under PR, regional elections have offered new openings. They have an added attraction to ecologists as a meaningful arena since their ideology has stressed regionalism. Although in the 1986 regional elections, the *Verts* as a political party were too new and disorganised to make more than a marginal impact,[10] the 1992 results were a major triumph for French ecologists (see Table 3.2). Together the *Verts* and GE attracted nearly 3.5 million electors (15 percent of votes cast), the best ecology result to date. The election was contested under optimal conditions. The environment remained a salient issue. The reputation of the Socialists had suffered in office from policy failures and scandals, leading some Socialist voters to lodge a protest vote with non-right-wing parties. In multi-constituency regional elections, the presence of two parties enlarged the appeal of political ecology in qualitative and quantitative terms. This was because both radical and reformist variants were on offer, whilst together two small parties could ensure greater coverage of the great number of seats to be contested than one alone. The *Verts* were dismayed, however, to find that GE, the new arrival on the scene, won more votes than them. Moreover their voter percentage dropped three points relative to 1989, with about a quarter of their 1989 vote transferring to GE

---

[10] For details, see Sainteny (1987).

(Sainteny, 1993: 56). The better performance of GE resulted from a combination of moderate policies and more experienced personnel. A survey by Boy, Roche and Le Seigneur (1992) showed that 44 percent of the successful candidates of GE had previously held an elected position, compared to only 21 percent of the *Verts*. In the 1998 regional elections, the *Verts* did not put up independent candidates, but campaigned jointly with the *gauche plurielle* (discussed below).

Meanwhile CPNT received 2.6 percent of votes in 1992 and returned twenty-nine regional councillors, rising to 2.7 percent and thirty-one respectively in 1998. Although these were small proportions of total votes, they were concentrated in a limited number of councils and allowed its representatives to put pressure on the mainstream right.

In municipal and departmental elections, small parties are beset with practical difficulties. Firstly, a very large number of candidates is required. This has revealed a 'structural weakness' (Villalba, 1996a: 82) within the *Verts*, as they have found it impossible to put forward candidates across France. In relation to those municipalities which they contested, their poll was approximately 8 percent in 1989 and 5 percent in 1995, with 1,369 and 1,226 candidates returned respectively. Secondly, these elections involve a high degree of personalisation: incumbents often enjoy a notoriety premium, whereas new parties usually lack *notables* (prominent local politicians). Departmental elections favour established politicians, as votes are cast for named individuals and not party lists. Thus in 1992 GE did better than the *Verts*, since it had recruited a number of established politicians who achieved reelection. But with only four departmental seats won in 1992 and eight in 1994, ecologists had to decide which elections to prioritise. Further, they had to capitalise on their breakthrough in second-order elections and make an impact at national level.

Table 3.2 Results of political ecologists in regional elections

Year	Party	Votes cast	% of total vote	Seats
1986	Various	658,949	2.4	5
1992	GE	1,744,350	7	
	Verts	1,666,161	6.7	
	Others	184,916	0.7	
	Total	3,595,427	14.4	213

First-order elections

Although French national elections apparently exclude new players, the reality is more complex. Contesting the presidency may seem pointless for small parties when 'defeat' is certain, but participation itself confers benefits. Requiring only one candidate and campaign trail, the presidential election is the least onerous contest in terms of personnel and logistics. A party having a charismatic candidate can offset organisational hurdles encountered elsewhere in the political system. For fledgling and cash-starved parties, the presidential campaign is a cheap and efficient way to access the national media (especially television), to publicise ideas and engage public opinion. It can be cost-effective, since candidates are eligible for refund of campaign expenses from the public purse.[11] Further, the fact of surmounting a 5 percent threshold of votes constitutes a form of democratic legitimisation and offers a springboard to inclusion elsewhere in the political system. Championing issues for national debate counts towards political agenda-setting and puts pressure on subsequent executives. Finally, minor candidates have regularly been co-opted into subsequent coalition governments.

Political ecologists have contested all four presidential elections since 1974. In proportional terms, Brice Lalonde's performance in 1981 was the most successful, with voter percentages slipping since (see Table 3.3). The 1974 Dumont campaign enjoyed the benefit of freshness, but had no electoral momentum behind it. The 1981 elections promised better, although gains were constricted by the closeness of the contest between the incumbent President

Table 3.3. Results of ecology candidates in presidential elections

Year	Candidate	Votes cast	% of total vote
1974	Dumont	337,800	1.3
1981	Lalonde	1,126,254	3.9
1988	Waechter	1,149,642	3.8
1995	Voynet	1,010,681	3.3

[11] Candidates polling less than 5 percent of votes were eligible for reimbursement of up to 7.2 million francs; those polling over 5 percent for up to 32.4 million, whilst second-round candidates were reimbursed 43.2 million. See Cole (1995).

Valéry d'Estaing and Socialist challenger François Mitterrand, which drew 'new left' votes away from the ecology candidate, Lalonde. The 1988 candidate, Antoine Waechter, was respected as a naturalist but considered a lacklustre campaigner. In 1995 three ecologists – Lalonde, Waechter and Voynet – initially proposed to stand.[12] Only Voynet could collect the necessary 500 endorsements from elected politicians. However, the infighting confirmed the negative image that hung over from the 1994 European elections. In a context where the electorate was more concerned with employment than the environment, Voynet's campaign barely stabilised the green vote.[13] But her major success lay in opening a dialogue with Lionel Jospin of the Socialist Party, which lead to an electoral alliance.

Despite the poor outlook in parliamentary elections (due to the 'first past the post' system), in 1997 political ecologists won eight seats, with roughly half their votes of 1993 when they won none (see Table 3.4). Analysis of the two elections will clarify this counter-intuitive outcome. In 1993, the alliance between the *Verts* and GE allowed ecologists to put forward candidates throughout France. In the context of a landslide in seats for the mainstream right, their alliance received 7.6 percent of votes, with the total green vote being 10.8 percent. Thus far from being a 'disastrous performance' (Shull, 1996: 235), the green vote in a 'first-order' election had more than doubled on its previous best and held up well in relation to the 'second-order' elections of 1989–92. Yet the ecologists were bitterly disappointed that voting forecasts of 15–20 percent translated into a poll that only allowed two candidates into the second round – Dominique Voynet (*Verts*) and Christine Barthet (GE) – neither of whom won a seat. Explanations included inexperience in major elections, overconfidence due to high polls, poor communication of programme and policy objectives, ambiguity over political positioning with contradictory statements made by Lalonde and Waechter,[14] and voter confusion caused by large numbers of 'independent' green candidates.

The disappointment led to a power struggle within the *Verts* and a major shift in strategy. In the late 1980s and early 1990s, with Antoine Waechter as de facto leader, the *Verts* were unwilling

---

[12] For details, see Roche (1995).

[13] For study of candidate interactions in the 1995 presidential election, see Szarka (1996).

[14] Roche (1993: 39–40) provides illuminating examples.

Table 3.4. Results of ecology parties in parliamentary elections

Year	Party	Votes cast	% of total vote	Seats
1978				
1st round	Various	621,000	2.2	0
1981				
1st round	Various	270,792	1.1	0
1986				
Single round	Various	393,041	1.2	0
1988				
1st round	Various	77,795	0.3	0
1993				
1st round	*Verts* & GE	1,944,674	7.6	0
1997				
1st round	*Verts*	910,253	3.6	7
	other Green	677,997	2.7	1

to entertain an alliance with a major party, campaigning on a 'neither left nor right' ticket (discussed below). Wresting dominance from the Waechter group in late 1993, Dominique Voynet's faction pushed for the abandonment of the non-alignment strategy. Gradually, the *Verts* came round to the idea of alliances within the left – firstly with fringe parties and in 1997 with the Socialist Party. Realism had entered the political analyses of the leadership: ecologists could not push forward their agenda by self-imposed isolation. Further, an alliance with the Socialists was no longer the poisoned chalice refused in 1993, when the electoral fortunes of the Socialists were at their low point. By 1997, the Socialist Party were again a credible political force. Yet although the right-wing Juppé government was deeply unpopular, the elections proved too close to call. Thus the Socialists' strategy was to garner the widest vote possible by entering into a multipartite coalition of the left – called the *gauche plurielle* – embracing communists, left-wing radicals, the *Mouvement des Citoyens* and the *Verts*.

This alliance explains the successful outcome of the 1997 parliamentary elections. The Socialists' agreement to stand down in a number of constituencies in favour of the *Verts* provided the opening for victories otherwise impossible under the majoritarian system. Not only did ecologists enter parliament for the first time, but the electoral pact extended to the distribution of ministerial portfolios. Voynet was able to exchange the political capital accrued in 1995 for the post of Minister for the Regions and the Environment. In spite of the large fall in electoral support in the mid-1990s, the 1997 outcome gave the *Verts* the possibility of making a policy impact at national level.

Converting Electoral Capital into Policy Capability

Just as the transition from a loose green movement to structured ecology parties proved fraught, so the translation of electoral victory into policy results was to prove limited. In participating in representative institutions, ecologists have implicitly accepted the 'democratic premise'. Hofferbert (1974: 234) defined this concept as 'the assumption that the behaviour of those in office is somehow a response to or at least conditioned by the desires or needs, or both, of those who participated in one way or another in electing them'. Thus the 'democratic premise' postulates the existence of clear links between the preferences of their electors and the issue appeals and subsequent policy initiatives of elected politicians. However the multi-dimensionality of environmental demand has resulted in problems for political ecologists. In seeking to attain their ambitious policy goals, the *Verts* have been hindered by three major obstacles: the ambiguities of their political positioning, their shifting and uncertain electoral base, and their limited influence as partners in government.

The ambiguities of political positioning

In the early years of the green movement, ecologists situated themselves off the right-left continuum, favouring a posture of non-alignment. Key slogans were '*ni droite, ni gauche mais devant*' (neither left nor right but ahead), '*faire de la politique autrement*' (conduct politics differently) and '*être ailleurs*' (being elsewhere). Lalonde (in Ribes, 1978: 28) had stated that 'in ecology, the notions of right and left have no relevance',[15] and he used this dictum to justify working with *both* the left and the right in the 1990s. But, as developed by the *Verts* between 1986 and 1993, it meant working

---

[15] 'En écologie, ces notions de droite et de gauche ne sont pas pertinentes.'

with *neither* the left nor the right. Developed under Waechter's leadership, the non-alignment posture in this period proved a distinctive characteristic of the *Verts*.

However, tension arose between their need to operate *inside* the French party system – based on left-right polarisation – whilst propagating an ideology that situated them *outside* it. Working within the party system involved the development of positional issues, coalition building and the targeting of adversaries. Although the electoral programmes of French ecologists called for major socioeconomic reform, they were light on precise environmental policy propositions, whilst offering no indication of how they would build alliances to attain their goals. This opened the door to parties such as CPNT and the *Nouveaux Ecologistes* to target positional issues, such as management of the countryside and animal rights. Moreover, CPNT was able to lobby for precise objectives in a manner which has largely eluded the *Verts*. Thus a hidden cost of non-alignment was that the *Verts* gifted away political capital, and left themselves exposed on their right flank. They suffered thereby the disadvantages of political polarisation without benefiting from its advantages. Advocacy without coalition proved an untenable posture which undermined their electoral support and political influence.

Non-alignment proved a futuristic strategy which anticipated an end to traditional left-right polarisation and a reform of the party system. In the 1986–93 period, electoral flux and the decline of the major parties of government suggested that a breakdown of the existing party system might be imminent. Were a broad realignment to occur, the *Verts* could expect to be in the vanguard, with the opportunity to change the political 'rules of interaction' within their grasp. But to date, left-right polarisation in France has not disappeared. At most, it had its sharp edges blunted by three phases of powersharing (*cohabitation*) between President and government of opposing political parties.[16] Moreover, after the massive victory of the right in 1993, the *Verts* found themselves firmly in the opposition. With their own survival under threat, they were forced to adapt to the party system, rather than change it. Meanwhile, the decline of the PS, the marginalisation of the PCF and the collapse of GE reconfigured the political space on the

---

[16] President Mitterrand and the Chirac government, 1986–8; President Mitterrand and the Balladur government, 1993–5; President Chirac and the Jospin government, 1997 to the time of writing.

left. These developments led to the abandonment by the *Verts* of the *'ni gauche, ni droite'* positioning in winter of 1993 and the subsequent *rapprochement* with parties of the left. But the protracted phase of hesitation postponed their entry into government. It also confused their electoral appeal.

The problems of a volatile and heterogeneous electorate

Whilst awareness of environmental issues increased among the general public (as seen in Chapter 2), the green electorate remained small, indicating the limited extent to which parties were able to convert environmental concern into actual votes. Extrapolating from elections over a decade, the core vote can be estimated as lying between 5 percent and 8 percent of the electorate, with protest votes and floating voters swelling the poll cyclically. The green vote has often been a negative vote expressing dissatisfaction with the political system or governing parties, rather than a positive vote expressing commitment. In the early 1990s, about half of votes for ecology parties were based on a positive preference (Sainteny, 1993: 51). The remainder was made up of protest voters of two kinds, one group voting against the established political system, the other protesting against the Socialist Party. Over the 1985–95 period, increasing numbers of voters grew disaffected with the Socialist President and government from whom they had expected radical change but got little. These *déçus du socialisme* progressively abandoned the PS. In the 1989 European elections, almost half of the green vote came from former Socialist voters, with almost no defections from centre or right-wing parties (Rüdig and Franklin, 1992: 43). The strong showing in the 1992 regional elections was likewise explained in terms of a vote against the incumbent Socialist government, with 50 percent of votes for GE and 43 percent of votes for the *Verts* being motivated by dismissal of other options available (Bréchon, 1992; Sainteny, 1993). Exit polls in 1992 revealed that 35 percent of Green voters situated themselves in the centre and 34 percent on the left (Sainteny, 1993: 51). Further, a third of those surveyed declared no interest in politics (Bennahmias and Roche, 1992: 172–3). These data point to the existence of several subgroups of ecology voters: the left-leaning, the moderates of the centre, a pool of the politically apathetic (the so-called *marais*), and a small proportion of 'non-aligned' voters. Moreover, ecology parties were unable to attract *right-leaning* voters: the emergence of CPNT capitalised on this inability.

Yet voters are prone to return to their roots, as in the 1994 European election, where Boy and Roche (1995: 104) noted a correlation between losses in the ecology vote and gains for mainstream left candidates (Rocard, Chevènement, Tapie). In addition, electoral support has tended to be for environmentalism rather than for ecologism. In 1992, 56 percent of voters for the *Verts* and GE were swayed by propositions on the environment but only 15 percent were attracted by a desire to reform society (Sainteny, 1993: 58). Due to these multiple ideological fractures, the green electorate is hard to mobilise and retain, and difficult to respond to once in office.

In brief, popular opinion and the ballot box had given a mandate for reform, but not for radical change. The green vote in France has been characterised by its complementary nature: it supplemented rather than replaced. It was complementary firstly in adding an environmental dimension to policy concerns. Secondly, a vote for green parties at regional and European elections did not always carry over to departmental, parliamentary or presidential elections. By applying a two-tier voting strategy, voters indicated policy preferences and applied pressure to incumbents, but their vote often constituted a temporary substitution rather than a lasting commitment. The final aspect of the complementary vote was that polls from the early 1990s onwards showed that a majority of French people wished to see ecologists as a component of government (Sainteny, 1993: 62). However, the role of junior partner has sat ill with the vast aims of the ecologists.

Towards new policy ambitions?

Entry into the *gauche plurielle* in 1997 represented a new stage of the ecologists' learning curve, born of the realisation that the green movement itself was plural, not pure. Party strategy had to reflect this if the 'democratic premise' was to be respected. Ironically, the ensuing 1997 coalition with the left meant that the radical *Verts* took over the reformist strategy of GE.

In participating in coalition government, the new dilemma for the *Verts* was to reconcile their role as a communicator of new values with the capacity to manage the policy process. The weakness of the party in the latter respect had been acknowledged by militants (Bidou, 1985: 79; Voynet, 1994). Though elected to a number of local and regional offices, only the *Verts* in the Regional Council of Nord-Pas de Calais had had the opportunity to develop 'hands-on' competence.[17] The shortage of political and administrative experience presented difficulties for Voynet in nominating her ministerial private office, with her first *directeur de cabinet* being designated by Prime Minister Jospin (Villalba, 1997: 131). Measures to address these problems by offering training programmes had been slight (Villalba, 1996b), partly because of limited resources but also because of resistance to professionalisation.

Since acceding to coalition government, the *Verts* have become ambivalent over their identity,[18] but have grown acclimatised to the culture of power acquisition. They have competed for influence with the *gauche plurielle*, seeking to establish themselves as the senior coalition partner of the Socialists. In the 1999 European election, the party came out three percentage points and three MEPs ahead of the PCF, which had previously counted as the second largest member of the government coalition. In subsequent weeks, the *Verts* called for a ministerial reshuffle and more posts, trying to extend the principle of proportional representation in elections to proportionality in attribution of ministerial portfolios, but with limited success. Moreover, the *Verts* have sought to broker a range of policies extending beyond the environment: they have been strong supporters of the Jospin government's measures for a 35 hour week and equal political opportunities for women. By the year 2001, the extension of the issue appeal of the *Verts* depended on the success of initiatives with no direct bearing on environmental questions.

Conclusions

Green parties have proved to be a paradoxical and chameleon political force. In the 1990s, they achieved a moderate level of electoral success, becoming a potential source of exogenous change in environmental policy subsystems. Because the French political system is relatively open, green politicians have participated at almost every level of the polity – with mayors, representatives in the councils of the *départements* and the regions, members of

---

[17] For details see Holliday (1993) and Boy *et al.* (1995).

[18] Speaking about the *Verts*, Voynet commented (*Le Monde*, 9.1.2000: 6): 'nous sommes à moitié un parti de gouvernement et à moitié un parti de contestation'.

parliament and MEPs. Even presidential elections, though impossible to win, furthered the green cause by providing a national forum at modest cost and a trampoline to ministerial office.[19] Thus greens have been able to make a direct impact (by entry into executives at local, regional and national levels) and an indirect impact (by a measure of agenda setting and influence on other parties). These developments give the lie to two received ideas. Firstly, contrary to the complaints of many ecologists, the French political system does not automatically exclude small parties from political life, or even from the legislature and the executive. Secondly, green parties have demonstrated sufficient longevity and impact to constitute more than 'a flash in the pan', even if their future prospects remain uncertain.

Yet political contests also revealed the major limitations of the green cause. Firstly, the mirage of a 'soft consensus' on the environment evaporated. Although green parties paid a high price at the ballot box for disunity, their internal disputes reproduced deep cleavages within environmental opinion. In conditions of fluid electoral competition, the distinct outlooks of individual parties resulted in an extreme form of political deconstruction of the environment, namely the fragmentation of the environmental cause. Secondly, like iron filings in a magnetic field, its shattered fragments reconfigured along the existing political poles, traditionalists being drawn to the right, political ecologists to the left. In the process, the political fortunes of each strand came to mesh with those of the mainstream, leading to relations of dependence. Thirdly, the abandonment of the 'non-alignment' stance by the *Verts* acknowledged that reconfiguration of the French party system could not be expected in the near future.

The realist acceptance of the political status quo drastically curtailed the ambitions of the ecologists. Although the aim of changing the 'systemic governing coalition' (Sabatier) had been attained, the minority position of ecologists constrained the pursuit of radical options. With the *Verts* party leader in ministerial office, calls for unconventional protest and civil disobedience remained muted, although the grass-roots maintained ambivalence over party institutionalisation. Access to the corridors of

---

[19] A total of four Environment Ministers have been former presidential candidates, two from the ecology movement (Lalonde, Voynet) and two from beyond (Crépeau, Bouchardeau).

power highlighted the constraints imposed on a small party. On the one hand, human resources and executive competence were in short supply. On the other, the ability to set an agenda was constrained by variability in the salience of environmental issues, the changing political climate and electoral cycle, the problems of power broking in coalition government, and the existence of established policy communities. These factors highlight two distinct challenges facing new parties: one is to make an electoral impact, the other is to make a policy impact.

In practice, converting a measure of success in the political system into an impact on the policy process proved fraught. The wider programme of the *Verts* was not abandoned, as will be seen later (particularly in Chapter 9). But top-down policy making involved entry into the logic of 'bureaucratic incrementalism' which resulted from the functioning of institutions, the need for interaction with a wide range of powerful actors, and ensuing policy compromises. Each of these aspects will be developed in turn, with the next chapter discussing the development of institutional capacity for making environmental policy.

4

THE FRENCH POLITY, INSTITUTIONAL CAPACITY BUILDING AND THE ENVIRONMENT

Introduction

Given the significant, if waning, importance of the 'statist' paradigm in France, this chapter considers environmental policy systems from the perspectives of national and subnational authorities, assessing their prerogatives and limitations. The building of institutional capacity in the environmental domain involved development of both the will and the means to effect policy change along three interrelated dimensions: the political, the administrative and the territorial. The chapter's first section deals with the growth of *political capacity* within central government. It explores the development of the French Environment Ministry, the flux to which it was subject over two decades and its relative stabilisation during the 1990s. The aim of analysing its role and key policy orientations will be to gauge the strength of political will to develop environmental policy. The second section considers the extension of *administrative capacity* by reviewing the internal organisation of the Environment Ministry, its regional field services and its main agencies. Here the concern is with means, namely the question of whether the scale of resources committed to environmental policy has been adequate to the tasks enjoined. The third section reviews the development of *territorial capacity.* It focuses on the shifting relationships between central and subnational tiers of government, on the change process brokered by the 1982–3 decentralisation reforms, and its effects on the distribution of environmental competencies. Because environmental policy implementation requires cooperation between politicians and administrators at national, regional and local levels, the exploration of their particular responsibilities and their interrelationships pulls together the themes of political will and practical means.

The Development of Political Capacity

The creation of an Environment Ministry in France was the result of an evolutionary process whose origins can be traced to developments both within France and on the international scene. Increasing concern over industrial pollution and the disappearance of nature led to new laws in the 1960s on water, air and national parks. Yet though the powerful Agriculture Ministry included a department for Nature Protection, specialised environmental agencies did not exist. Various interministerial committees related to the environment were progressively set up, with the most significant work being done by the *Délégation à l'aménagement du territoire et à l'action régionale* (DATAR), which had responsibility for regional planning and development. In 1969 it produced an influential policy document entitled *Cent mesures pour l'environnement* ('one hundred measures for the environment'). Meanwhile the environmental movement was making an international impact. Capacity to deliver environmental policy remained weak, however, prompting a number of countries to establish specialised institutions. The US Department of the Environment was set up in 1969, which was also European nature protection year. In France, President Pompidou set up the Environment Ministry (EM) in January 1971.

The Environment Ministry in search of a direction

The brief of the EM consistently proved problematic. After difficult negotiations,[1] it took over attributions from five different

---

[1] See Poujade (1975: 31–3).

ministries (industry, agriculture, transport, culture, regional development). It was charged with overview of national and regional parks, policy coordination regarding water resources, the licensing of hunting and fishing, the protection of national monuments and the inspection of *installations classées* (licensed industrial sites). As stated in the Ministry's founding decree, its remit was 'to reconcile economic growth and the improvement of the quality of life',[2] but a credibility gap quickly opened up between grandiose intentions and the capacity to act, leading the EM to be nicknamed as the *Ministère des Beaux Parleurs* (Ministry of Fine Speakers). Numerous obstacles lay in the EM's path. Its objectives were vague and its resources minimal. The long-established and more powerful ministries who had lost some of their attributions to the EM considered it a rival, and were prone to undermine it. The right-wing politicians in power tended to view the green movement as a hotbed of subversion, and considered the Environment Ministry as ideologically suspect on a priori grounds. Consequently it was kept at arm's length from the sensitive domain of energy policy, against which ecologists had mounted a frontal attack (see Chapter 2). In the face of these challenges, the EM proved weak and unstable. Its early history can be summarised as firstly, a struggle for survival, secondly, confusion over identity and thirdly, uncertainty over role.

In the 1970s and 1980s, the EM traversed vicissitudes which almost led to its disappearance. As indicated in Tables 4.1 and 4.2, it lost its independent status at several points, being merged with larger ministries such as Culture or *Equipement*.[3] Each phase of merger put a question mark over the EM's capacity to act. Further, the environmental portfolio was usually given to a little-known politician of low ministerial rank. Poujade and Carignon were nominated *ministres délégués* (Junior Ministers) in 1971 and 1986 respectively, and the even lowlier rank of *secrétaire d'Etat* was repeatedly assigned.[4] Only in the 1990s was a full cabinet position

---

[2] 'concilier dans un même mouvement la croissance économique et l'épanouissement de la qualité de la vie'.

[3] For a detailed account, see Prieur (1994).

[4] As relatively junior appointments, *ministres délégués* and *secrétaires d'Etat* do not attend meetings of the *Conseil des Ministres* unless an issue within their remit figures on the agenda. By contrast, in Britain the title 'Secretary of State' designates a high-ranking Cabinet member: Secretaries of State for the Environment have included Michael Heseltine and John Prescott, both deputy party leaders.

consistently allocated. Frequent changes of minister also contributed to lack of direction. In addition, several incumbents had little or no party base to draw on for parliamentary support. Between 1981 and 1992, none of Mitterrand's appointees were members of the Socialist Party. Three of them (Crépeau, Bouchardeau, Lalonde) had stood against him in a presidential campaign and counted as erstwhile rivals. Voynet, the leader of the *Verts*, was a minor candidate in the 1995 presidential election where Chirac and Jospin were pitted against each other, but in the 'cohabitation' period after 1997, she was given a enlarged portfolio to include regional planning (see Table 4.3). Due to these factors, the EM has in general been a marginal institution, headed by a low-ranking minister with little political clout.

The frequent changes in the EM's name – indicated in Tables 4.1

Table 4.1 Environment Ministers during the Pompidou and Giscard presidencies

Year	Prime Minister	Title of Environment Minister	Name of Minister
1971	Chaban-Delmas	Ministre délégué auprès du PM, chargé de la protection de la nature et de l'environnement	Robert Poujade
1973	Messmer	Ministre de la protection de la nature et de l'environnement	Robert Poujade
1974	Messmer	Ministre des affaires culturelles et de l'environnement	Alain Peyrefitte
1974	Chirac	Ministre de la qualité de la vie	André Jarrot
1976	Chirac	Ministre de la qualité de la vie	André Fosset
1976	Barre	Ministre de la qualité de la vie	Vincent Ansquer
1977	Barre	Ministre de la culture et de l'environnement	Michel d'Ornano
1978-81	Barre	Ministre de l'environnement et du cadre de vie	Michel d'Ornano

Sources: Assemblée Nationale (1996a, 1996b)

and 4.2 – reveal the influence of rival constructions of the environment and contributed to a lack of clarity over the ministry's identity. In its first incarnation, the emphasis was placed on nature conservation. But as the economic crisis of the 1970s deepened, the stress fell on the quality of life of French citizens. Later an ill-defined link was made with culture, before switching to an emphasis on living conditions (*cadre de vie*). In the 1980s, concern over natural disasters and technological hazards led to the assignation of a separate portfolio for these, but in the 1990s they were brought back within the EM. These repeated hesitations over the EM's remit suggest that the executive had no clear idea of what it was committing itself to.

Ambiguity over the EM's identity led to uncertainly over its role. Established ministries – such as Agriculture or Industry – are considered to be *ministères régaliens*, a telling phrase which evokes the sovereign prerogatives associated with central government. In practice, this means that they combine the functions of policy development, the preparation of legislation, a spending programme along with, where appropriate, the enforcement of a regulatory framework. In French terminology, this type of institution has been labelled as an *administration de gestion*, indicating the managerial nature of its remit. On the other hand, an *administration de mission* serves analytic, proselytising or coordinating functions,[5] and is akin to a task-force in that its organisation is neither rigid, hierarchical nor permanent.[6] As noted by Poujade (1975: 27), President Pompidou envisaged the EM as 'un ministère de coordination, d'impulsion, de mission', placing the stress on interministerial cooperation and raising public awareness. Consequently, few 'management' functions were initially attributed, few resources were deemed necessary and the EM found itself hemmed into narrow policy areas by well-endowed ministries. Being short of political influence and resources, Environment Minister Poujade (1975) ruefully dubbed his office as *le ministère de l'impossible*. For him, the EM portfolio proved a 'mission impossible' because it lacked the means to be a *ministère de gestion* nor yet had the legitimacy to be a *ministère de mission*. If in its infancy the EM represented an example of symbolic politics, the question was whether it would remain so.

[5] Pisani (1956) originated these terms. Their development was traced by Autexier and Heppenheimer (1971).

[6] For discussion of the implications, see Dupuy and Thoenig (1983: 183) and Rigaud and Delcros (1984: 147–213).

Table 4.2 Environment Ministers during the Mitterrand presidencies

Year	Prime Minister	Title of Environment Minister	Name of Minister
1981	Mauroy	Ministre de l'environnement	Michel Crépeau
1983	Mauroy	Secrétaire d'Etat auprès du PM, chargé de l'environnement et de la qualité de la vie	Huguette Bouchardeau
1984	Fabius	Ministre de l'Environnement	Huguette Bouchardeau
		Secrétaire d'Etat auprès du PM, chargé de la prévention des risques naturels et technologiques majeurs	Haroun Tazieff
1986	Chirac	Ministre délégué auprès du Ministre de l'équipement, chargé de l'environnement	Alain Carignon
1988	Rocard	Secrétaire d'Etat auprès du Premier Ministre, chargé de l'Environnement	Brice Lalonde
		Secrétaire d'Etat, chargé de la prévention des risques naturels et technologiques majeurs	Gérard Renon
1989	Rocard	Secrétaire d'Etat, auprès du Premier Ministre, chargé de l'environnement et de la prévention des risques naturels et technologiques majeurs	Brice Lalonde
1990	Rocard	Ministre délégué auprès du Premier Ministre, chargé de l'environnement et de la prévention des risques naturels et technologiques majeurs	Brice Lalonde
1991	Cresson	Ministre de l'environnement	Brice Lalonde
1992	Bérégovoy	Ministre de l'environnement	Ségolène Royal
1993	Balladur	Ministre de l'environnement	Michel Barnier

Table 4.3 Environment Ministers during the Chirac presidency

Year	Prime Minister	Title of Environment Minister	Name of Minister
1995	Juppé	Ministre de l'environnement	Corinne Lepage
1997	Jospin	Ministre de l'aménagement du territoire et de l'environnement	Dominique Voynet

The Environment Ministry in search of a policy

The constraints imposed on the EM in fighting for survival, resolving its identity dilemma and carving out a role meant that during the 1970s and 1980s environmental policy was developed in reactive mode, being dominated by rushed responses to unexpected crises. Only in the 1990s did ministers pursue a proactive agenda.

Poujade targeted two core components of environmental demand for rapid action. By the start of 1974, a nature conservation act had been prepared (Poujade, 1975: 147), with a bill on industrial pollution control having a similar genesis. These proved to be important damage-limitation initiatives, and will be discussed in Chapters 6 and 7. But the EM's work was quickly overtaken by external developments. The oil crisis of the mid-1970s exposed structural weaknesses in Western economies, leading to recession and major imbalances of payments. Almost from the EM's inception, the objection arose that environmental protection was an expensive irrelevance in times of economic crisis. In reaction, the ministry put forward a policy discussion document (Gruson et al., 1974) which provided an economic rationale for environmental protection, so setting en example that became a tradition. In a context of oil and raw materials price hikes, the need to reduce excessive consumption – *la lutte contre le gaspillage* – offered a composite policy platform. The Gruson report's insistence on the husbandry of rare resources was in tune with the 'limits to growth' thesis (Meadows et al., 1972). In stressing clean production and highlighting the problems of intensive agriculture, it anticipated some of the theses of ecological modernisation.[7] Proposals such as increased flexi-time and distance working were ahead of their times, but recommendations for reductions in energy use (by improved building insulation and better public transport) were speedily implemented. The concern with excessive consumption also led to the 1975 act on waste – though it related mainly to disposal, doing little to encourage recycling.

However, a general pattern emerged whereby the influence, salience and cabinet ranking of the EM rose and fell in line with swings in electoral support for political ecologists (Sainteny, 1998b). During the Giscard presidency (1974–81), the right-wing executive's concern with the environment proved intermittent and opportunist. With the 1978 parliamentary elections expected to be closely run and with ecology candidates increasing the salience of green issues, Giscard's 'Charter for the Quality of Life' proposed a council for information on the nuclear electricity industry, an agency to combat atmospheric pollution, environmental impact studies, public hearings for major infrastructural proposals, as well as an annual statement on the state of the environment in France. However, once the right won the 1978 elections, the environment was again assigned a low priority.

This pattern repeated itself after the 1981 presidential and parliamentary elections. Despite their electoral promises to review their predecessor's nuclear energy policy, the largely Socialist executive disappointed ecologists by the decision to pursue it. Only limited signs of commitment towards the environment emerged. The Josselin report (1983: 6) was critical of environmental policy in the 1970s due to 'its lack of continuity, its over-restrictive conception of the environment, inadequate resources, its emphasis on repair rather prevention and weaknesses in research and training', and proposed greater democratic participation, a better urban environment and improved risk and pollution prevention. However, in the 1983 cabinet reshuffle the EM was downgraded, with Huguette Bouchardeau nominated as *secrétaire d'Etat*. Her arrival in office coincided with a public outcry over the illegal dumping in France of barrels of the toxic chemical dioxin, subsequent to the 1976 explosion in Seveso, Italy. The search for the barrels monopolised her time, and revealed a

---

[7] Discussions of 'ecological modernisation' can be found in Weale (1992), Spaargaren and Mol (1992) and Mol (1997).

culture of secrecy around environmental risks which even a government minister found hard to penetrate.[8] The reactive policy mode continued after the right's narrow victory in 1986 and the formation of the Chirac government. The environment portfolio was entrusted to a Junior Minister, Alain Carignon, with a reduced budget and housed within the *Ministère de l'Equipement*, which was generally associated with the promotion of new construction projects rather than the protection of the environment. When in 1986 a cloud of radioactive fallout from the Chernobyl explosion passed over Europe, Carignon simply denied that France was affected – in the face of scientific evidence to the contrary. After the *Assemblée Nationale* voted itself rights to receive accurate information on nuclear matters, the parliamentary decision was abrogated by executive order, perpetuating the culture of secrecy.

By the end of the 1980s, policy developments in neighbouring countries, the regulatory output of the European Community and an increase in the scope of international agreements opened out the environmental agenda. In 1988, Mitterrand was reelected President, followed by a narrow victory for the left at the parliamentary elections. The new Prime Minister, Michel Rocard, proved supportive of environmental issues, the profile of the French EM was gradually raised and a period of proactive policy making began. He appointed Gérard Renon as Junior Minister for the prevention of major natural and technological hazards, a decision which responded to public alarm over the Seveso dioxin barrels, Chernobyl nuclear fallout and severe flash floods in France. Moreover, the appointment of Brice Lalonde as Junior Minister for the environment meant that for the first time a political ecologist was co-opted into government.[9]

Emulating countries such as the Netherlands, Denmark and Canada, Lalonde drew up a national 'green plan' in 1990.[10] It listed the shortcomings of French environmental policy over the previous twenty years as unambitious targets, excessive state centralisation, a weak and marginalised EM, and a narrowly French (rather than international) view of environmental policy making.

[8] For details of this episode, see Denis-Lempereur (1983), Bouchardeau (1986), Vesseron (1988) and Nicolino (1990).

[9] Rocard and Lalonde belonged to the same political generation, with common roots in the *Parti Socialiste Unifié*.

[10] For details, see Theys and Chabason (1991). For cross-national studies of green planning, see Dalal-Clayton et al. (1996), and Jänicke and Jörgens (1998).

It recommended new legislation, greater decentralisation and cooperation between the central state and local authorities, more democratic procedures, and a more international outlook. Hatem (1991) criticised the plan for its lack of clear priorities, evasiveness over costs, and continued stress on the central state. Innovations such as the inclusion of environmental rights within the constitution and environmental tax reforms were absent. Yet despite its limitations, the plan was distinguished by its long-term commitments. As regards policy outputs, new water and waste acts were put forward during Lalonde's period in office, and a reorganisation of the EM and its field services effected (discussed below). Although Lalonde outlined a ten-year horizon for policy development, political deadlines were far shorter. With the popularity of the Socialists plummeting, he resigned in 1992 to improve the prospects of his political party – *Génération écologie* – in the 1993 parliamentary elections (discussed in Chapter 3).

The electoral calendar and outcomes subsequently brought choppiness to environmental policy making. His successor, Ségolène Royal, had barely a year in office. At the 1992 Rio Conference, she promised French support in combating the enhanced greenhouse effect, greater protection of biodiversity and forests, and increased development aid (Royal, 1994). However, practical measures were modest, if sometimes spectacular, such as the unilateral halting of imports of waste from Germany. In 1993, the victory of the right led to the formation of the Balladur government, with Michel Barnier appointed as Environment Minister. Policy proved a mixture of the reactive and the proactive. In the wake of the 1992 recession, the Balladur government put forward a limited reflation package, which included 1.3 billion francs for rehabilitation of polluted sites and burial of EDF's power cables. It authorised 500 million francs of spending on the urban environment, and allocated 200 million francs for the creation of 'green' jobs (Ministère de l'Environnement, 1994). Barnier's measures were largely piecemeal, such as the establishment of *Operation Gardes de l'Environnement* within each *département* to police the natural environment, the introduction of 'green national service' (permitting conscripts to work on environmental projects), and the 1994 national debate on energy sourcing (twenty years after the executive's decision in favour of nuclear energy). His major contribution lay in pushing forward Agenda 21, notably through the 1995 *loi Barnier* (discussed in Chapter 9).

After Chirac's victory in the 1995 presidential elections, Prime Minister Juppé appointed Corinne Lepage to the environment portfolio. Unlike her predecessors, she was not a career politician, but a prominent environmental lawyer. Her office was marked by two legislative initiatives. The 1996 Air Quality Act responded to new problems of atmospheric pollution and is discussed in Chapter 8. A bill to institute a *code de l'environnement* was intended to reinforce French environmental law, since its application was acknowledged to be insecure. However the bill was mauled during its parliamentary reading, and the early dissolution of April 1997 placed it in limbo. Having little backing from Prime Minister Juppé, and being a co-opted specialist rather than an elected representative, Lepage found that she lacked the political power base necessary for ambitious reform.[11]

The surprise victory of the left in May 1997 opened the way for Dominique Voynet, leader of the *Verts*, to be appointed as *ministre de l'Aménagement du territoire et de l'Environnement*.[12] The enlargement of the portfolio to include regional planning in principle gave greater capacity to formulate effective policy. Further, unlike Lepage, Voynet had political experience and capital. But backed by only eight green MPs, opportunities to direct policy proved limited. The electoral pact signed between the *Verts* and the Socialist Party provided a contractual basis for the support of Prime Minister Jospin, but within the government coalition strategies of cooperation and persuasion were of the essence (see Chapter 3). But in comparison to her predecessors, Voynet was better placed to formulate a proactive policy, launching an ambitious bill on sustainable development (discussed in Chapter 9).

In summary, the highest levels of the French executive have rarely demonstrated political leadership in environmental matters, at best preferring the surrogate of co-opting ecologists into government. Ministerial appointments have often been short-lived and expendable, since they were rarely political 'heavyweights' either in electoral terms or within the ministerial hierarchy. Nevertheless, over the long term, commitment to the environment was asserted by the stabilisation of the EM and an increase in its political capacity, marked by a clarification of its remit and a degree of proactive policy making in the 1990s.

---

[11] A sense of frustration is evident throughout her memoirs: see Lepage (1998).

[12] This combined portfolio had already been recommended by Poujade (1975: 271).

The Growth in Administrative Capacity

In this section we review the administrative arrangements for the implementation of environmental policy, which are largely organised within and around the Environment Ministry.

The organisation of the Environment Ministry

To improve effectiveness, the structure of the EM, the organisation of its field services and its relationships to environmental agencies have repeatedly been modified.[13] By the 1990s, three directorates corresponding to the core remit of the Ministry had assumed a certain longevity – the Directorate for Nature, the Directorate for the Prevention of Pollution and Risks, and the Directorate for Water. In turn, field services and specialised institutions report to these directorates, though associated environmental agencies enjoy considerable independence.

From originally having no field services, the EM now has two sets. In his 'green plan', Environment Minister Lalonde made provision for the establishment in each of metropolitan France's twenty-two regions of a *Direction régionale de l'environnement* (DIREN) to represent the EM in the domains of nature conservation, architecture and town planning, and to exercise a coordinating role regarding water. The aim was to bring an environmental dimension to infrastructural and housing projects, as well as consolidate water and waste management. Further, a part of the field services of the Industry Ministry was given responsibilities for environment protection, and placed under the co-jurisdiction of the Environment Ministry, being relabelled as the *Directions régionales de l'industrie, de la recherche et de l'environnement* (DRIRE). As shown by Lascoumes and Le Bourhis (1997), the EM's field services developed the capability to operate in both a 'vertical' mode (collecting and disseminating information for planning purposes, implementing specific programmes) and a 'horizontal' mode (acting as a coordinator of public and private actors). This expansion in institutional capacity was to prove crucial in enforcing the widening raft of European legislation.

---

[13] An extensive literature exists on the development of France's environmental administration, notably Vallet (1975), Le Prestre (1981), Romi (1990a, 1992, 1997), Billaudot (1991), Laurent (1996) and Prieur (1996).

However, the impact of the reform was limited by several factors. Unlike other ministries, the EM did not have its own *grands corps* to champion policy. Its field services were small, with no organisation at the departmental level, making its officers dependent on colleagues attached to other ministers, such as those in the *Directions départementales de l'agriculture et de la forêt* (DDAF) and *Directions départementales de l'équipement* (DDE). Further, the division of labour between the DIREN and the DRIRE consecrated a long-standing political deconstruction of the environment into 'natural' and 'industrial' segments. In practice a number of resource utilisation issues – such as water – cut across this divide, but institutional compartmentalisation has hampered a transversal response.

The tendency to segmentation is evident too in the proliferation of consultative bodies and environmental agencies which report to the EM. Over a hundred interministerial committees exist. Advisory bodies include the *Conseil national de l'eau, Conseil national du bruit* and the *Haut Comité à l'environnement*. The EM oversees the *Office national de la chasse* (ONC) and the *Conseil supérieur de la pêche* (CSP), which have an active role in the management of hunting and fishing. The six *Agences de l'eau*, corresponding to the major river basins in France, are the leading institutions for water management. The *Agence de l'environnement et de la maîtrise de l'énergie* (ADEME) – the Environment and Energy Efficiency Agency – has branches in each of France's regions and levies a range of environmental taxes on industry, conducts research and sponsors investment in cleaner technology. Collecting statistical information on the environment, the *Institut français de l'environnement* (IFEN) was set up in 1991 as the French counterpart to the European Environment Agency. It relies on a vast range of research institutions, including the *Centre national du machinisme agricole du génie rural, des eaux et des forêts* (covering agriculture, water and forests) and the *Institut national de la recherche sur l'environnement industriel et les risques* (INERIS) which specialises in industrial hazards caused by pollution, explosion and fire. Along with the Industry and Research Ministries, the EM oversees the *Agence nationale pour la gestion des déchets radioactifs* (ANDRA) which is responsible for the management of nuclear waste, a rare instance of EM involvement in the sensitive area of nuclear energy.

The resources of the Environment Ministry and environmental agencies

Representing only a tiny fraction – 0.1 percent – of state spending (see Table 4.4), the resources directly available to the EM have been remarkably slim. As a proportion of government spending, its budget actually fell between 1980 and 1989, one indication of the limited priority accorded to the environment at that time. In the 1990s, the EM was better endowed, allowing incumbent ministers to report year-on-year proportional increases, but this has always to be related to the low base for comparison. Reasons advanced to explain increased environmental spending include tighter legislation, more environmental charges and public pressure (Ministère de l'Environnement, 1994: 31). The trend to improved resourcing continued under the Jospin government, with a 15 percent increase in the budget of the Environment Ministry programmed for 1999, taking the environment budget to 2.1 billion francs; with a further 1.8 billions for regional development, allowing 500 new posts to be created (*Le Monde*, 9.8.1998: 5).

It is instructive to place the EM's resources in the context of total public spending on the environment. In 1994, its budget was 1.6 billion francs, whilst environmental spending by other public bodies was some 63.6 billion francs, of which 49.5 was by local

Table 4.4. The budget of the French Environment Ministry

Year	Total state budget	Environment Ministry budget	as % of state civil budget
		millions of francs	
1980	562,450	629	0.11
1983	933,485	861	0.09
1985	1,059,623	817	0.07
1987	1,137,827	818	0.07
1989	1,420,364	882	0.06
1991	1,041,731	1,270	0.10
1993	956,787	1,614	0.16
1994	991,332	1,653	0.16
1995	1,268,613	1,756	0.13
1996	1,299,618	1,751	0.13

Source: Prieur (1996: 34)

authorities, indicating their key role.[14] The difference between EM and local authority funding is explained partly by environmental spending in other central ministries, but relates mainly to the activities of public sector environmental establishments and agencies. Table 4.5 gives a breakdown of the financial and human resources of the latter. The four largest – the *Agences de l'eau*, the ADEME, the ONC and the CSP – have independent revenues levied on their respective constituencies, namely water users, industrialists, hunters and anglers. The combined resources of the *Agences de l'eau*, the ADEME and the ANDRA stood at 12.7 billion francs in 1996 – roughly seven times the EM's budget – and are used to control pollution and manage waste. In contrast, spending on nature conservation by the *parcs nationaux* and the *Conservatoire de l'espace littoral et des rivages lacustres* (CELRL) was approximately 0.02 billion francs. In addition, the total employment in these agencies stood at 5,627, roughly double that of the EM itself which in 1995 counted some 2,300 employees, plus 743 in the DRIRE and 1,127 in the DIREN. This allocation of resources, with a much smaller share going directly to the EM than to its subordinate agencies, points up ambiguities over the capacity of the Environment Minister to see through policy reform which falls within the remits of its agencies. Because the *Agences de l'eau* and the ADEME both make charges and dispose of the proceeds,[15] they enjoy considerable autonomy from the EM.[16] The division of the environmental administration between the EM and a series of semiautonomous agencies prevents a concentration of resources and power.[17] Although this compartmentalisation arose for

[14] Data are from the internet site of the *Ministère des Affaires étrangères*, September 1995.

[15] Further details are provided in Chapters 7 and 8.

[16] In the 1990s, the EM had an arm's length relation to the ADEME which, in terms of resources and visibility, was close to constituting a rival. Consequently, Environment Ministers sought to influence the ADEME by the nomination of its chief executive.

[17] The ADEME combined three previously separate agencies: the *Agence française pour la maîtrise de l'énergie*, the *Agence nationale pour la récupération et l'élimination des déchets* and the *Agence pour la qualité de l'air*. However, an institution of the breadth of the Environment Agency of England and Wales (which brought together the National Rivers Authority, Her Majesty's Inspectorate of Pollution and the former local government Waste Regulation Authorities) was deliberately avoided. The inclusion of the *Agences de l'eau* in the ADEME was contemplated but ruled out, apparently on the grounds that the new institution would be too powerful (Pissaloux, 1995: 254).

Table 4.5. Financial and human resources of French environmental agencies

Agency	1995	1996	No. of employees (1996)
	millions of francs		
Agences de l'eau	10,260.3	11,376.4	1,321
ADEME	863.9	1,047.5	576
ONC	530.3	663.2	1,632
CSP	252.2	247.0	784
ANDRA	242.0	247.0	474
INERIS	119.7	125.8	407
IFEN	2.0	2.0	25
Parcs nationaux	15.0	15.0	372
CELRL	4.4	5.7	36
Total	12,289.8	13,729.6	5,627

Sources: République française (1996: 38; 1997: 42)

historical reasons, for example with the *Agences de l'eau* preceding the EM, its preservation appears to be politically motivated and designed to prevent 'empire building', and it raises questions over the effectiveness of environmental institutions, to which the case study chapters will return.

In summary, by the 1990s the responsibilities of the EM had stabilised to constitute what can now be termed 'classic' environmental policy: namely, nature conservation, industrial pollution control, and water and waste management. Consequently Chapters 6 to 8 will develop these domains in detail. Administrative capacity was increased to allow the ministry to play a two-fold role. Within its core competencies, it worked in a broadly 'managerial' mode, whilst in relation to cross-cutting issues, it coordinated the inputs of other actors. Thus over time the antinomy between the roles of *administration de gestion* and *administration de mission* gave way to a degree of complementarity. In appearance, the EM followed the top-down mode of policy making of a traditional *ministère régalien*. The normative, regulatory framework developed in European legislation likewise encouraged a 'command and control' policy style. But in reality the central authority was largely bereft of the resources to administer policy, being dependent on the cooperation of a range of private and public actors. We next turn to the key set that is formed by subnational authorities.

The Reform of Territorial Capacity

Consideration of environmental policy at local levels requires treatment of the competencies of subnational government, and examination of the interlocks between political and administrative channels in the field.

The French polity has often been characterised as having a unitary, highly centralised state, benefiting from considerable financial, administrative and human resources, and which historically proved capable of ambitious entrepreneurship. But by the 1970s, the 'strong state' thesis was already being disputed as interventionism reached its limits and the dysfunctions of centralisation became more apparent. Thus when Grémion (1976: 208) analysed 'la balkanisation de l'administration territoriale', he noted extensive competition between local politicians and civil servants, rather than a homogenous state bloc. In the 1980s and 1990s the powers and prerogatives of the central state declined further due to four main factors: the scale of public debt, the Maastricht convergence criteria for European monetary union, the accelerated integration of the national economy into a global order, and government reform at local and regional levels. For present purposes, it is this latter development which is of most relevance.

The tradition of 'crosswise regulation'

French local administration traditionally comprised two tiers: the *communes* (based on old parishes), and the *départements* (established by Napoleon). Local and national policy making was interconnected along two channels: one political, drawing its legitimacy from universal suffrage, the other administrative, based on technical expertise. In descending hierarchy, the political channel was formed by President, parliament, the *Conseil général* (*département* level) and the *Conseil municipal* (*commune* level). The administrative channel was formed by central government ministers, high ranking civil servants in Paris, and the departmental *préfet*. Like Siamese twins, the two channels were joined at either end in that ministers were generally (but not exclusively) elected politicians, whilst the key figure in the *commune* was the mayor, who was both an elected representative *and* an agent of the state. In principle, once parliament had passed enabling acts, major regulatory decisions were made in central government ministries and took the form of instructions communicated by ministerial circulars. These were transmitted to the *préfets* who were enjoined powers of policy implementation, since they exercised local oversight of central ministry field services such as the DDAF or the DDE.

The existence of two vertical channels, one political, the other administrative, each connecting the centre with the periphery, and each having its own hierarchy, raised questions about the prerogatives and influence of each, as well as about their interrelationships. Political sociologists such as Crozier and Thoenig (1975) and Thoenig (1978) theorised these issues under the concept of *régulation croisée,* arguing that regulation occurred crosswise, that is across channels. Thus where competition over resource allocation (notably central state funding) produced blockages either among elected officials (such as mayors voicing parochial interests) or administrators (bearing on a policy sector), powerful individuals from one channel could exercise adjudication and coordination over the other channel by drawing on personal networks. In the case of outstanding politicians (the *notables*), this was achieved by the accumulation of offices (*cumul des mandats*) at local and national levels, giving access to a plurality of political spheres. Conversely, administrators could appeal to the prefect or the heads of the *grands corps* (*Corps des Mines, Corps des Ponts et Chaussées* etc.) to which they belonged in attempts to encourage 'Paris' to resolve the conflict in their favour. The beauty of this 'honeycomb' system was that it generated interdependence, produced a series of checks and balances, and gave prizes to all players without loss of face for any. Its main disadvantages were defensive strategies (leading to stalemates and secrecy) and the exclusion of ordinary citizens (fostering non-conventional styles of protest). These problems was exacerbated by the cumbersome nature of French territorial administration, based on a legacy of ninety-five *départements* and over 36,000 (mostly rural) *communes.*

Decentralisation as a new political framework

Reforms which regrouped small, ineffective units into larger, more meaningful ones, whilst responding to the problems of the conurbations (which had grown massively in the postwar period) were acknowledged as essential from the 1960s on. A number of initiatives were taken – the 1959–69 decrees creating twenty-two regional administrative areas, the regional reforms of 1964–8, General de Gaulle's 1969 referendum on regional organisation, the 1971 Marcellin law on regrouping of communes, the 1972 law on regional reform – but, due to the strength of vested interests and the complexity of centre-periphery relations, they met with outright failure or limited success. Gradually, however, a regional tier of administration took root with the *établissements publics régionaux* and the *comités de développement économique régional* (CODER). With the arrival to power of the Socialists in 1981, local government reform became a major ambition. Named after their architect, the 1982–3 *lois Defferre* set in motion a major wave of decentralisation. An overview of the reform will be presented in order to outline the contexts in which environmental policy is implemented.[18]

In cameo, decentralisation resembled a transfer of powers from Paris to the provinces, but closer inspection reveals a different physiognomy. The reforms involved a complex remodelling of local and regional institutions, involving a strengthening of the political channel *vis-à-vis* the administrative channel. For the first time, regional councils were designated by universal suffrage, exercising competencies in relation to economic and social development, including secondary school education, transport, infrastructures and development (*aménagement du territoire*). Also, the office of regional prefect was instituted. Resources from regional taxation have been scant, hence regions are heavily reliant on the redistributive mechanism of the *contrats de plan Elul-région*, whereby agreed development objectives are jointly financed (although the influence of the state is predominant given that regions bid for central funding). The *départements* and *communes* have retained most of their previous responsibilities, including departmental roads and collective facilities for the former, and a large range of social services and enforcement powers for the latter. No major change was made with regard to the taxes they levied. Yet although three levels of elected subnational government now exist, no hierarchy obtains among them. In principle, each level acts independently within its allotted competencies, and is not subordinated to any other. Not only are the

---

[18] For broader evaluations of decentralisation see Loughlin and Mazey (1995).

territorial units of government held to be functionally separate, the franchise of elected representatives has been augmented in relation to state representatives. Thus Balme (1995: 186) commented: 'the prefect's technical-bureaucratic legitimacy is now subordinated to the political legitimacy of the elected councillors', in particular to the chair of the relevant assembly (*président du conseil régional, président du conseil général*). Further, ministerial field services, which report locally to the *préfet*, were also placed at the disposition of elected politicians. This development represented one facet of the *déconcentration* process which accompanied decentralisation.[19]

A number of consequences of these processes are worth stressing. Firstly, unlike previous initiatives, they took root and *local government* – as opposed to *territorial administration* – developed to a substantial extent. Gaston Defferre who, as Mayor of Marseille, was a grandee of French local politics, had calculated that if the traditional prerogatives of local politicians were enhanced rather than disturbed, then they would make the reforms work. Indeed the reforms were partly prompted by political entrepreneurship in the cities, and encouraged yet more. Secondly, decentralisation stopped short of regionalisation. Although political currents (such as the ecologists) favouring strong regions exist in France, regionalisation alarmed mainstream sensibilities. As Mény (1987: 58) emphasised: 'France demands of the constituent parts of the nation an exclusive allegiance which tolerates no duality of political identity'. The concept of 'region' carried cultural and ethnic undertones considered problematic by traditionalists since those areas of France with the strongest regional identity harboured separatist movements.[20] Thirdly, as noted by Le Galès (1992: 19), the 'decentralisation reforms have reinforced the dominant institutions of the French local system, cities and *départements*'. Fourthly, the rise in prominence of the *notables* was accompanied by a decline in the authority of the *préfet*, whose very name (temporarily) disappeared in the early 1980s.

The powers devolved to the periphery by the decentralisation process are significant for three reasons. The first and obvious reason is that they strengthened subnational government *vis-à-vis* the

---

[19] Diederichs and Luben (1995: 3) define *déconcentration* as 'une redistribution des pouvoirs au sein de l'Etat'.
[20] Principally these have been Corsica, the Basque country, Brittany and – to lesser degrees – 'Occitania', French Catalonia and Alsace.

centre. The second is that they contributed to a reform in local political culture. Whereas in the postwar period the interlocks between *notables* and *préfets* that threatened to produce stalemate were overcome by the impulsion of a standardising, *dirigiste* central state, the social and economic problems of the 1980s and 1990s required locally sourced political entrepreneurship. Reform has encouraged local politicians 'to give up their habits of being secret mediators and to act as dynamic entrepreneurs' (Michel, 1998: 159), cross-linking the interests of different social groups. Thirdly, these innovations opened out the closed policy communities that traditionally prevailed in France. Thus according to Duran and Thoenig (1996) the model of *régulation croisée* has to an extent been superseded in recent years by 'a model of institutionalised collective action'[21] in which, as part of the decentralisation process, the French state no longer dictates policy but organises the conditions for interaction and negotiation among a broader range of actors than previously used to be the case. An overhang of *régulation croisée* has persisted, but the ability of the prefect to act as counterbalance to overenthusiastic local politicians has been reduced, whilst new interlocutors have progressively found a place. As a result of these developments, it is the coherence of the French state which is open to question, but not its continued influence.

Local government reform and the environment

In principle, the Defferre laws allotted each tier of subnational government distinct competencies, whilst the 1992 law on territorial administration, invoking the principle of subsidiarity, gave central government those national responsibilities which cannot be devolved. In environmental matters, the central state had a near monopoly until the 1982–3 decentralisation laws; thereafter environmental protection became a shared competence between national and subnational governments. But how clear is the distribution of competencies in practice? Administrative lawyers such as Romi (1993a) and Rouyère (1996) have concluded that the legal demarcations of environmental responsibilities are insecure. Further, a survey of the *directeurs généraux de l'environnement* who head up the DIREN revealed that the separation of responsibilities proved unclear in the field (Deveze and Sanson, 1993). In reality,

---

[21] 'un modèle de l'institutionalisation de l'action collective'.

environmental competencies under decentralisation were not so much redistributed as diffused, producing overlaps and ambiguities.

The *communes* shoulder a wide range of environmental responsibilities, notably the provision of drinking water, sewerage and the collection of household waste.[22] The mayor exercises what is known as *police municipale*, namely powers of enforcement of water, air and noise regulations. Since 1982 mayors draw up planning documents, known as *plan d'occupation des sols* (POS), and participate in the approval of construction permits.[23] Communes are enjoined to draw up *chartes pour l'environnement*, to which we return in Chapter 9. However, with both planning documents and environmental charters, a measure of coordination is implied with other layers of subnational government.

On one reading, the *département* has been considered the 'natural' unit for environmental policy, but in practice its competencies have provided limited scope for environmental initiatives.[24] It manages the fire brigade, draws up plans against hazards, has responsibilities for tourism, manages nature sites, and maintains roads and thoroughfares. (Though even with footpaths, coordination is required with *communes*.) The *conseils d'architecture, d'urbanisme et d'environnement* bring together elected representatives of the *départements* and *communes* for construction planning. A few départements (Isère, the Landes and Gironde) have taken a proactive approach by drawing up environmental plans themselves (Alphandéry, Bitoun and Dupont, 1991).

On an alternative reading, the region's geographic size offers the most appropriate territorial unit for environmental policy. During the initial stages of decentralisation, it seemed that the region was indeed destined to be a major actor in environmental matters, but in practice it acquired limited formal powers.[25] It has co-responsibility with the state in environmental matters through the *contrats de plan Etat-régions*, though Romi (1993a: 53) observed that these favoured economic development rather than environmental

---

[22] For detailed presentation of the mayor's legal authority in environmental matters, see Zimeray (1994).

[23] See Booth (1998) for a useful analysis of POS.

[24] For discussion of the problems associated with devolving environmental responsibility to *départements*, see Romi (1990b).

[25] See Prieur (1985) for details on early anticipated trends, and Bodiguel and Buller (1995) for review of developments in environmental policy in the regions.

protection. Regional authorities manage coastlines, ports and waterways and are enjoined with a duty to preserve nature, notably through the *parcs naturels régionaux* (PNR). However, for PNR approvals, the regional authorities have to reach agreement with *communes*, whilst the EM takes final decisions. Some regions have ranged wider in their activities, with Provence-Alpes-Côted'Azur, Midi-Pyrénées and Picardie establishing their own *agence régionale pour l'environnement* (Prieur, 1988: 93).

Over and against local government powers are set the environmental competencies of the administrative channel, which have been maintained subsequent to decentralisation. To explain this continuity, Romi (1993a: 53) stressed 'the traditional distrust towards local authorities in environmental matters'.[26] Thus a number of enforcement duties known as *polices administratives spéciales* persist which lie within the jurisdiction of the prefect and supersede the general enforcement powers (*police générale*) of the mayor. Specifically, prefects have retained their prerogatives in relation to licensed industrial sites, mines and quarries, to the designation of nature conservation sites, and to the fixing of the opening and closing dates of the hunting season. Further, the 1992 territorial administration act reinstated the prefect's role in the coordination of regional planning and economic development. Because of these extensive powers, Mousel (1995: 66) concluded that 'the departmental prefect is the main implementer of environmental policy'.[27] However, certain decisions require ministerial approval in Paris, including the establishment of hunting reserves and the designation of monuments. Moreover, legislation subsequent to decentralisation, such as the 1985 Mountain Act and the 1986 Coastline Act, stressed the prerogatives of central government in relation to the sensitive issues of tourism and construction in upland and coastal areas. These latter factors introduced a measure of 'recentralisation' into the environmental policy equation.

Bringing some order to this tangled skein, Jégouzo (1995: 50) summarised the schedule of competencies by qualifying environmental protection as the 'quasi-monopole de l'Etat', whilst the management of services (such as water and waste) falls to subnational authorities. Decentralisation's complex institutional mix has

---

[26] 'la traditionnelle méfiance envers les collectivités locales en matière d'environnement'.

[27] 'le préfet de département est l'exécuteur principal de la politique de l'environnement'.

produced uneven outcomes. The functional isolation of each devolved assembly has proved to be largely a legal fiction, with political overcrowding favouring the multiplication of log-jams. Meanwhile the administrative channel was expected to exercise surveillance over the political channel, but its relative weakening proved problematic in a context where environmental policy remained predicated on a centralised approach. Although buttressed by a measure of recentralisation, its powers are tightly circumscribed; the EM's regional field services, the DIREN and the DRIRE, remain relatively weak actors. All of this limits the ability of the EM to exercise a 'command and control' type of intervention, a theme to be developed in later chapters.

Yet the question remains as to why decentralisation and environmental policy have proved ill-assorted bedfellows. A far-reaching explanation is offered by the 'model of institutionalised collective action' (Duran and Thoenig, 1996). It indicates that issue areas no longer correspond to predefined and stable politico-administrative territories.[28] Water, waste, atmospheric pollution, and other environmental problems besides, each require their own space of reference and accompanying policy network. Viewed from this perspective, the diffuse distribution of environmental competencies under decentralisation is the consequence of the lack of constant administrative counterparts for issue areas having differing territorial boundaries.

Conclusions

A paradox for French environmental policy arose from the need to develop institutional capacity for sectoral intervention in a period when the 'Colbertist', centralising state was entering decline. From the 1970s on, European integration, accelerated globalisation and the prevalence of market norms led governments to scale back interventionist and redistributive public policies. Top-down policies orchestrated in the traditional mode by a would-be *ministère régalien* had increasingly to be complemented by bottom-up, territorial policies, and coordinated with 'horizontal' or sectoral policies at European and international levels. In the process,

---

[28] According to Duran and Thoenig (1996: 611), 'il est de plus en plus vain de vouloir à tout prix faire correspondre les circonscriptions politiques et administratives avec les espaces de gestion des problèmes publics'.

power was parcelled out to fragmented political, administrative and private spheres, pitting a large number of actors against each other in a jostle for predominance, with the danger of stalemate rarely distant.

'Classic' environmental policy was born into this crowded house. Environmental policy makers, faced with urgent problems, tried to harness the old policy modes for new ends. Initially, to accord with the traditions of the *dirigiste* state and the new requirements imposed by European directives, this involved a 'command and control' style of environmental policy. Ironically, the new institution of the EM spent over twenty years growing central state competence and resources in a period when the prerogatives of the nation-state were being whittled away from below (by decentralisation) and from above (by European integration). But because the development of the EM went against the trend to 'roll back the state', its available resources were disproportionately small in relation to problems in the field and left it vulnerable within the established networks of power in France's conflictual government and administration. In addition, the *déconcentration* of ministerial field services suffered from the limited relevance of politico-administrative boundaries to environmental problems. It was also caught up in the vestiges of *regulation croisée*, and the latter's tendencies to policy dilution in the field. The territorialisation of major environmental actors, especially the *Agences de l'eau* and the ADEME, created specific forms of decentralisation and subsectoral closure, as well as raising awkward questions over their degree of independence from the central institution of the EM. Thus the French case provides support for Weale's reservations over the assumption that 'environmental problems could be dealt with adequately by a specialist branch of the machinery of government' (1992: 75).

Yet if the shortcomings of the French EM loom large, they should be related to the steep learning curve in which it was engaged, and to the large-scale, unanticipated changes in public institutions which occurred. Although no single institution could master the gamut of environmental issues, entrepreneurial Environment Ministers could constitute an indispensable force to act as standard bearers and carry forward the policy process. Conversely, in periods when the EM was particularly enfeebled, important initiatives failed to emerge. Over time, the case for an *administration de gestion* piloting the major functions of environmental protection became accepted by all political persuasions. In addition, the new policy climate of the late 1980s engendered a different variation on the theme of an *administration de mission*. From a Jacobin mode of coordination of central ministries, the new requirements for the EM were to integrate within its policy space both semi-independent environmental agencies and subnational levels of government, as well as to make France an active player at European and international levels. By the 1990s, a complex model of governance had emerged in which a multiplicity of public and private actors – international, European, national and subnational – interacted to take top-down, lateral and bottom-up initiatives.

5

EUROPEAN ENVIRONMENTAL POLICY AND FRANCE

Introduction

The European Community (EC) is often considered a source of exogenous change in the shaping of domestic environmental policy. Haigh stated that 'in the environmental field the extent of the legislation is such that it is now impossible to understand the policies of any EC Member state without understanding EC policy' (1992: 229). Yet whilst the importance of European legislation is undeniable, a simple input-output model – in which Brussels decides and member states follow – is inapplicable. European policy making involves a large number of actors engaged in iterative and protracted negotiations having top-down, bottom-up and lateral components; moreover, the direction of influence is reciprocal rather than linear.

To try to capture this multidimensionality, the present chapter will explore different perspectives on European policy making and on French approaches to the process.[1] The first section provides an overview of the development of European environmental policy. In order to ascertain why it has arisen at all, the second section assesses a range of competing theories which aim to explain the behaviour of key actors in policy negotiations. To review why policy has not always achieved its ambitions, the third section sets out reasons for implementation deficits. The fourth section

[1] Discussion of the detail of legislation will be held over for the case study chapters.

concentrates on France's twofold strategy towards Europe. On the one hand, that strategy has been characterised by a long-term pursuit of national interests at the Community level and has sought to make Europe more French. On the other, European legislation was incorporated into domestic frameworks in such a manner that its foreign origin was usually lost, so reducing conflicts and diluting its impact. This sequence of analyses will argue that, due to the processes by which European policy is produced and because of France's twofold strategy towards them, the European Community was not so much a source of exogenous shocks on French environmental policy as an interactive arena encouraging political renewal and a constraining influence which reshaped choices between *existing* policy modes.

European Environmental Policy: an Overview

The 1972 Stockholm conference on the environment disseminated the realisation that effective environmental policies required international coordination. According to Environment Minister Poujade (1975: 237–8), France brokered a European environmental policy by the convening of a summit in Paris in October 1972. The summit produced a joint statement proposing to reduce pollution, improve urban and natural environments, address resource depletion and promote environmental education. This initiative led to the development of five 'action programmes' (see Table 5.1) which, though not legally binding, provided an EC environmental policy framework. Ambitious declarations were translated into a substantial body of legislation, whose legal foundation was strengthened by revision of the European treaties.

The early development of European environmental policy is all the more impressive in that its legal bases in the 1957 Treaty of Rome were slim. In the absence of explicit reference to the environment and despite periodic questioning, articles 100 and 235 were regularly invoked to support legislation. Beraud (1979: 38) contended that their extended use was a sign of political, rather than legal, audacity. Nevertheless, when in the 1980s European leaders set about reinvigorating a 'common market' overcome by 'Eurosclerosis', the opportunity to consolidate environmental policy was seized. Thus the 1987 Single European Act (SEA) included a chapter on the environment, whose measures were augmented by the 1992 Treaty of European Union, signed in Maastricht. Article 130r of the latter indicated that 'community policy on the environment shall aim at a high level of protection taking into account the diversity of situations in the various regions' and stipulated its objectives as 'preserving, protecting and improving the quality of the environment; protecting human health; prudent and rational utilisation of natural resources; promoting measures at international level to deal with regional or world-wide environmental problems'. The treaty reiterated three long-standing environmental principles – the polluter should pay, rectification at source and preventative action – and added the precautionary principle. The need to integrate environmental protection requirements into other policies was stressed. Article 100a of the SEA introduced qualified majority voting within the Council of Ministers for measures completing the internal market, including some environmental issues. However, article 130s of the Maastricht treaty maintained the principle of unanimity in decision making on taxation, planning and land use, and energy sourcing. Consequently much environmental policy making in the 1990s continued to require unanimous agreement. The 1997 Amsterdam Treaty extended joint decision making between the Council of Ministers and the European Parliament to environmental policy, implying a new regime for the future, though the latter's impact will be limited *inter alia* by the fact that the unanimity rule continues to apply to taxation (unless new amendments are made). The Amsterdam treaty also reinforced the scope for individual nations to introduce more stringent environmental measures than those enacted under EU auspices, though unilateral action has to be justified to the European Commission on the basis of new scientific evidence.

European environmental legislation has mostly taken the form of directives rather than regulations,[2] with well over a hundred directives in place. Nature conservation has been a salient concern. Water was made a priority, with quality standards set at European level for drinking water, bathing water, fresh water and sea water. Likewise air pollution was attacked from several angles, including vehicle emissions, pollution from large combustion plants and a (failed) proposal for a carbon tax. Issues such as industrial hazards, waste disposal, noise and genetically modified food have all received attention. The reinforcement of the legal

---

[2] Regulations are directly applicable in their entirety, whilst directives require transposition into domestic law.

Table 5.1 European environmental policy: five action programmes

The first programme: 1973–7
- developed pollution abatement measures;
- required that the polluter should pay to repair damage and correct at source;
- was mainly concerned with single media – air, water, soil – though the problem of cross-media transfers was recognised.

The second programme: 1977–82
- augmented the policy framework by stress on rational utilisation of natural resources;
- extended pollution control to include toxic and radioactive wastes.

The third programme: 1982–6
- called for the integration of the environment into economic and structural policies;
- stated the prevention principle;
- recommended environmental impact assessment for major industrial, energy and tourist development projects;
- stressed improved access to information, and better environmental education.

The fourth programme: 1986–92
- was conditioned by the SEA in that the single European market required harmonisation of environmental measures;
- encouraged enhancement of competitiveness by high environmental standards (the 'ecological modernisation' thesis);
- emphasised the improvement of policy execution, given known 'implementation deficits'.

The fifth programme: 1993–2000
- introduced the theme of sustainable development;
- called for international cooperation within the framework of Agenda 21;
- aimed at long-term measures (previous programmes had been short term to medium term);
- included climate change, acidification and biodiversity in priority themes;
- stressed better environmental policy integration in five key sectors: tourism, industry, energy, transport and agriculture;
- broadened the range of policy instruments to include 'green taxes'.

foundation of Community environmental policy, and the breadth and technicality of its individual measures have created a comprehensive policy framework. Yet both policy negotiation and implementation have proved contentious and problematic.

Theories of European Environmental Policy Negotiation

Why have member states subscribed to the demanding framework of European environmental policy? A simplistic assumption found in the media is that European environmental legislation is merely imposed on countries, companies and consumers by the European Commission. But in practice the processes of policy development are complex, encouraging practitioners and scholars to put forward a range of competing theories to explain them. Reviewing the spread of interpretations will give insights into the behaviour of key actors in European negotiations, but will also lead to a questioning of the bases on which characterisation of member state environmental policy strategies has often been made.

The European Commission's model

In official EC publications, four reasons have been advanced to explain the development of environmental policy:[3]

- the pressure of public opinion;
- a commitment to raising standards of living dating from the Rome Treaty;
- the international character of environmental problems, given *inter alia* the greater incidence of cross-border pollution;
- a commitment to free trade and the ending of trade barriers, including distortions caused by differences in national technical norms.

Although these are valid starting points for explanation, they present an incomplete picture. The opinion poll data cited in Chapter 2 indicated that public concern was multifaceted, ambivalent and provided only general pointers for policy. The

---

[3] See for example Commission of the EC (1984).

dash for economic growth in the postwar period increased the level of household incomes but also led to more environmental harm. In generating tension between attaining higher standards of living and enhancing the quality of life, it provided no clear mandate or blueprint for environmental policy.

The transboundary nature of environmental problems has no doubt encouraged policy making at European and international levels. Yet many environmental problems are local in nature. Golub (1996a: 11–13) showed that a number of issues dealt with at the EC level, including noise, waste disposal and environmental impact assessment, have no transboundary implications; certain problems of water and air pollution are geographically restricted, whilst half the species listed in the 1979 'Birds directive' are non-migratory. Where uniform European legislation has been enacted, its suitability to local situations has been variable.

On the other hand, the concern with free trade is at the heart of the European project. From the 1970s, the need to ensure compatibility between economic and environmental objectives was perceived, and the danger of nation-specific environmental norms creating barriers to trade recognised. In addition, the opportunity was seized to accelerate policy learning by pooling scientific knowledge and practical experience. In the late 1980s, the development of the 'single market' made the coordination of economic initiatives and environmental policies more urgent. As the dynamics of economic integration spread to embrace not only monetary union but also political union, the logic of bringing the cross-cutting domain of the environment within the European remit became irresistible. The inclusion of the environmental chapter in the SEA, and its extension in the Maastricht and Amsterdam treaties, was more than a legal exercise: it also flagged up the increased scale of European ambitions. Yet if these four generic reasons reveal mainly economic and political motivations (and contain a highly instrumental construction of the environment), explanation of the strategic behaviour of key players and of outcomes is missing.

The 'leader–laggard' thesis

The perception that certain countries are more environmentally 'advanced' than others has been frequently expressed. Sbragia (1996: 236) argued that 'the policy process in the environmental arena is typically driven by a small number of member states which are significantly more environmentally progressive than the rest'. The leaders were identified as a 'green troika', composed of Denmark, the Netherlands and Germany, with the remainder classified as 'laggards' (Spain, Britain) or 'neutrals' (such as France). Later analyses have, however, given only moderate support for this thesis. Liefferink and Andersen (1998) reviewed the strategies of reputedly 'green' member states, namely the 'troika' just mentioned, together with Sweden, Finland and Austria after their accession. In principle, these 'forerunner' countries set the pace for others to follow, but in practice the translation of national preferences into Community policy proved less than straightforward. Liefferink and Andersen found 'leader' strategies were not homogenous, spanning a range of behaviours between constructive 'pushing' and defensive opt-outs, whilst consistent alliance building among themselves proved elusive. Moreover characterisations in terms of degree of 'greenness' had not remained consistent over time, with Germany in the 1990s sliding towards a more passive posture than in the 1980s. Similarly, Knill (1998: 11) found in the German case 'a dominant pattern of ineffective implementation as a result of administrative resistance to change' regarding four major environmental directives.

The explanatory power of the 'leader-laggard' thesis is constrained by several factors. An inbuilt problem is that a good or bad reputation is ascribed to a nation as a whole, rather than in relation to policy actors on an issue at a particular time. A stress on high national levels of environmental expenditure can give a biased presentation of 'green' commitment, since they present the clean-up costs of heavy pollution. However, locations with an unspoilt environment do not figure in this accountancy. Successful agenda setting likewise leads to distortions in perspective. The specific environmental problems of southern Europe, such as water shortages and forest fires, emerged late on the collective European agenda and have remained in a lower position than those of the heavily industrialised north. Thus Weale (1996: 605) concluded that 'national differences in policy making style and priorities are not simply a lagged response by countries at different levels of economic development to a common set of environmental problems, but reflect the fact that national environments differ and so their policy needs differ'. The characterisation of national environmental strategies along a 'leader-laggard' continuum contains the unproved assumption that European convergence in the environmental domain is an inevitable process.

However, with the environment – as in the economy – competition rather than convergence may be the defining factor.

The 'regulatory competition' thesis

The thesis of 'regulatory competition', as put forward by Héritier (1996) and Héritier, Knill and Mingers (1996), proposed that member states have a vested interest in promoting components of their national regulatory systems to the Commission as policy 'gatekeeper' such that they form the basis for European law. A 'first mover' strategy in initiating future directives averts an exogenous regulatory shock, avoids adaptation costs (whether borne by firms, or by legal and institutional systems), and may confer competitive advantage where export markets are opened to existing products and technologies. It was also argued that member states take turns in influencing European policy, leading to qualified characterisations of their strategies (rather than ascribing a single shade of 'light' or 'dark' green).

Whilst some of the specific examples it offers are compelling, the theory leaves implicit the limiting conditions under which it operates. The identification of the origin and subsequent tracking of opportunistic initiatives require that they be: (a) distinctive in terms of national policy traditions, (b) faithful in their substantive content to their domestic model, and (c) sufficiently problematic to other nations to provoke open disagreement and competition. Examples such as the 1988 Large Combustion Plant directive and the 1993 Eco-Audit directive meet these criteria, since the German influence in the first case, and the British in the second, were patent. However, few environmental directives meet these conditions. Much information on specific inputs is not recorded, or if filed remains secret. Consequently many national 'stories ' are not told. Further, member state policy preferences, where they exist, are commonly eroded by low-profile players in the lobbying and 'commitology' stages where national interests give way to highly technical, sector-specific considerations. In summary, the 'regulatory competition' thesis is insightful in relation to the cases studied and avoids the pitfall of assuming that degrees of 'greenness' among member states remain constant. But in being a more sophisticated version of the 'leader-laggard' thesis, it shares some of its drawbacks, particularly in its stress on government advocacy. In practice, ministers can experience difficulties in articulating a unified national interest, whilst competition is tempered by requirements for coalition building and compromise at the EC negotiating table. To develop the latter points, two further models will be considered, which stress differentiation inside the policy process, albeit at different levels.

The 'slack cutting' thesis

The hypothesis of 'slack cutting' put forward by Golub (1996b: 21) emphasised differences *within* national executives: 'environmental ministers enjoy interministerial slack when cutting deals in Brussels which have been blocked domestically by traditionally powerful ministries such as Finance, Trade and Industry, or Agriculture'. Tighter regulations than government colleagues would have countenanced are agreed in the European Council of Ministers, in sessions where only environment ministers deliberate. On this view, the member state is envisaged not as a unitary actor pressing a parochial interest in Brussels, but rather as a collection of internal divisions between national ministries which spawn rival policy priorities. Environmental ministers are assumed to find more common cause with their European counterparts than with cabinet colleagues at home.

Yet the former do not operate as free agents, but must respect a negotiating brief largely set by hierarchical superiors. To address this objection, Collier and Golub (1997) suggested further reasons to explain willingness to sign, including expected non-compliance (the belief that targets are more to be aimed at than hit), the limitations of intergovernmentalism (a persistent national veto is unacceptable within the European partnership) and issue linkage (where negotiations lead to trade-offs across sectors). Whether environmental issues are linked positively or negatively to other domains, and how linkage actually occurs, could be elucidated further within this thesis. Nevertheless, its positioning of environmental questions within broader European agendas provides a reminder of heterogeneity within national priorities, and of interaction between levels of European decision making.

The 'issue networks' thesis

Mazey and Richardson (1993) and Bomberg (1998) drew on Richardson's own early work and on the 'Rhodes model' of a network continuum (outlined in Chapter 1) to explore the multilevel procedures operating within the EC. Here policy is considered as the output of 'open' issue networks spanning a transnational set of agents, rather than of the limited policy communities which used to characterise domestic policy making. Richardson (1996: 27) defined the European 'actor based model' as one in which 'the extreme openness of decision making to lobbyists and the considerable weight of national politico-administrative elites within the process, create an unstable and multidimensional policy making environment.'

On this view, pressure groups enjoyed a greater role at European than at domestic levels, due to the 'promiscuity' of the Commission. In the environmental field, this greater openness was explained by the fact that interest groups could mobilise resources and provide technical information that the understaffed Directorate-General for the Environment, Nuclear Safety and Civil Protection lacks. To exploit these opportunities, environmental groups – notably Friends of the Earth, WWF and Greenpeace – set up offices in Brussels and developed close ties at the European level (Marks and McAdam, 1996: 119). Thus interests which were marginalised at the national level promoted their agenda in the transnational European forum, pushing out the boundaries of policy subsystems. These analyses sought to prevent a slide down the pluralist slope by stressing the importance of European institutions – the Commission, Council of Ministers, European Parliament (since the development of the co-decision procedure) and the European Court of Justice (ECJ) – and the unequal spread of influence among actors and institutions. A major consequence of these complex interactions is that even large states and powerful transnational interest coalitions – let alone modestly resourced environmental groups – can lose the ability to direct policy agenda and content.

Although the 'issue networks' approach has been taxed with being descriptive, it identifies important effects. Multilevel interaction creates fluidity, uncertainty and unpredictability. Fluidity leads to the erosion of member-state autonomy, with the attendant need for researchers to be wary of overestimating the influence of national interests at the policy formulation stage. Uncertainty means that governments as European policy implementers do not always know what they are signing up to, precisely who will be affected or how much it will cost. Unpredictability has the consequence that policy integrity and effectiveness can be impaired.

In conclusion, the theories of European environmental policy negotiation surveyed here are divided in their assessment of the ability of national governments to control the policy agenda at European levels. This disagreement stems from the diversity and plasticity of issues areas debated at European level, and from inconsistencies in actor behaviour. Because of these empirical factors, each theory throws light on particular circumstances and outcomes but, by the same token, an eclectic synthesis of their positions is ruled out. However, this does make the consistent ascription of a 'green' or a 'brown' reputation problematic. The problems are compounded by variations not only at the policy formulation stage, but also in terms of the real impact of European legislation, which often falls short of its targets. This, in turn, raises questions about the extent to which European policy effectively shapes national responses.

Explanations of European Environmental Policy Shortfalls

A whole series of 'implementation deficits' has been caused by the EU's complex system of multilevel governance and by the nature of its policy outputs. As analysts such as Majone (1996) and Mény (1995) have stressed, the preferred policy mode of the European Community has been regulation, with little recourse to stabilising or redistributive policy modes generally, and none in the environmental domain. With regard to the environment, 'new regulatory policy' has been defined as 'curbing negative external impacts on the public or the work force from productive activities and individual consumption' (Héritier, Knill and Mingers, 1996: 9). The consequence is that 'the environment is being defined in normative, scientific rather than cultural terms' (Buller, Lowe and Flynn, 1993: 192). European directives are prescriptive in content and frequently premised on the existence of 'command and control' regimes within the nation-state, presupposing and encouraging a centralisation of environmental administration. However, this bias has proved problematic because of the limits on institutional capacity, because of recent trends towards decentralisation and because of the characteristics of particular issue areas (such as the division of responsibilities between public and private sectors in relation to water, or the presence of opposed interests in relation to nature conservation). Moreover, a single policy mode – regulation – cannot respond to all categories of problems, needs and ambitions. In consequence, deficiencies regularly arise in the implementation process.

Complex preparations and poor draughtsmanship

The institutional and procedural features of European policy making entail decision processes lasting many years, with some measures never seeing the light of day. Coordination between policy domains is particularly elusive, despite integration between environmental and other policies being a stated aim in the treaties. The practical problems of European legislation continue once it is couched on paper. The House of Lords Select Committee on the EC (1992: 47) noted that 'too much legislation is formulated and drafted with insufficient attention to its eventual implementation'. The European Commission proposes legislation, but the small size and limited resources of the Directorate-General for the Environment have posed problems, leading to questioning of the scientific basis of some environmental directives, such as the limit values for water quality.

The inconsistencies of 'implementation'

The difficulties of 'implementation' start with inconsistent use of the term itself. In the legal literature, it refers to the transposition into national legislation of directives decided at the Community level (together with a report to the Commission that this has been done) whilst 'enforcement' indicates the steps taken by the European Commission to ensure full and correct transposition.[4] However, outside of the domain of European law, this use of terminology can be misleading. Thus Glim (1990: 2) distinguished between 'formal compliance', namely transposition of directives into national law, and 'practical compliance' or 'what has been done in reality to put the laws into effect'. Similarly, the House of Lords Select Committee on the EC (1992: 8) stated:

> There are three main stages of implementation or compliance, each of which can give rise to problems. The first is the development of the legal obligation. This involves policy formulation, its

[4] For discussions, see Wägenbaur (1991), Collins and Earnshaw (1992), Macrory (1992) and Sbragia (1992).

embodiment in Community legislation, and the transposition of such legislation where necessary into the legal systems of each Member State. Second is the establishment of national policies, administrative mechanisms and sanctions to give effect to legislation in practice. This involves the establishment of arrangements for monitoring, inspection and review. And third is enforcement under the processes of the law so as to rectify omissions or defects.

To reduce the ambiguities, the following conventions are proposed for current purposes. The conversion of Community directives into national law will be referred to as 'transposition', whilst checks by the Commission to ensure conformity of national texts with their European sources will be termed 'compliance'. The practical application and observance of law will be termed 'implementation'. The process whereby public officials ensure the conformity of the behaviour of regulatory targets with the law (and notably the instigation of sanctions for non-conformity) will be termed 'enforcement'. The term 'implementation deficits' is used as a generic expression to cover all these modes.

The realisation that shortfalls existed in all four areas was widespread by the end of the 1980s, with attention being directed firstly at inadequate transposition and compliance, and latterly at failures of implementation and enforcement.[5] The range and complexity of domestic legal systems caused problems in the *transposition* of European legislation, since the latter tended to cut across national traditions and concepts. Reconciliation of existing law with European innovations involved delays due to consultation procedures and the need to find acceptable phrasing. For example, Collins and Earnshaw (1992: 217) noted that in the UK some twenty items of legislation were needed to transpose the directive on environmental impact assessment. This complexity in turn leads to problems of *compliance* since the reporting of the transposition to Brussels can prove over-complex, or fail to materialise. In such cases, the Commission has the option of invoking an escalating scale of sanctions against the member state under article 169 of the Rome Treaty.[6] At the *implementation* stage, directives can be subject to political constraints. Government may favour a new measure but be denied an easy passage where a powerful interest group considers its prerogatives threatened (Mény and Chérel,

---

[5] See From and Stava (1993) and Kunzlik (1994: 115–16).

[6] For reports on the application of community law, see Commission of the EC (1996a, 1997, 1998).

1988: 298–304). Extra complications set in where governments blame unpopular measures on the EC. Finally, at the *enforcement* stage, national regulatory agencies encounter practical difficulties in the field, as will be seen in later chapters.

The failures of 'concurrent decision making'

The model of 'concurrent decision making' proposed by Weale (1996) elegantly combines a characterisation of the procedures of European environmental policy making with identification of their intrinsic shortcomings. On this view, sets of institutional and functional actors at national and Community levels share authority and engage in negotiation, leading to aggregation and modification of the objectives of European environmental measures. Because decisions are typically subject to the veto of powerful players, the policy style is one of protracted accommodation. Transaction costs are high, reducing the scope for policy innovation and favouring the status quo. Major hurdles are constituted by the need for the European Parliament and Council to agree a common position, and by the difficulties of integration between environmental policy and sectoral policies, particularly in relation to industry, transport and agriculture. Weale concluded that concurrent decision making was intrinsically ill-adapted to the environmental domain, where the need was not for 'bargaining' but for 'problem-solving'. On this reading, the potential for European environmental policy to constitute a major source of exogenous change at the national level is diminished. The range of 'implementation deficits' listed supports that view.

Extrapolating from this review of theories of European environmental policy negotiation and explanations of implementation deficits, the conclusion is drawn that the reality of member state activity is refractory to general categorisation, being highly context-specific and the result of a broad range of interactions. If nation-level strategies vary in relation to issue areas and over time, then characterisation is hazardous. Accordingly, a summary comparison of France's degree of 'greenness' to that of her neighbours will not be attempted. Rather, a different hypothesis will be explored, namely that national strategy towards the Europeanisation process constitutes a guiding framework which conditions the handling of individual sectoral policies, whilst allowing leeway for contingent solutions. Thus rather than limit the analysis to the mesolevel of environmental policy per se, the next section contextualises the latter within the macroperspective of France's European policy.

France and the 'Naturalisation' of Europe

France has favoured the 'naturalisation' of Europe, rather than embrace the 'Europeanisation' of France. Since the 1950s, her European strategy has consistently pursued national goals by European means, and political ambitions by economic methods.[7] The idea of *une Europe à la française* – a policy of making Europe more French – was cherished by General de Gaulle and his heirs.[8] This constituted the top tier of what is labelled here as the 'naturalisation' of Europe, namely the bestowing of French 'nationality' or identity on the European sphere.

As a co-founder of the EEC, France exercised leadership in setting the rules and agenda for the European 'club'. This orientation continued in the recent period, during which President Mitterrand gave priority to European construction, acting as one of the architects of the 1992 Maastricht Treaty, whilst President Chirac pushed France towards the single currency in the late 1990s, despite his reservations in previous decades. Their aims have focused on the defence of French interests (such as agriculture through the Common Agricultural Policy), enhancing Community *acquis* and promoting French competitiveness through industrial and research policy, the Single Market and monetary integration. Economic developments contained an inbuilt political dimension in that they sought to moor Germany to Europe. Through the single currency, the French aimed to increase their role in European economic and monetary policy by wresting influence from the Bundesbank.

In the early years, French public opinion concurred that the benefits of membership outweighed the drawbacks.[9] However, by the 1990s, French leadership had diminished as a result of German

---

[7] For discussion, see Duchêne (1996) and Moreau Defarges (1996).

[8] As Claude Cheysson, a former French Minister for European Affairs, tellingly remarked 'il n'y plus d'affaires étrangères (. . .) il y a une traduction extérieure des politiques intérieures' (quoted in Lequesne, 1987: 290).

[9] Guyomarch, Machin and Ella (1998: 94–102) provide detailed discussion.

reunification and the downgrading of such traditional French priorities as agricultural policy and industrial policy (Kassim, 1997). In a context of rapid decline in French influence,[10] rising Euroscepticism was confirmed by the narrow 'yes' vote in the 1992 Maastricht referendum.[11] The public's disenchantment was exacerbated by the deflationary economic policy adopted in the period 1995–7 to meet the convergence criteria for monetary union. Due to the trimming of public services and the welfare state, the deep unpopularity of Prime Minister Juppé's policies led to the right's electoral defeat in 1997. Yet if these outbursts of discontent constituted a questioning of the European project, the lateness of their occurrence testified to the success of 'unification by stealth' (Hayward, 1996).

The pursuit of key national interests by European diplomacy was accompanied by political realism over the need to make accommodations in secondary policy arenas. Environmental policy has been considered one such arena, with the French approach being low key. France's concern with the 'high politics' of European integration resulted in a measure of attention displacement away from the 'low politics' of environmental regulation, treated as an instance of humdrum negotiation distinct from history-making decisions. Viewed from Paris, European environmental policy was one of the smaller pieces of a large and complex jigsaw. In lower priority arenas, the second tier of the French strategy of 'naturalisation' was to lose the foreign origin of European policy by low-profile assimilation into domestic frameworks.

In a context of rapid European and domestic change, the tensions generated by this strategy led to modifications not in the direction but in the details of France's approach. These will be considered in the following subsections which deal with the manners in which the French adapted their policy style and administration to Europe, whilst domesticating European policy and legislation.

Adapting French strategies to Europe

Gerbet (1969) noted that France's early policy style in European negotiations was to rely on centralisation within the French

---

[10] This led Kramer (1994) to pointedly ask *Does France Still Count?*

[11] Cameron (1996) showed that the waning of the popularity of European integration with French opinion set in at the start of the 1990s. For discussion of the increase in French Euroscepticism see Drake and Milner (1999).

administration, notably by the establishment of the *Secrétariat général du comité interministériel pour les questions de coopération économique européenne* (SGCI). The aim was to press national interests in a harmonised and consistent manner by European agenda setting at the highest intergovernmental levels, with a marked role reserved for the French president.[12] This was well suited to the EEC 'club of six', dominated by France and Germany and their shared legalistic policy *formulation* mode, but the context evolved rapidly with the admission of Britain and Denmark, both of whom were preoccupied with effective policy *implementation* and negotiated strenuously to that end (Mény, 1985: 10).

Not only did the French approach prove less suitable with the arrival of more members and procedural changes, but the coordinating role of the SGCI was limited to the negotiating phase and had no part in following through the transposition of legislation. This task fell to the specialist ministry in question, with the SGCI involved only when the Commission took action in a case of noncompliance. In the 1980s, France was one of the countries with the poorest compliance record (Carnelutti, 1988: 532), leading to a high number of article 169 infringement proceedings by the Commission. Mény (1985: 19) commented that 'France is a past mistress [sic] in the art of evasion which allows her to apply numerous measures *in extremis*',[13] whilst French public officials were reported as still following Tocqueville's dictum that 'rules are rigid, but practice is soft'.[14] Consultations within the administration were often inadequate; thus field services responsible for enforcement were usually not involved in policy formulation, either by the European Commission or by their ministry in Paris.[15]

---

[12] As indicated by Lequesne (1993: 123): 'cette situation reflétait de manière significative une conception qui a longtemps prévalu au sein de l'appareil politico-administratif de la France: la construction communautaire nécessite que l'on s'adapte à la phase « noble » de la négociation, mais non à celle de l'exécution des décisions'.

[13] 'La France est passée maîtresse dans cet art de l'esquive qui lui permet d'appliquer de nombreuses décisions *in extremis*.'

[14] 'La règle est rigide, mais la pratique est molle', quoted in Siedentopf and Hauschild (1988: 553).

[15] Siedentopf and Hauschild (1988: 549) reported that 'en France, l'application des actes juridiques du droit communautaire relève des compétences de divers niveaux administratifs, en particulier de l'administration centrale et des services extérieurs. Le rapport français fait ressortir le manque de communication entre les uns et les autres comme une faiblesse structurelle particulière'. Mény and Chérel (1988: 291–4) and Carnelutti (1988: 15) pointed to similar shortcomings.

Moreover, with the measures on qualified majority voting contained in the SEA, national interests could not be supported solely by negotiations at the Council of Ministers stage, but required lobbying the Commission during the drafting stage, a practice belatedly encouraged by Prime Minister Cresson. These shifts in European procedures necessitated a change of policy style from hierarchical centralisation to a more diffuse policy network approach (Lequesne, 1995: 149–50). The Clausade inquiry (1991) was set up to meet the urgent need to update the French strategy. These 'downstream' modifications will be discussed next.

Adjusting European legislation to France

Just as France aimed to secure optimal outcomes at the negotiation stage of European policy, so she sought to exploit leeway in its transposition, implementation and enforcement in order to reduce adaptation costs. In environmental policy this was facilitated by the diversity and flexibility of *existing* national measures. As noted by Héritier, Knill and Mingers (1996: 2): 'France . . . has long disposed of a "requisite variety" of instruments, a broad range of multifarious environmental regulatory tools facilitating instrumental compliance with European requirements. France has accordingly taken little initiative to influence European policy and has needed little effort to conform with European rules'.

However, the room for manoeuvre did not remain constant. Over time, France found herself more hemmed in by the technical constraints of European law and pressures from Community institutions, notably the Commission and the ECJ. Directives constitute the usual instrument and in principle allow a degree of flexibility in transposition. Article 189 of the Rome Treaty states that 'a directive shall be binding, as to the result to be achieved, upon each Member State to which it is addressed but shall leave to the national authorities the choice of form and methods'. This invites the assumption that the 'form and methods' for attaining results stipulated by directives are a matter of national preference. However, practice has shown that the requirements are highly restrictive. Correct transposition poses varying levels of difficulty depending on the nature of the directive, the complexity of its incorporation where national legislation already exists, and the particular procedure by which it is effected. Because the stipulations of directives often leave little scope for modification of wording, the usual practice of Greece, Ireland and Luxembourg is transcription, namely a word-for-word translation into national legislation.[16] This is not a welcome solution in states such as Britain and France, where great emphasis is placed on sovereign rights.

In France, two routes to transposition exist: the parliamentary and the ministerial. Article 34 of the 1958 constitution specifies those areas in which parliament legislates by statute (*loi*), whilst article 37 indicates that in all other matters the executive legislates by regulation (*règlement*). In general, the prerogatives of parliament during the Fifth Republic have been limited in comparison with earlier periods of French history, or in nations such as Britain. Parliament was further sidelined by European integration since it had no direct input into the formulation of European legislation.[17] Its role has been limited to adapting directives to national contexts, prompting concern that its powers of law making have been reduced.[18] In reaction it has sought to exert more influence, albeit with limited success. Since the establishment of a *Délégation nationale pour les Communautés européennes* in 1979, parliament receives by right information on Community legislative proposals.[19] Discussion in the early 1990s of the 'democratic deficit', as well as irritations over the perceived incursions of the ECJ, resulted in a renewed wish for greater influence.[20] The Pezet (1992) parliamentary report complained that the elected chambers had been converted into 'registration offices' which transcribed European law; it made the proposal that directives be made into framework laws to allow debate and flexibility. The French parliament, however, is not empowered to change European procedures, only French ones. Thus a 1992 constitutional amendment (article 88–4) was made allowing parliament to vote resolutions

[16] See Collins and Earnshaw (1992: 218).
[17] For detailed review see Pierré-Caps (1991) who noted 'le pouvoir réglementaire devenait parallèlement 'le pouvoir normatif exclusif' dans l'exécution du droit communautaire, la compétence législative ne subsistant qu'au titre d'une compétence liée'.
[18] For a summary of the problems, see Mény and Chérel (1988: 279–83). A typical complaint is the comment by parliamentarian Nicole Catala that the transposition process 'conduit le législateur à recopier parfois mot pour mot des articles entiers du texte européen' (quoted in Pierré-Caps, 1991: 251).
[19] For details on its establishment and procedures, see Cottereau (1982).
[20] See Guillaume (1992) and Sauron (1995: 66–74).

on EC matters.[21] It can now do so on a limited range of matters (foreign policy and security, European cooperation in justice and the setting of agricultural prices are all excluded), and must intervene in timely fashion.[22] These resolutions have no binding force on the government during Council of Ministers negotiations but can be persuasive nonetheless. For example, parliamentary opposition to the Commission's proposals for a European tax on carbon emissions stiffened the resolve of the French government to oppose them.[23]

On the other hand, ministerial and executive powers have been in the ascendancy. For a law voted by parliament to take effect, the government must subsequently edict implementation decrees (*décrets d'application*). However, years may pass between one and the other.[24] Further, most European directives have been transposed not by parliament but by ministers using their powers under articles 21 and 37 of the French constitution (Simon and Rigaux, 1991: 293). A parliamentary report (Ligot, 1991: 20) noted that of some 1,000 European directives in effect in 1991, only seventy-five had been transposed by act of parliament. Though pragmatic, the ministerial route has its problems. Firstly, in the event of overlapping remits between ministries, internal negotiations slow down the process. Secondly, European environmental law has largely been subsumed under French administrative law (Huglo, 1992. 11). This reduces democratic debate, and tends to exclude concerned third parties and public scrutiny. Thirdly, the technical inadequacies of ministerial transposition have been stressed.[25] The administration used to favour ministry circulars because, like

---

[21] See Délégation de l'Assemblée nationale pour les Communautés européennes (1994).

[22] French Parliamentary procedure is slow in European matters. Favret (1996: 100) noted that it usually takes two days for Community documents to reach the UK Select Committee on European Legislation, but two months to arrive before French parliamentarians. A notable cause of delay is the *Conseil d'Etat* which forwards only those European documents that it considers to be within Parliament's remit.

[23] Opposition to the carbon tax was based on the view that it would disadvantage the French electro-nuclear industry (which produces little CO_2). See the Senate report prepared by François (1996).

[24] Mathieu (1992: 25) noted that some of the *décrets d'application* for the 1964 Water Act were not enacted till 1983.

[25] For discussions and examples of this problem, see Simon and Rigaux (1991), Niang (1992) and Romi (1993b: 136–40).

directives but unlike other French legal instruments, they laid down detailed, technical instructions (Mény and Chérel, 1988: 295). However, the objections ranged against them included insufficient legal force, excessive interpretative latitude (with amendment or repeal possible with a change of minister) and inadequate information to beneficiaries of directives bestowing rights. The ECJ has repeatedly ruled that circulars and guidance notes were inadequate as a means for transposition, and that laws or regulations must be passed and published in an official journal.[26] Since 1991, this ruling has been accepted (Krämer and Kromarek, 1994: 216–17). The elimination of circulars indicates that, despite the wording of article 189, the selection of legal means does not entail a free choice. Finally, French decrees and statutes do not make consistent reference to root directives, and reporting on transposition to Brussels can be sketchy. The Commission has repeatedly complained about the difficulty of ascertaining compliance due to the latter two problems and has sought to shame guilty parties by greater publicity.

European directives have limited visibility to French citizens due to these transposition processes. Buller (1998: 80) labelled this low profiling of European inputs as 'internalisation', a process whose result is that 'state agencies rarely deal with Commission texts directly but await their incorporation into national law while individual lower tier local authorities are often unaware of the European origin of environmental rules'. In contradistinction to Britain where European environmental policy has sometimes been branded as alien, the process of 'naturalisation' in France lessened the scope for controversy, but also produced delays and reduced public awareness of the impact of European measures.

The shortcomings of national transposition procedures have to an extent been compensated by the rulings of the ECJ. The legal force of directives has been increased by its doctrine of 'direct effect' which holds that, where the provisions of a directive are 'unconditional and sufficiently precise',[27] European law has primacy over national law. The highest administrative court in France, the *Conseil d'Etat*, was long considered unwilling to acknowledge the precedence of international treaties over national

---

[26] Krämer (1988: 24) reviews this issue.
[27] The quotation is from the case law of the ECJ and figures in Krämer (1991: 40), where 'direct effect' is discussed in detail.

law and to accept the 'direct effect' of directives. In the 'Nicolino' case of 1989, however, the *Conseil d'Etat* acknowledged the supremacy of European law. Moreover, the ECJ reinforced its case-law relating to 'direct effect' by its 1991 'Francovich' ruling, leading the *Conseil d'Etat* to accept the direct applicability of directives (Huglo and Mafoua Badinga, 1993: 94). As Roseren (1992) indicated, the underlying difficulty had been the reluctance of French courts to undertake judicial review of statutes, considering their role to be limited to the application of law enacted by parliament as sovereign body. As this reluctance was gradually shed, first by judicial then by administrative courts, so conformity of national provisions with Community law increased, bringing France more into line with practice across Europe in relation to derived law.

As a result of these developments, European legislation has been instrumental in pushing out the boundaries of French environmental policy, and filling in a series of normative objectives related to environmental quality. As pointed out by the IFEN (1994), French environmental policy making in the 1990s was in large part a process of updating national law in line with European measures. The OECD (1997: 211) indicated that, as at 1995, France had transposed almost all European environmental directives into national legislation and had notified Brussels that it had done so in relation to 118 directives out of 125. Examples include: the 1992 Water Act; the 1993 Landscape Act (which brought environmental considerations within the purview of building planning regulations); the 1992 Household and Industrial Waste Act; the 1992 Noise Abatement Act; the 1992 Biotechnologies Act; the 1993 Public Inquiries and Environmental Assessment Act (which transposed the 1985 European directive regarding public information and evaluation of cross-border impacts); the 1993 Quarries Act (placing quarries in the category of 'licensed sites ' regulated by the Environment Ministry); parts of the 1995 *loi Barnier* and the 1996 Atmospheric Pollution Act. Further, as stressed by Buller (1998: 78), the exuberance of European environmental legislation has empowered the French Environmental Ministry, resulting in an increase in its visibility and importance.

But by 1998 France was once again falling behind on her European commitments, leaving herself open to article 169 proceedings, including more citations before the ECJ than any other nation, most of which were in the environmental domain (*Le Monde*, 16.10.1998: 13). Indeed, former Environment Minister Lepage (1998: 141) declared that 'a number of Community texts have purely and simply been ignored in French law'.[28] In addition, few traces can be found of France acting as a pace-setter in European environmental policy. An early exception was the initiative of Environment Minister Michel d'Ornano in launching what became the 1979 Birds directive. However, as will be developed in Chapter 6, in arousing the ire of the French hunting lobby, the directive backfired. Having burnt her fingers, France seemed satisfied in the 1980s and 1990s to accompany environmental initiatives by countries taking a more proactive stance. This intermediary position makes generalisations regarding French strategy problematic. In European environmental policy France has not set the pace, acts of defiance can be identified but are rare, nor yet can she be considered 'neutral' since over time significant commitments can be traced. Moreover, France's uneven responses towards Community environmental policy are one manifestation of the tension between a grandiose European design and an ad hoc stumbling towards progress on practical issues, and need to be evaluated within the context of that tension, rather than on a simplistic spectrum of 'greenness'.

Conclusions

Although ambitious and comprehensive, European environmental policy has developed in an unsystematic manner. Theories of policy formulation reflect this diversity, being fragmented rather than cohesive, but in spanning a great number of actors, aims and strategies, they contribute to our understanding of uneven outcomes. In addition, the typology of policy modes and their application reveals fault-lines within Community environmental policy. Having few redistributive or stabilising policies, the EU is largely a regulatory state, and exclusively so in environmental domains. This lopsidedness explains some of the 'implementation deficits' observed within environmental policy. The production of regulations is a relatively cheap option, requiring few resources at the European level. However, their implementation requires substantial resources at national and subnational levels. Traditionally, national polities combined policy

---

[28] 'Un certain nombre de textes communautaires sont purement et simplement occultés en droit français.'

modes: stabilising and redistributive policies shifted resources in tandem with regulatory responses to fresh initiatives, new requirements and external shocks. An emblematic instance of this combinatorial strategy was the Common Agricultural Policy. The composite approach to policy allowed bargains to be struck among socioeconomic groups involving transfers of costs and sharing of burdens. If gains did not always offset losses, conflicts of interest could be diluted to socially non-critical levels.

European environmental policy, however, has operated under a set of dissymmetries. Firstly, its introduction into national systems produced immediate and evident costs, but long-term and diffuse benefits. Secondly, it displaced burdens but redistributed no resources. Thirdly, no clear rationale emerged for burden sharing among member states, and between producer and consumer interests, leading to improvised reactions which reproduced local and national particularities. Finally, as stressed by Weale (1996), negotiations over a common environmental policy, being anchored in the ideology of 'convergence', were directed at European compromises rather than at geographically-specific problem solving. Meanwhile, an optimal level of subsidiarity proved an unfindable grail.

The major consequence at national levels was a tortuous process of incomplete adaptation. The reactions of member states proved diverse, as is to be expected given the variation in salience of environmental issues, the variety of geographical conditions, available resource bases, institutional frameworks and political capacity. In France's case, the strategy of 'naturalisation' was attractive because in the field of 'high' politics she could shape the Community agenda to a profitable extent (particularly in the early years of the European club), whilst in the field of 'low' politics the costs of compromise were, by definition, contained within secondary arenas, and could be diffused and defused at domestic levels. Thus France tried to 'export' her policy preferences to the European level, whilst rebadging European 'imports' for home consumption. The danger of exogenous shocks was thereby minimised. Moreover, because of historically entrenched French leadership, national autonomy was maintained for a comparatively long period.

However, once the European Community welcomed more members and embraced new policy objectives, complex relations of interdependence emerged and national autonomy was ceded across a range of sectors. In the 1990s, the recognition of dwindling

French influence in European affairs, together with greater awareness of the costs of political and monetary integration, encouraged
Euroscepticism. The constitutional reforms necessitated by the
Maastricht and Amsterdam treaties sharpened recognition of the
domestic impact of the EU. In response France adjusted the 'naturalisation' strategy. In practice this meant that France aimed to propel and direct the transition to a single European currency, act in
concert regarding foreign and military affairs, whilst quietly maintaining national preferences in secondary arenas such as the
environment. Here the 'naturalisation' of Community directives
ensured that the French public was largely unaware of the impact
of European measures on national policies, apart from rare
instances where measures proved controversial (as with nature
conservation) or costly (as with water). In these cases, the reactions
of entrenched special interests posed serious problems to the political management of the environment.

To meet the challenges, the French authorities cushioned the
weight of regulatory burdens by exploiting the leeway for adjustment of European environmental legislation to local circumstances, and by maintaining flanking policies of distributive and
redistributive kinds, for example via hypothecated taxation. By
the late 1990s that leeway had certainly receded and the flanking
policies required review, but, because of the clumsiness of European policy processes and the artfulness of France's two-tier strategy of 'naturalisation', a slim margin for manoeuvre was
maintained. In environmental policy, the process of adjustment
was facilitated by two sets of domestic factors: the presence of a
'requisite variety' of instruments, both at transposition and
implementation stages, and by the 'absorptive capacity' of the
French polity to embrace diverse environmental policy streams
and accommodate conflicts of interests. However, as the case
study chapters will show, over time the freedom to choose
between instruments was to be progressively reduced, whilst the
polity's 'absorptive capacity' would be tested to its limits.

PART II

CASE STUDIES

6

THE NATURAL ENVIRONMENT:

Conserving Nature or Protecting Special Interests?

Introduction

Beneath current views of nature, two archetypes persist. One is the bountiful mother and giver of plenty who must be respected and protected; the other is the baleful father and source of destruction, against whom people and property require protection. This ancestral ambivalence finds its translation into individual behaviours and public policies. Yet instrumental responses to nature's dual stimulus betray a common characteristic, which is the urge to dominate nature: crudely in one case, by the neutralisation of threatening forces; subtly in the other, since the conservation of nature, whether as bread bowl, game reserve or sanctuary, always expresses preferences for particular landscapes and life-forms.

French responses to nature stem partly from geographical and ecological factors, partly from social and cultural ones. With its extensive mountain ranges, lowlands, beaches and shores, France is particularly varied in its geographical characteristics. Richly endowed in terms of climate types and biodiversity, France has around 40 percent of flora in Europe and, after the former Soviet Union, has the largest number of mammalian species (Le Grand, 1994). Given this scale and variety, it would be impossible to cover all of France's natural environment in one chapter. Attention will be focused on a cross-section of representative cases illustrating social attitudes to nature and their conversion into public policy. After a review of policy actors, a section is devoted to nature conservation, where the response model is largely nurturing. The problems raised by the hunt lobby are then investigated. Here the response pattern to nature is inherently aggressive, and policy arrangements are meso-corporatist in character. The final section considers responses to natural disasters which have been inherently defensive, with the central state setting up mechanisms to encourage solidarity.

This cross-section of analyses will illustrate the multiplicity of constructions of the natural environment, and the diversity of attempts to reconcile conflicting social, economic and environmental interests. In exploring the need to integrate resource allocation, rule-making and problem-solving modes of policy making, the argument is made that nature conservation – and environmental policy in general – depends on the striking of equitable societal bargains.

The Range of Policy Actors

In France, a great number of actors and agencies are involved in the management of the natural environment. Over the past twenty-five years, tension has prevailed between the central state and local authorities as to who is the better steward. As a result of this tension, a measure of both decentralisation and recentralisation has emerged. The core policy makers are parliament and the central government. Within the French Environment Ministry, the *Direction de la nature et des paysages* has responsibilities for the conservation of flora and fauna, landscapes and also listed buildings. The relevant field services are the DIREN, which are organised at regional level, but have no departmental layer, unlike the field services of the *Ministère de l'Equipement* and the *Ministère de l'Agriculture*, upon whose cooperation the DIREN are often reliant. In addition, within the Environment Ministry the *Direction de la prévention des pollutions et des risques* coordinates policy on natural and technological hazards.

Turning to the tiers of decentralised government, the regions now have responsibility for regional nature parks, but otherwise their nature policies have remained limited. Baldock, Holzner and Bennett (1987: 13) noted that the *départements* have developed conservation programmes funded by the *taxe départementale pour les espaces verts*, which is earmarked for conservation objectives. However, at the end of 1993, only sixty-three *départements* levied this tax (Prieur, 1996: 407). In terms of land-use planning, the key actors are the *communes*. Since the decentralisation laws of 1982–3, the municipality (not the prefecture) draws up the planning document known as the *plan d'occupation des sols* (POS) on the basis of which building permission is given. Thus on a day-to-day level, the decision to conserve natural spaces or develop them is taken by the mayor. In principle, the prefect exercises a posteriori supervision and can defer suspected cases of illegal granting of planning permission or illegal construction before the courts, but in practice this is an infrequent resort. As arbiters between diverging interests, councillors encounter constant pressure from property developers to sacrifice nature conservation for economic gain, whilst environmental groups, having few financial resources, seek to maximise the leverage theoretically afforded by law. The result is a series of highly conflictual situations, whose unravelling requires as much attention to social and political processes as to the natural world itself.

Conserving the Natural Heritage

In practice, nature conservation is an interventionist policy which addresses two sets of competing issues: one is broadly scientific, related to the maintenance of biodiversity, the other is socio-economic and related to development issues. As noted by Thiebaut (1988: 86), a major dilemma facing policy-makers is whether to prioritise the conservation of the past or the rights of future generations: the first can lead to conservatism and a reactionary defence of privilege, whilst the latter can give licence to unbridled exploitation. Policy makers have tried to steer their craft between these two reefs, but in the absence of clear values often lack a rudder. The result has been a series of ad hoc interventions, stemming from particular opportunities to accommodate conflicting interests, but whose ecological value in terms of habitat and species preservation is open to question.

The 1976 Nature Conservation Act

Overexploitation of nature has resulted in a number of measures to ensure the survival of flora and fauna. The 1930 National Heritage Act provided for the listing of some 7,500 architectural and natural sites on aesthetic, historic or scientific grounds, but in practice it offered inadequate protection. To tackle the deficiencies, the 1976 Nature Conservation Act was drawn up. The vastness of its ambitions can be gauged from its first article, which summarily made nature conservation *en bloc* a matter of 'public interest'.[1] However, the generality of its aims has proved problematic. Although nature conservation became an official objective, nothing in the act and its subsequent interpretation suggested that it had become a priority. As one among many conflicting sets of values and interests, doubts have perennially arisen as to whether conservation concerns are considered equal to economic or social ones. Although the 1976 act received near-unanimous support in parliament, little consensus emerged regarding its enforcement, nor have its ambitions been matched by the allocation of corresponding resources.

Some specific measures were nevertheless instituted by the act. Notably, environmental impact assessments were made compulsory for construction projects liable to cause harm, such as airports, roads, canals, dams and power stations. The study was to be paid for by the promoter, and required a survey of the initial state of the site, the damage and nuisance caused, as well as measures taken to minimise these or provide compensation. This was a bold move, but as the text was couched in ambiguous terms it led to divergent interpretations. Since the promoter draws up the assessment, it has frequently been used as a marketing exercise. Local authority development plans have been excluded from its terms. However, an important innovation was to increase public participation by enabling state-recognised environmental groups to bring complaints before the courts.

In addition to the 1976 act, a series of targeted measures were developed to extend the scope for nature conservation; here too the political deconstruction of the environment has been the prelude to action.

Nature parks and conservation sites

In order to achieve greater efficacy in nature conservation, the classic response has been to designate specific sites as worthy of

---

[1] The article read: 'La protection des espaces naturels et des paysages, la préservation des espèces animales et végétales, le maintien des équilibres biologiques auxquels ils participent et la protection des ressources naturelles contre toutes les causes de dégradation qui les menacent sont d'intérêt général'.

protective measures. Using Lowi's (1972) terms, this constitutes a form of 'distributive' policy, namely a policy characterised by a primary allocation of resources. Although the beginnings of nature parks can be traced to Fontainebleau in 1861, Sept-Iles in 1910 and the Camargue in 1927, most have been established from the 1960s on, with France following belatedly in the footsteps of the USA, the UK and continental neighbours in establishing conservation sites.[2] A wide typology of sites now exists.

The creation of national parks was enabled by the 1960 parliamentary act. Currently there are seven: Vanoise (set up in 1963), Ile de Port-Cros, (1963), Pyrénées occidentales (1967), Cévennes (1970), Ecrins (1973), Mercantour (1979) and Guadeloupe (1983). These parks each comprise an outer 'buffer' zone, and (except in the case of the Cévennes) a central zone where human inhabitation is prohibited in order to attain high levels of conservation. Together they cover some 3 percent of French territory and, with the exception of Port-Cros, lie in mountain areas. This skew is explained by the instrumental role played by forest owners in mountainous regions in the creation of national parks (Gerbaux, 1988: 150), and by low population densities (mountain areas cover about 20 percent of French territory but account for only 7 percent of population).

Management of each national park is undertaken by a public agency receiving state subsidies. Efforts have been made to make parks self-financing through agriculture, tourism and scientific research. The tension between nature conservation and economic development has been recurrent. In 1969, a proposal to build a ski resort in Vanoise prompted one of the first environmentalist outcries in France (Raveneau, 1986). Conflicts over development have since resurfaced perennially. In 1998, the Environment Minister's refusal of permission for an underground ski conveyor in Vanoise once again exercised local promoters (*Le Monde*, 2.12.1998: 12). Given the restrictive regulations in force in national parks and the hostility they can arouse, other forms of park have also developed.

Between their inception in 1967 and 1995, twenty-seven *parcs naturels régionaux* (PNR) were established. Comprising some 3,610,00 hectares, they cover approximately 9 percent of France, having a resident population of some two million people, being extremely varied in their physical characteristics and the flora and

[2] Viard (1990: 90–107) provided an interesting discussion of these developments.

fauna they harbour (Laurens, 1995: 342). Large variations in size exist among the PNR: they range from 260 square kilometres and covering nineteen *communes* to 3,480 square kilometres and 129 *communes*. Their hybrid brief is to conserve nature, provide information and education on wildlife as well as to promote economic and social development. Laurens (1995) and Gorgeu (1992) gave optimistic accounts of PNR success in promoting extensive agriculture aimed at sustainable development. Whilst Lanneaux and Chapuis (1995: 532) agreed that the PNR had been successful in their education and tourism aims, they also stressed that results were mixed as regards nature conservation.

Nature reserves were created by the 1976 Nature Conservation Act. Reserves are small in area but large in number – over a hundred – and can be publicly or privately owned. In 63 percent of cases they are managed by environmental groups (Mosse, 1996: 21). However, nature reserves tend to be under-financed, making it difficult to attain a high standard of conservation. Complementary measures include biotope protection areas – of which there are over 400 – which are established by order of the departmental prefect to prevent harm to specific species or their habitats. Similarly, the 1979 European 'Birds directive' provided for the creation of bird sanctuaries known as *zone de protection spéciale* (ZPS), of which there are ninety-nine. France has designated eleven sites under the 1971 Ramsar Convention on the conservation of wetlands, though systematic drainage has continued elsewhere.[3]

A nationwide inventory of outstanding areas of natural heritage has been compiled, known as *zones naturelles d'intérêt écologique, faunistique et floristique* (ZNIEFF). By 1995, some 15,000 areas have been identified (CFDD, 1996a, 153). Although designation as a ZNIEFF does not give automatic legal protection, it has been used in court to demonstrate the ecological value of a site (Coulombie, 1992: 7). However, concern has been voiced over the correlation between existing nature reserves and the habitats of endangered species. Whilst protected areas include a significant number of ZNIEFF (and therefore had been set up in the right places), many ZNIEFF lie outside the patchwork of protected areas. Consequently, to conserve biodiversity the ecologically coherent network of sites proposed under the European Community's 1992 'Habitats directive' and Natura 2000 scheme

---

[3] Data are from IFEN (1996c).

has relevance for France. The directive provided for the conservation of 172 natural habitats, fifty-seven species of flora and eighty-three species of fauna, with the Natura 2000 network of protected sites to have been drawn up by 30 June 1995. Progress was slow, however. European classificatory criteria were different to those of the ZNIEFF, and French databases had to be modified. Moreover, as with other nature conservation issues, rival constituencies emerged. Hunters resisted the establishment of Natura 2000 sites, believing that hunting would be banned within them. Farmers sought to reschedule or amputate potential sites, in order to preserve their flexibility in planting cereal crops such as maize. In response, the right-wing Juppé government froze the directive's implementation in 1996. In 1997, the incoming Jospin government reopened the issue, proposing a management fund – the *fonds de gestion des milieux naturels* – in the 1999 Finance Bill to pay for the implementation of Natura 2000 (*Le Monde*, 11.9.1998: 7). Environment Minister Voynet sought to make up for lost time, but her list of designated sites was struck down in October 1999 by the *Conseil d'Etat* on a technicality. At the time of writing the 1992 'Habitats directive' had not been formally transposed into French law, whilst its substantive measures remained to be implemented. The European Commission has made several referrals to the European Court of Justice, with the threat of large fines and withholding of structural funds possible. The stakes are high since France has one of the largest and most biodiverse national territories in the Western world, and has a major role to play in European nature conservation.

Policy towards sensitive natural areas

If nature conservation is to go beyond the demarcation of a limited number of sites, it needs to encompass larger expanses of countryside, coasts and mountains.

Generally speaking, landscapes are not protected by legislative or regulatory measures. Sainteny (1999) argued that the marked decline in the quality of French landscapes due to urban building, construction of infrastructures and changes in agricultural usage (hedge removals, drainage of wetlands etc.) called for a more assertive landscape policy. The 1993 Landscapes Act represented a measure of progress in that it aimed to preserve and improve the aesthetic qualities of urban and rural scenery, by encouraging 'sympathetic' construction, limiting the erection of billboards and providing for underground ducting of power cables.

Additional measures have been taken in relation to forests. Contrary to popular belief, woodlands in France have actually increased in area. Although historical data suffer from gaps and idiosyncrasies (traditionally forests were subject to taxes, hence owners had an incentive to underestimate their size), the occurrence of a 'forest transition' has been demonstrated, with a nadir in forest depletion near the start of the nineteenth century and major increases in forest cover thereafter (Mather, Fairbairn and Needle, 1999). Woodlands covered some 9.1 million hectares in 1879, rising to 14.3 million hectares in 1995 (IFEN, 1996b: 45). The criticism has been made that intensive forestry methods resulted in the planting of coniferous rather than deciduous trees, so changing the character of the countryside. The brunt of this criticism has been borne by the *Office national des forêts* (ONF), a public sector organisation charged with woodlands conservation and commercial forestry, which thereby acts as an instrument of 'distributive' policy. It is responsible for the management of 4.4 million hectares of publicly owned woodlands in metropolitan France and 8 million hectares in the overseas dominions. It has been criticised by conservationists for the clearing of tropical forests in New Caledonia and Guyana (Kempf, 1994: 64–5). The 1985 Forestry Act sought to reduce excessive tree felling and improve forest management, with better preventive measures against fires. Public subsidies are available for owners of woods covering more than 10 hectares who maintain agreed standards. Overall, if forestation trends have been broadly positive, specific problems persist and the economic future of the sector is itself under review due to international competition (Barthod, 1998).

Mountain areas constitute a particular set of challenges. France has five mountain ranges – the Alps, the Pyrenees, the Vosges, the Jura and the *Massif Central* – covering about a quarter of the country. As demonstrated by Gerbaux (1988), public policy on the use of mountains areas started in the nineteenth century. Formerly conducted in concert with farmers and foresters within a corporatist framework, recent reforms have opened out the policy community, giving greater scope for entrepreneurial mayors to develop their *communes*. New legislation (the 1985 *loi Montagne*, the 1994 *loi Bosson* and the 1995 *loi Barnier*) provides a framework for the reconciliation of three types of interests – hillside agriculture and forestry, tourism, and nature conservation – but without establishing a hierarchy among them or fixing norms of conduct (Lascoumes, 1995). According to Vigouroux (1996), each modification in the legislation has reduced its coherence and effectively made economic development easier, as evidenced by the expansion in France's winter tourism industry. But after a period of decline, the population in mountain areas has stabilised and the need for a sustainable pattern of development acknowledged.

France's coastline stretches some 5,500 kilometres, and is used for a wide number of purposes: fishing, seafood cultivation, agriculture, tourism. Social and economic pressures on land use are high. In the interests of nature conservation, the Coastal Conservatory – *Conservatoire de l'espace littoral et des rivages lacustres* (CELRL) – was set up in 1975. Loosely modelled on the British National Trust, the CELRL is a public body which buys up land adjacent to seas and lakes. In a telling instance of 'distributive' policy, only outright purchase was considered sufficiently effective to overcome laxity and abuse (Faucon, 1992: 271). Thus the CELRL is an instance of state intervention to overcome local stalemates. However, once purchased, land is turned over to local authorities for management and opened to the public. Mosse (1996: 15) noted that by 1995, the CELRL had acquired some 45,000 hectares of land (corresponding to 622 kilometres of coastline, 11 percent of the total). Its modest financial resources are provided solely by central government (see table 4.5). Sites near the sea are prey to speculative building projects, pushing up prices and making public purchase more difficult. A policy alternative to outright acquisition was embodied in the 1986 Coastline Act which regulates development schemes in 1,124 coastal *communes* whose scenery is considered 'remarkable'. Based on a series of principles contained in 'soft law' (Calderon, 1994), such as the 1973 Council of Europe resolution on coastal zones and the 1981 European Coastline Charter, the act aimed to achieve integrated management of coastal areas by reconciling economic and environmental objectives. It made construction illegal on a 100 metre band from the sea (measured at high tide levels) and imposed restrictions in relation to the next 400 metre strip. However, other measures introduced into the legislation, such as the 'get-out clause' referring to 'new hamlets integrated into the environment',[4] provided leeway for property developers.

---

[4] 'hameaux nouveaux intégrés à l'environnement'.

A recognised problem is that buildings mushroom with scant regard for legality. Examples include extensions to ski resorts such as Vaujany (Alps), construction at Somport in the Pyrenees national park, or the bridge between La Rochelle and the Ile de Ré. In such instances, and subsequent to court actions by environmental groups, the administrative and judicial authorities have been known to rule that property development was in breach of regulations, yet proved powerless to undo it. Indeed, given the overhang of 'crosswise regulation' (discussed in Chapter 4), prefects tend to prioritise the preservation of good relations with mayors over the exercise of their powers of a posteriori supervision. Coulombie (1992) gloomily concluded that in practice coastline conservation was left 'abandoned by politicians . . . betrayed by the administrators . . . and a victim of lawyers'. The evaluation of the 1986 Coastline Act made by the 1999 Gressier report was more positive, though this too acknowledged that new construction proceeded apace with over 10 percent of coastal *communes* not conforming with the law (*Le Monde*, 25.2.1999: 13).

In summary, a wide range of measures has been implemented in France to conserve nature, but due to conflicting priorities the results have been uneven. Distributive measures which set up dedicated conservation sites have proved most effective, but have been limited in extension due to lack of resources and local stalemates. On the other hand, the drawing up of a framework of rules to balance environmental and economic priorities has proved less satisfactory in a context marked by the 'managed rurality' perspective (discussed in Chapter 1), which accords greater weight to the preferences of farmers and hunters than to conservationists.

Protecting the Hunt Lobby?

Three major issues have emerged in relation to hunting in France: the preservation of biodiversity in relation to protected or threatened species, the adequacy of arrangements for culling of proliferating and harmful species, and the allocation of amenity between social groups where one – the hunt lobby – exercises ascendancy by its privileges and use of firearms. Developments around the French hunt lobby illustrate the difficulties surrounding the renegotiation of a social bargain in the interests of better environmental policy. Further, because the meso-corporatist model found in hunting is clear-cut, it helps elucidate some of the scenarios discussed in later chapters.

The legal and institutional framework

French law follows Roman law in considering game as *res nullius*, meaning that it has no owner.[5] This legal predisposition has profoundly influenced French attitudes to wildlife and to hunting. The 1964 *loi Verdeille* established hunting areas managed by so-called ACCA (*associations communales de chasse agréées* - registered municipal hunting associations) in twenty-eight *départements* with the aim of controlling pests. In these areas, landowners with holdings of less than 20 hectares are forced by law to join the ACCA. Small landowners are powerless to prevent hunting on their property, nor are they offered compensation for nuisance caused by hunters. In effect, the *loi Verdeille* set hunting rights above their property rights. Large landowners, however, can enclose their property and set up fee-paying game reserves.

Management of the hunting sector constitutes an example of meso-corporatism as defined in Chapter 1. The meso-corporatist system granted a monopoly over management of a sector to interested parties in exchange for keeping order within it and accepting official supervision. The authority responsible for the regulation of hunting is the Environment Ministry and within it the National Hunting Office (*Office national de la chasse* – ONC). The latter is colonised by hunting federations which were instituted under the Vichy government in 1941 and offer an example of state-sponsored corporatism (Vadrot, 1986: 107; Mathieu, 1987: 56–7; Darbon, 1997: 135–43). Obtaining a hunting permit requires payment of a fee and entails membership of the departmental hunting federation, which receives most of the proceeds. The national association of departmental federations acts as a pressure group in relation to the ONC which, in any case, is chaired by a prestigious member of the hunting fraternity. The ONC employs a body of *gardes-champêtres* (wardens) to enforce regulations. In principle, they are public employees but in practice they report to

---

[5] Jaffeux (1990: 149) highlighted the consequences in comparing: 'l'idée plutôt latine où les chasseurs considéraient que la faune leur appartenait et qu'ils pouvaient l'exploiter, à l'idée anglo-saxonne où la faune appartient à la société toute entière qui ne concède l'exploitation de la faune sauvage par les chasseurs que dans un cadre strict et limité'.

the chair of the departmental hunting federation, who produces a yearly appraisal of 'his' staff.[6]

In effect, the hunt lobby has captured the state regulator and pays itself to exploit 'free' wildlife. In defending hunting 'rights', it pushes for maximalist interpretations of open seasons, sidelines nature conservationists, ignores the property rights of small landowners and refuses compensation for its appropriation of resources. Using Lowi's (1972: 300) terminology, policy towards hunting can be characterised as having both 'distributive' components, due to private appropriation of the 'commons' (here wildlife), and 'constituent' components, since the meso-corporatist framework established an 'environment of conduct' based on log-rolling.[7]

Concerns have been voiced perennially over problems within the sector. Environment Minister Poujade (1975: 151) stated that the 'hunting education of many hunters was zero'.[8] Thus in 1976 an examination was introduced as a requirement for a hunting licence. The examination is run by the departmental federations, covering the identification of wildlife and knowledge of regulations. Reports by ONC officials have repeatedly questioned the adequacy of training given in relation to safe handling of firearms (*Le Monde*, 11.9.1999: 11). According to ONC figures, in the 1997–8 season forty-five people were killed in a total of 224 accidents, with the number of serious accidents rising in 1998-9 to 259, the highest figures for twenty years (*Le Monde*, 3.5.1999: 11; 9.6.1999: 12). The commonest cause was the flouting of safety measures. In 89 percent of cases, hunt participants were the victims, but householders within ACCA and ramblers suffered too. Deliberate attacks on wardens have also been recorded.

Hunting constitutes a differentiated phenomenon not only because of the variety of practices and behaviour, but also because of its changing social and cultural bases. As Fabiani (1982, 1985) showed, representations of hunting have evolved

---

[6] Romi (1990c: 392–3) noted that *gardes-champêtres* had even been obliged to put up election posters for the party of their hunting federation's choice, namely CPNT.

[7] Darbon (1997) argued that this neocorporatist model came under stress due to conflicts within the ranks of the hunting community, particularly since the rise of the CPNT, which has resorted to electoral pressure rather than the traditional administrative arrangements, but nevertheless acknowledges the model's persistence.

[8] 'l'éducation cynégétique de beaucoup de chasseurs était nulle'.

through numerous historical phases: aristocratic privilege, agricultural necessity, a republican 'right', rural tradition, a modern 'sport'. The legitimacy of each has been contested as social and political conditions changed. The most recent phase of questioning stems on the one hand from the ethical questions raised by bloodsports and, on the other, from ecological issues, since the survival of game is in doubt in a context where habitats and the reproduction of species are threatened by environmental pressures (notably, intensive agriculture, with its use of pesticides and herbicides, and rapid urbanisation which is reducing green spaces). Hunters have responded by setting up breeding centres for game (such as hybrids of boar) and releasing animals back into the wild. However, in a Darwinian twist, some new varieties have proved too successful. The population of boars has exploded in southern France, causing mounting damage to crops (*Le Monde,* 4.12.1998). The trend to substitute bred animals for 'natural' game has gathered pace over several decades. These factors contextualise the argument put forward by the hunt lobby that its activities are sanctioned by time-hallowed 'tradition'. In reality, its stress on the preservation of rural identity constitutes a recent variant in a long line of legitimatisations of hunting. It is no coincidence that this representation has crystallised at a time when the institutionalised privileges of hunters are being challenged.

Mobilisation against European rule-making

The power of the French hunt lobby is revealed by its ability to block European nature conservation legislation. Its opposition to the regulatory framework instituted by the 1979 'Birds directive' – which banned the hunting of migrating birds during their reproductive season – is now infamous. Co-sponsored in the drafting stage by French Environment Minister Michel d'Ornano,[9] the directive was unanimously agreed in the Council of Ministers. The decision was a classic example of the need for transboundary cooperation in environmental policy, given that bird migration patterns embrace the whole of Europe and extend into Africa. It designated forty-eight species of bird that could be hunted, if

[9] Already in 1969, measures to limit the hunting of birds had been introduced by the French government, with a failed attempt to ban the hunting of turtle doves in spring. These measures prompted a strategy of civil disobedience by hunters from the 1970s on.

states so ruled: France drew up the longest list (thirty-seven species), whilst Belgium and the Netherlands had less than ten, and Luxembourg had none (Mathieu, 1987: 207). France has the longest open season in Europe (over six months), as well as the largest number of hunters, some 1.6 million (Darbon, 1997: 51).[10]

Enforcement of the directive has been passionately resisted by hunters, with widespread flouting of its provisions, frequent mass demonstrations and political pressure at local and national levels. Since 1983, a series of cases brought forward by environmental groups has been heard by French and European courts.[11] The hunt lobby put forward various arguments to justify its actions. Firstly, it contested the legal basis of the 1979 directive, arguing that the Treaty of Rome did not give EC organs the authority to legislate in this area. Whilst the legal base for the environmental legislation of the EC prior to the 1987 Single European Act was acknowledged as indirect (namely articles 100 and 235 of the 1957 Rome Treaty, which made no specific reference to the environment), the ECJ nevertheless ruled that it was sufficient. Secondly, the hunt lobby claimed that the timing and length of its preferred open seasons presented no ecological dangers to the reproductive habits of listed species. It applied political pressure to prefects – who set the relevant calendars – into accepting their view. Typically this means permission to hunt in February. These prefectoral decisions have repeatedly been overturned by administrative courts, including the *Conseil d'Etat*, to little effect. Thirdly, in the 1980s hunters organised themselves as a political force. The establishment of a single-issue party *Chasse, Pêche, Nature, Tradition* (CPNT) allowed them to contest elections at local and European levels (see Chapter 3).

Whilst its anti-European stance is not shared by all members of the French hunting and fishing fraternities, CPNT has acted as a lightning rod for diffused discontent and resistance to European integration, particularly in southwest rural areas where agricultural reform has proved problematic. The party channelled one element of the anti-Maastricht vote in the 1992 referendum. Proportional representation gave it a foothold in regional

---

[10] The number of hunters is in decline, having stood at 2.3 million in the early 1970s (Vallet, 1975: 209).

[11] Administrative lawyers have produced a copious literature on these disputes: see Malafosse (1981), Untermaier (1988), Romi (1989, 1990c), Janin (1991) and Vignier (1995).

assemblies and the opportunity to exert pressure on the mainstream right which, being squeezed by both the left and the far right, has been willing to strike political bargains. Thus in February 1997, Alain Juppé, as Prime Minister and Mayor of Bordeaux (close to French hunting heartlands), promoted André Goustat, a CPNT leader, to a government position as 'Rural Commissioner'. However, polls have shown that French public opinion is largely opposed to the positions of hunters, with 49 percent of respondents 'disapproving' of hunting as a sport to 39 percent 'approving', whilst 83 percent support a close season during animal reproductive periods; moreover hunting remains a minority activity, pursued by 4 percent of respondents as compared to 16 percent who fish and 30 percent who ramble (IFEN, 1998b).

The hunt lobby has been virulent in its defence of 'traditional' hunting methods,[12] and repeatedly forced the authorities to cave in to its demands. Not only did it successfully resist the implementation of the 1979 'Birds directive', but it obstructed the 1992 'Habitats directive' in the belief that the policy would set up sanctuaries in which hunting was prohibited. Charbonneau (1996: 449) commented that their emotionally charged behaviour was based on 'misinformation' and 'paranoia'. The lobby reacted violently to the appointment of Dominique Voynet as Environment Minister in 1997, since she was a *Vert*, a member of the Anti-Hunt Rally (*Rassemblement des opposants à la chasse*) and determined to implement both the 'Birds' and the 'Habitats' directives. A demonstration was organised in Paris in February 1998 to protest yet again against the 1979 'Birds directive', and against Voynet's decision to enforce it. The event illustrated the long-standing hostility between hunters and ecologists, and its translation into political polarisation. It had the specific aim of pressurising parliamentarians to modify French legislation. In July 1998 a private member's bill was passed tabling a longer open season (mid-July to end of February), so 'legalising' prefectoral decisions to allow hunting in February and, in principle, preventing administrative courts from ruling such decisions illegal. This decision was all the more surprising since, as indicated in Chapter 5, European law takes precedence over national law, and it set a collision course with the EU. The Commission responded by issuing a 'reasoned

---

[12] These include the use of nets and glue to capture birds. Another technique involves pouring waste oil on the ground to attract boars, then shooting them as they roll around drowning their fleas (Piétrasanta, 1993: 147–8).

opinion' in August 1998, and referred the case to the European Court of Justice in December 1998. Further, the ruling by the *Conseil d'Etat* of the 3 December 1999 again confirmed the precedence of European law over national law, effectively striking down the 1998 act as illegal. In a different action, the European Court of Human Rights in April 1999 ruled against the *loi Verdeille* on three counts: violation of property rights, denial of freedom of association, and discrimination in relation to small landowners. To find a compromise, Socialist MP François Patriat was appointed by Dominique Voynet in July 1999 to make recommendations for a new law to revise the *loi Verdeille,* reform hunting institutions (notably the ONC), review hunting practices (including safety issues), and enable conformity of the French open season with European legislation.

In summary, hostility aroused by rival claims on resource allocation produced a political impasse. Confrontations between hunters and ecologists illustrate the difficulty of promoting nature conservation policy in France, due not to government inertia but to the power of special interests. The conflict demonstrates the obstructionism of the meso-corporatist policy community. Over time, the bargains struck to maintain social order fossilised into a stubborn defence of privilege. Attempts to modify policy by 'new' social actors were handicapped by their exclusion from the policy community and the violent demonstrations of extremists. In response, new 'advocacy coalitions' of nature conservationists and small landowners emerged, seeking to replace old 'deals' with new 'rules', notably via the intermediary of European directives and court rulings. However, the enforcement of legislation remained a problem when national and local authorities were divided over priorities, and where the vagaries of electoral politics encouraged short-term concessions.

Defending against Natural Disasters

As with hunting, the desire to dominate nature emerges strongly in relation to natural disasters, which have preoccupied humanity since time immemorial. Modern technologies have held out the hope that nature could at last be tamed. In reality, many disasters – such as earthquakes and tidal waves – cannot be averted. Ideally, the combination of prediction and prevention would allow evasive and damage-limiting action. However, the ability to predict is limited, whilst alternative zones for habitation and defensive barriers are often found wanting, meaning that many communities must live with high levels of risk. In addition, excessive faith in technological prowess, inattention to natural cycles, together with negligence and greed, have frequently aggravated problematic situations, transforming natural phenomena into human tragedies.

The varied topography of mainland France, combined with the distinctive geographical features of its widely-spread overseas territories, provide for the occurrence of most forms of catastrophe: floods, forest fires, gales, avalanches, earthquakes, tornadoes, even volcanic eruptions. In Martinique, the eruption of Mount Pelée in 1903 caused some 20,000 deaths, and in Guadeloupe a tornado killed 1,200 in 1928 (Ledoux, 1995: 17). When the river Tarn burst its banks in 1930, 200 people died. The recent period has brought is own swathe of disasters. In October 1987, the gales which uprooted trees and tore off roofs in southeast England crossed to Brittany, with similar consequences including two deaths. The storms of December 1999 were even worse, with widespread damage to property, 3.4 million people without power and fifty-seven deaths. The droughts of 1989–1993 led to increased occurrence of forest fires, especially in Provence-Côte d'Azur. Yet floods constitute the largest single source of danger in terms of frequency and harm (Morin and Caragonta, 1988: 13), with the period of 1992–4 seeing a large number, and the events of November 1999 leaving twenty-six dead in Aude, Tarn and Midi-Pyrénées.

The 1982 Natural Catastrophes Act

In the early 1980s, policy on natural disasters attained new prominence. Haroun Tazieff was appointed to head a committee on natural disasters and make recommendations. The ensuing 1982 Natural Catastrophes Act provided a belated response to the generous sentiments of the 1946 constitution, proclaiming the solidarity of the French people in sharing the burden of natural calamities. It introduced a mixed regime in which private insurance companies sold policies to householders and were liable for losses, but with the state acting as underwriter of last resort; thereby compensation was given to victims on the basis of a national redistributive system (Jullien, 1998). Though initially focused on compensation mechanisms, parliamentary debate also identified potential perverse effects. The new insurance regime offered incentives to unscrupulous promoters since building in at-risk zones was profitable (due to depressed land values), whilst the cost of 'naturally-caused' damage could be discounted since insurers (and finally the taxpayer) would pick up the bill.

To reduce untoward outcomes, the act proposed preventive measures based on *plans d'exposition aux risques* (PER). The latter defined areas most exposed to natural hazards, with construction being banned (in principle) from central, high-risk zones and subject to tighter building regulations in buffer zones. However, their implementation encountered various obstacles. Firstly, scientific knowledge was fairly well developed in relation to some dangers (e.g. floods), inadequate in relation to others (gales) or considered too sensitive for public dissemination (tremors).[13] Further, cartographic representation of risk – which is essential for zoning measures – is variable in accuracy. Secondly, the scale of the operation posed problems. An initial survey suggested some 10,000 *communes* (almost a third of the total) might be involved, entailing protracted and expensive surveys (Peyret, 1986). Thirdly, an experimental phase revealed local resistance. The PER were to be drawn up by the state, and involved an unwelcome measure of recentralisation. Property values in at-risk zones systematically fell. Subsequently progress slowed to a crawl, with only 347 PER approved by 1995 (Dequéant, 1995). Fourthly, floods – the most frequent form of disaster – are worsened in intensity and impact by urbanisation, raising sensitive questions about where and how to build. The construction of buildings and roads leads to major reductions in soil permeability and radically alters conditions of water run-off. Consequently, areas which were once thought safe can be put at risk of floods by subsequent, ill-considered construction.

The limits of prevention

This last point is supported by the disasters in Nîmes and Vaison-La-Romaine. The flooding of Nîmes on 3 October 1988 affected 45,000 people, with a death toll of nine; 3,500 businesses, 9,500 cars and many buildings suffered serious damage (Jez, 1989). The cause was a six-hour rain-storm which, though exceptionally

---

[13] Over 1970–80, specialists drew up so-called ZERMOS maps indicating risks from tremors; these are not made available to the public (Ledoux, 1995: 392–3).

heavy, was not a unique occurrence. Historical investigation subsequently revealed that such extreme events recurred approximately once every hundred years (Hémain, 1989: 427). However,
this knowledge had been lost from collective memory. Further, in
the contemporary period, intensive urbanisation on the steep hillsides near the city had removed natural channels for water run-
off. Under centennial conditions, the deluge poured down the
valley basin, sweeping cars and trees before it.[14]

The flash-floods in the town of Vaison-La-Romaine (Provence)
on the 22 September 1991 presented a similar case. When the river
Ouvèze burst its banks, it deposited large quantities of mud and
rubbish on the town, causing thirty-seven deaths. Although the
immediate cause was natural, the scale of destruction was magni-
fied by human activities: the river-path had been artificially
diverted, jerry-built housing erected in the flood-plain, and a
recent extension of vine growing on hillsides had led to soil
erosion.[15] These events led to a questioning of the adequacy of
traditional engineering methods for the control of natural waters
(such as dam-building and river diversion), and exploration of a
wider range of factors in flood prevention.

For the people concerned, these disasters demonstrated the
value of the compensation provisions set up by the 1982 act.
However, the preventive component of the act transpired to be a
failure (Ledoux, 1995: 120). Indeed commentators such as Decrop
(1991) raised fundamental questions about the potential for this
type of policy to have preventive effects. Drawing lessons from
previous shortcomings, the 1995 *loi Barnier* simplified preventive
procedures, which were renamed *plans de prévention des risques
naturels prévisibles* (PPR). These contain stringent building regulations suited to local conditions, and are drawn up locally by the
prefect. The law instituted better maintenance of water courses
liable to cause hazard; and gave the state the option of making
compulsory purchase orders on high-risk property, allocating
funds to finance them (Legrand, 1996). These measures once again
provided technical, engineering solutions supported by redistributive mechanisms and attained a degree of success. By 1999, 1,692
out of some 10,000 at-risk *communes* had drawn up a PPR (*Le
Monde*, 15.4.1999).

[14] Detailed accounts can be found in Fabre et al. (1989) and Gilbert (1990: 121–37).
[15] For details, see Mennessier (1992).

Complementary options have also been recommended. Romi (1993c: 35) concluded that the need was not to multiply regulations, but to encourage responsible behaviour and so prevent the amplification of adverse events. Whilst this is undoubtedly true, restrictive approaches stressing individual responsibility are problematic given the diversity of social situations. In a well-known cycle, at-risk areas tend to be populated by the poor, since devalued housing attracts impoverished residents. Thus as Barraqué (1994: 144) argued, risk management requires collective responsibility at the local level in order to implement equitable and broad-based solutions. Policy frameworks dominated by a technical orientation can evade the social and political dimensions of the issue by stressing large-scale construction projects (dams, dikes, etc.).[16] Nîmes constitutes a case in point, since after the flood the drilling of underground tunnels was preferred to changes in housing policy.

In summary, although preserving the social status quo simplifies the lives of decision makers in the short term, the wider reforms required for long-term improvements to protect against natural hazards remain underexplored. No doubt redistributive arrangements based on household insurance and preventive schemes based on engineering solutions have softened the blows. But in relation to housing and development in at-risk areas, the terms of the underlying social bargain are deliberately left untouched, since politicians are chary of the possible consequences of renegotiation. In view of the frequency of recent disasters, and the increased likelihood of gales and flooding due to climate change, it seems inevitable that this policy will be revisited in the future.

Conclusions

Social constructions of nature have taken a variety of forms, each carrying particular cognitive and emotional charges, and entailing different categories of policy response. Some constructions express aesthetic or spiritual satisfaction derived from the grace

---

[16] This is not to ignore the importance of sound engineering practices. Indeed, particular circumstances require their upgrading. Nice and the Côte d'Azur face significant hazards from tremors, yet only 5 percent of buildings comply with relevant norms (Morin and Caracostea, 1988: 18).

and beauty of creation. They yield the nurturing impulse, a wish to conserve nature. But since the natural heritage has been extensively remodelled by human activity, this impulse blends into the anthropocentric desire to preserve cultural history and artefacts. Alongside these conceptions has emerged an ecocentric stress on the maintenance of biodiversity. This too has yielded multiple concepts: a scientific understanding of the interdependence of the natural world, an ethical concern with the survival of non-human life-forms together with their habitats, and a diffuse awareness of humanity's dependence on the biosphere. These relatively new world-views have impacted upon popular consciousness in France, yet older visions carried by rural ancestry remain prominent. For some, nature is there to be aggressively hunted. For others, nature remains a threat against which human beings must defend themselves. Overall, defensive and aggressive patterns of response are dominant in France, whilst nurturing – though present – is recessive. The 'managed rurality' perspective, with its connotations of traditional agricultural practices, rural retreats and homespun values, grows from this underlying configuration of responses to nature. But in a context of cultural change, a rift has opened between those seeking to conserve and those seeking to exploit nature.

To embrace this duality, French environmental policy has greatly expanded over the last three decades. Legislative responses to the conflicts provoked by the natural environment have not aimed at imposing 'solutions'.[17] Rather they have provided frameworks within which social conflicts can be contained and managed, if not necessarily resolved. However, the scales of the law are not evenly balanced, having a tendency to tip towards economic interests. Thus nature policies in France have needed to extend beyond formal, legal frameworks and accommodate resource allocation issues. But bringing in resource allocation also brought in the central state. This is because the French state has a unique ability to mobilise different types of resource: it alone can be an 'insurer of last resort' (an economic resource), act as a property holder of integrity (a moral resource) or have the legitimacy to strike social bargains (a political resource).

---

[17] As Lascoumes (1995: 407) indicated: 'Cette politique n'est donc pas faite de systèmes de contrainte unilatérale qui imposeraient d'autorité aux acteurs sociaux des règles directes de comportement vis-à-vis de l'environnement'.

In order to characterise these varied French policies towards the natural environment and identify their defining kernel, Table 6.1 summarises public initiatives by drawing on Lowi's (1972) policy typology. From the preceding discussion and the spread of policy modes, it emerges that France has concentrated on constituent, distributive and redistributive policies: these policy modes all mobilise resources in specific directions. Regulations, however, provide an enabling, rather than a directing, framework. In consequence, policy has mostly taken the form of 'deals' supported by 'rules' – rather than the reverse. Each of the three major areas under review contains a social bargain. In relation to nature conservation, it is based on the collective management – and sometimes ownership – of areas of outstanding importance. In relation to natural disasters, it is based on societal burden sharing legitimatised by the republican principle of national solidarity. But in relation to hunting, precedence is given to the prerogatives of the hunt lobby over the property rights of small landowners or the amenity rights of ramblers. This defence of special interests constituted exceptional treatment, and as such contained the seeds of social conflict. It proved doubly problematic once European nature policy developed, since the latter gives primacy to a 'rule-based' approach, unlike the predominantly 'deal-based' French approach. This constitutes the underlying reason why European nature directives have provoked adverse reaction and an apparent policy impasse.

The problems have been aggravated by constraints on state action, which has been curtailed by its decreasing ability to mobilise resources, and its distance from local problems. As regards the hunt lobby, a historical deal was superseded by a

Table 6.1. Categories of policy towards the natural environment

Policy type	Domain	Territorial level	Policy subsystem
Regulatory	Wildlife conservation	Europe	Transnational policy networks
Constituent	Hunting	National	Meso-corporatist policy community
Distributive	Protected areas	National/ regional	Decentralised policy networks
Redistributive	Natural catastrophes	National/local	Centralised policy community

European rule under conditions of minimal consultation with a central and powerful actor. The new rule impacted on the allocation of resources, since the appropriation of wildlife by hunters was curtailed (though not banned as their lobby sometimes claims). The shock proved traumatic in that the 'absorptive capacity' of the French polity – here its ability to soften unwelcome blows – was exhausted by the lopsidedness of the existing social bargain. In France, much wildlife was already classified as game, and game was freely available for hunting. Thus the authorities were left with few residual resources to trade. The result was a stalemate between advocacy coalitions for and against the European framework for wildlife protection.

The general conclusion drawn from the evolution in policy modes is that environmental policy will *fail* if it is inattentive to existing social bargains, incapable of mobilising resources, or unable to strike a new deal. In other words, 'new rules' are no substitute for 'old deals'.

7

THE INDUSTRIAL ENVIRONMENT:

'Command and Control' or Corporatist Policy
Making?

Introduction

This chapter focuses on public policies bearing on industry
which have the aim of promoting 'environmental protection'
or, more specifically, controlling pollution and preventing hazards. Concerns over these problems were aggravated by the wave
of industrial expansion that characterised the postwar period.
From the 1960s on, industrial emissions to air, water and soil
became major policy issues, whilst highly publicised disasters
focused public attention on the large-scale hazards of certain processes. Public policy adapted gradually to changing contexts.
Since the nineteenth century, French policy has been characterised
by a mix of statutory and administrative controls, and by the use
of a 'requisite variety of instruments' (Héritier, Knill and Mingers,
1996: 2) to manage industrial impacts on the environment whilst
preserving the play of market forces. But from the 1970s, environmental protection – particularly as set out in European Community directives – has been predicated on regulatory norms
related to emissions standards and hazard prevention, and based
on an apparent 'command and control' policy mode.

The question then arises of how this top-down orientation can
be reconciled with the claim made by Larrue and Chabason (1998:
74) that 'the main characteristic of the implementation of French
environmental policy is that it is based on consensus rather than

on imposition of constraints'. In response to this question, it will be argued that the state has maintained the appearances of an authoritarian policy mode, whilst in reality negotiating policy content with industry representatives. This duality is the result of the interaction between the French 'statist' tradition (expressed particularly at the policy formulation stage), and a system of corporatist intermediation (operating mainly at the implementation stage). As discussed in Chapter 1, the 'variety of corporatism' in question here is that of 'meso-corporatism', defined by Cawson (1986: 38) as 'a specific socio-political process in which organisations representing monopolistic functional interests engage in political exchange with state agencies over public policy outputs which involves those organisations in a role which combines interest representation and policy implementation through delegated self-enforcement'.

To show how this system has worked in practice, the first section investigates the regulatory framework bearing on industrial pollution control, and notes the latitude enjoyed by industrialists and regulators in their negotiations. The second section examines the framework for the prevention of major technological hazards, where 'command and control' does pertain, but takes particular inflections. A third section, reviewing the use of environmental taxes as a flanking policy to regulation, shows that the imposition of financial charges was tempered by hypothecation, meaning that industrialists largely recouped taxes paid in by receiving subsidies for environmental investments. Taken together, these features constituted a state-industry bargain which delivered environmental performance improvements, but was characterised by the in-built limitations of meso-corporatism.

Industrial Pollution Control

France has often been associated with an authoritarian policy style. The Economist Intelligence Unit report (1990: 25) described the French approach to the environment as administrative, and imbued with scientific and technocratic confidence. Likewise Trilling (1981: 74) pointed to the importance of the 'active, *dirigiste* state' and claimed that the adversarial mode characterising the USA did *not* pertain in France: 'unlike its American counterpart, the French state is a unitary, administrative state which makes the strategy of playing off checks and balances . . . of playing the judiciary or the legislative against the executive, and vice versa, a much less potentially fruitful, and hence a much less important strategy for French environmentalism'. Policies for environmental protection have indeed displayed a technocratic and bureaucratic approach, which concentrated decision making within a policy community restricted to central government ministries, civil servants, enforcement agencies and industrialists. Yet the Environment Ministry, as a new arrival in the institutional landscape, was unable to implement a *dirigiste* model, although it needed to keep up appearances by espousal of top-down policy formulation. In practice, administrative sectorisation and interdepartmental rivalries within the state, together with the economic power of industrialists, were the preconditions for the development of 'French-style corporatism' (see Chapter 1). These factors invite reconsideration of the 'statist' and *'dirigiste'* view of French environmental protection policy. In addition, it will be seen that over time the separation of executive, legislative and judicial powers in France proved a more potent source of policy reform than anticipated by Trilling.

The legislative framework and its implementation

Legislation regulating the environmental performance of French firms has developed over nearly two centuries. The aim was never to outlaw damage caused by industry, but rather to achieve compromises between the interests of industrialists, the workforce, the local community, clients and consumer groups, whilst promoting economic expansion and social harmony. In practice this involved a form of bureaucratic incrementalism, which involved gradual adjustments between distinct societal interests (Lascoumes, 1994: 271). The legislation is punctuated by the three key texts of 1810, 1917 and 1976.

The 1810 decree imposed the need for permission to undertake specific industrial activities, creating the category of *installations classées* ('licensed sites') for the most polluting or hazardous plants. Although only immediate neighbours to the industrial nuisance had rights of complaint and redress on the grounds of insalubrity, local variations in strictness of application created uncertainties for manufacturers. The 1917 act continued to stress health and safety, but also aimed for national standardisation of regulatory enforcement, whilst placating industrialists by offering them a secure and predictable statutory environment. An inspectoral corps was created, called the *Inspection des Installations Classées* ('Licensed Sites Inspectorate'). Initially, inspectors were few in number, part-time and under-trained. Already in these early forms, French environmental protection legislation sought to reconcile entrepreneurial freedoms with public supervision (Lascoumes, 1989: 317).

By 1971 when the Environment Ministry was established, the 1917 statute was clearly outdated, as a result of the large-scale industrialisation of the postwar period. Environment Minister Poujade responded to rising levels of anxiety by initiating new legislation. The 1976 act on *installations classées* updated and strengthened the regulatory framework. For the first time, environmental protection was made an explicit requirement. The role of the Environment Ministry was confirmed, thus the regulatory authority was the central state exercising its *pouvoir régalien* ('regal power'). This phrase harks back to the absolute power of the French monarchy, and in principle means that the state has the legitimacy and means to impose its will in the public interest. The 1976 act reiterated the powers of administrative sanction in the event of untoward incidents (including temporary stoppage or even plant closure on the orders of the prefect) and increased the scope for prosecutions under criminal law. The licensing regime gradually brought in more categories of establishment and was made more rigorous.[1] Two categories of licensed sites were established, those requiring 'authorisation' (over 63,000) and those requiring a 'declaration' of their activities (over 500,000). In the case of 'authorisation', the process requires the preparation of an environmental impact assessment and an analysis of hazards (*une étude des dangers*) to be undertaken by the industrialist, as well as an audit of activities made by the *Inspection des Installations Classées*. A public enquiry has been compulsory since 1985. In exceptional cases, the decision to give 'authorisation' is passed up to the Environment Minister, but normally it is the departmental prefect who lays down a detailed licence. The latter specifies technical operating requirements in line with environmental and safety standards, stipulating pollution control methods and emission limits. For establishments subject simply to 'declaration', the prefect issues a list of standardised operating requirements.

[1] Large-scale, animal-breeding complexes and state sector firms were included within the 1976 act. The 1993 *loi Saumade* brought quarries within its scope and under the jurisdiction of the Environment Ministry (rather than the Industry Ministry, as was previously the case).

Although the 1976 act is characterised by its authoritarian provisions, Brénac (1985, 1988) showed that its implementation was marked by a meso-corporatist orientation. Prescriptions are negotiated between regulators and industrialists at two levels. General standards applicable to industrial sectors (e.g. pulp and paper production, iron and steel etc.) are negotiated at central ministerial level by industry representatives and ministry officials. Site-specific operating procedures are negotiated and adjusted to local conditions during the licensing process between plant managers, inspectors and departmental administrators. As a result of this negotiation 'secondary implementation norms are more significant than the original legislation' (Lascoumes, 1994: 169),[2] and questions related to the national or the European provenance of requirements fall by the wayside. In these processes, industrialists had the upper hand since they controlled access to information on operating procedures, associated costs, and on the consequences of operational changes geared towards better environmental performance. Crucially, environmental protection regulations are implemented by industrialists themselves operating in a regime of 'delegated self-enforcement' (Cawson, 1986: 38). By the very nature of their activity, no other actor can fully play this role – the context of application entails a 'structural monopoly' exercised by the regulatory targets themselves. Enforcement by the regulatory authority is a second-degree operation which ascertains compliance with environmental licences. However, enforcement is more than a matter of simply policing: it also requires that state agencies gain the confidence and cooperation of industrialists.

Enforcement and compliance

Environmental regulations on industrial and mining firms related to air, water and waste management are enforced by the *Inspection des Installations Classées*,[3] who report locally to the prefect and are bound by the latter's decisions. After the fire at the Feyzin refinery in 1966, the largely non-technical inspectors were replaced by highly trained engineers from the elite *Corps des Mines*, and their operations were transposed from the Industry Ministry to the

---

[2] 'les normes secondaires d'application se révèlent plus déterminantes que la législation de référence'.

[3] Licensed farming establishments are overseen by Agriculture Ministry inspectors.

Environment Ministry in 1971. However, inspectors retain allegiance to the Industry Ministry from whence their careers are largely managed, a situation which generates divided loyalties. Subsequent to Lalonde's 1990 'green plan' and the reorganisation of the Environment Ministry's field services, the inspectorate was housed within the DRIRE (see Chapter 4). The 1976 act enhanced the inspectorate's role, but resources remained scant, given the significant range of tasks with which it is enjoined. Inspectors participate in preliminary inquiries related to the granting of licences and draw up the technical prescriptions for regulated firms. They identify those establishments requiring operating permits that have not obtained one, and exercise surveillance over non-listed industrial and artisanal establishments causing pollution. They visit licensed sites, examine documents and operations to ensure conformity with regulations, identify infringements and are empowered to initiate court action (Fromageau and Guttinger, 1993; Ducasset, 1997).

The reality of enforcement raises practical and political issues. Environmental protection is conceptualised in terms of compliance with a licence, rather than in terms of environmental damage per se. As Fromageau and Guttinger (1993: 141) pointed out, industrialists are prone to view their licence as 'an established right to do harm',[4] regardless of changes in surrounding land use, or in terms of technological innovation. Colllot and Font Reaulx (1979) – both members of the *Inspection des Installations Classées* – painted a rosy picture of the inspector's ability to bring industrialists into line with more stringent operating requirements as more effective technology became available. Yet industrialists are not obliged by law to make new investments in process technology. Indeed, licensing procedures can act as a disincentive against the latter. Major changes in operating procedures affect the terms of an 'authorisation', requiring a resubmission and entailing a new public inquiry – a process of which industrialists can be chary.

In principle, industrialists do well to fear their regulators. Where licences are contravened, sanctions can be imposed under criminal law (with the possibility of imprisonment) or under administrative prerogatives (the prefect can suspend the operations of the firm). Over the years, the strictures have tightened,

---

[4] 'droit acquis à nuire'.

with harsher sanctions set out in the act of the 3 July 1985.[5] However prosecution is rare and a measure of last resort. Legal action can be interpreted as a sign of the inspector's failure to ensure compliance by normal means and is reserved for persistent contraventions. It is also uncertain in its outcome. Without solid proof of the infraction's existence and a demonstration of its gravity, the action will fail at the first hurdle, which is to convince the *procureur de la République* (broadly comparable to the British Crown Prosecution Service) that there is a case to be answered. Thus the inspector has to ensure that his technical analysis of the breach translates into a cogent legal argument. Successful prosecutions brought against non-compliant firms are infrequent occurrences. Throughout France there were 282 in 1984, 371 in 1986, 304 in 1989, 410 in 1990 and 358 in 1991 (IFEN, 1994: 323). Finally, such sanctions as are imposed by the courts are often less severe than expected (Charbonneau, 1992: 92–104), leading environmental lawyer and former Environment Minister Corinne Lepage (1998: 137–47) to argue that in France the letter of the law is one thing, but its application is another.

The resources of the inspectorate are paltry in relation to their remit. Inspectors are few in number – 680 in 1998 (MATE, 1999a), the equivalent of about one inspector to every 1,000 establishments in the licensing regime. Further, their work is not exclusively environmental, and on-site inspection is only one of many tasks undertaken. A document published by the DRIRE-Ile de France (1997) – the regional authority responsible for the greater Paris basin – indicated that in 1996 its seventy-five inspectors undertook 1,940 inspections (roughly one each per fortnight) and seventy-eight unannounced spot-checks (one each per year). A total of 261 administrative sanctions were imposed, of which nineteen resulted in a process shutdown. A total of 111 legal actions were initiated. Further, of the 5,248 plants requiring a licence, only 643 regularly communicated to the inspectorate data on their environmental performance. There is little in these figures related to one of France's most heavily industrialised regions to suggest a 'command and control' regime. It is true that, given their limited resources, the *Inspection des Installations Classées* prioritises firms which pose greatest hazards, namely those covered by the 'Seveso directive' (discussed below). But the limited ability of industrial

---

[5] But for a critical discussion of its limitations, see Littmann-Martin (1987).

inspectors to act as 'environmental policemen' can also be traced to other factors.

Negotiation and compromise

A measure of ambiguity persists in the remit of the DRIRE. As representatives of the Environment Ministry, but maintaining close links with the Industry Ministry, they seek both to ensure environmental protection and promote economic competitiveness. Though not automatically incompatible, these two aims can pull in different directions. Industrialists are concerned that distortions to competition be avoided. By stressing weaknesses in their actual or potential competitive position, they are prone to push for lenient standards of environmental performance. Inspectors, being responsible for drawing up licences and operating standards, interpret legislation and adapt it to local circumstances. This adaptation, however, is not purely a technical matter, but spills over into a wider scenario in which compromises are reached between divergent and competing interests, principally firms concerned with their costs base, and local authorities concerned with keeping the peace and maintaining continuity of political power. Further, inspectors are bound by the administrative and political processes in which they operate. Due to the overhang left by the system of *régulation croisée* (discussed in Chapter 4), complex relations of interdependence hold between prefects (to whom DRIRE inspectors are responsible) and elected politicians. In conditions of economic exigency, industrialists are prone to pressure politicians, who in turn lean on the prefect. Thus the DRIRE's dependence on the prefect can 'seriously limit the effectiveness of their action' (Charbonneau, 1994: 130).[6] Power relations among interested parties are uneven. Despite its reputation, the French state is not all-powerful, and its representatives can be constrained into compromise. The situation is particularly delicate where industrial equipment is outdated, where new investments are substantial and employment losses are used as a threat by recalcitrant owners (Ducasset, 1997). Confronted with the possible downturn or disappearance of the firms they regulate, inspectors have responded by a flexible interpretation of the manner in which norms are to be respected. The core of this policy

---

[6] In contrast, the *inspecteurs du travail* (Works Inspectorate), who enforce employment legislation, are independent of the prefect.

was put in place in 1978 by a ministerial circular written by Philippe Vesseron, then head of the Industrial Environment Service in the Environment Ministry, which stated 'we can and we must negotiate implementation timetables, but the objectives are non-negotiable'.[7] In practice, this policy meant nominally upholding statutory norms, but extending the deadlines within which compliance was to be attained.

However, the Protex case illustrates the failures of compromised adjournment. A manufacturer of hazardous chemical products located near Tours, the Protex company had been identified by the DRIRE as failing to meet environmental standards and posing a safety threat. Despite repeated warnings from inspectors over a period of years, Protex management persistently failed to implement *agreed* improvements in equipment and operating standards. An 'accident' was waiting to happen, yet no sanctions were taken. A major explosion and fire occurred on the night of 8 June 1988. The subsequent pollution of the Loire river by toxic waste caused the death of some fifteen tonnes of fish and prompted the decision to cut water supplies to Tours, a city of some 155,000 people, for a week.[8] Yet even after the accident, the company owner was not prosecuted for environmental breaches. Thus Lascoumes (1994: 95–6) in his analysis of the affair concluded that the *appel à l'Etat gendarme*, namely the intervention of a repressive public authority, had little basis in fact. Local economic and administrative factors, such as the apparent economic viability of the company and the power of the prefect, had conditioned an overly flexible mode of enforcement. Whereas the French policy style seemed authoritative at the level of formulation, at the level of implementation it was based on a consensus which exploited the 'absorptive capacity' of the polity.

The nature of the consensus should not mislead: rather than representing a broad-based societal arrangement, it is the result of a neo-corporatist bargain. The negotiation process is marked by the skewed membership of the policy community, which gives priority to industrialists and excludes representatives of civil society and elected politicians. As Hostiou (1990) pointed out, although mayors exercise general powers of enforcement of environmental regulations, they have no jurisdiction against a

---

[7] 'On peut et on doit négocier les calendriers, on ne doit jamais négocier les objectifs' (Vesseron, 1981: 68).
[8] For details of the handling of this crisis, see Gilbert (1990: 93–110 and 274–81).

suspect *installation classée*. The *police administrative spéciale* (or specific enforcement authority) exercised by the DRIRE and the prefect is a form of ring-fencing which protects industrialists from local politicians wishing to uphold existing regulations vigorously by recourse to their *police générale* (general enforcement powers). Given this division of responsibilities, characterisation of the pollution control system as an instance of the concentration of authority in the hands of central state representatives is formally valid. Yet the central authorities are unable to 'command and control' because of the economic influence of industry. Further, the consequence of the meso-corporatist orientation of the central government policy framework is to shield private firms from local government oversight, secreting a form of 'implementation deficit'. The prevalence of neo-corporatism and its attendant shortfalls is corroborated by analysis of the Environment Ministry's recourse to contract-based agreements.

Contractual arrangements

In the 1970s and 1980s, the 'pinnacle' of the Environment Ministry's negotiated approach was constituted by contracts drawn up with industrial representatives on a sectoral basis aimed at improving environmental performance; these were known as *contrats de branche*. The justification offered for this meso-corporatist approach was that policy would be more effective by tailoring measures to particular problems and incorporating cost-benefit analysis. The intention was not to replace the regulatory framework (since it provided the last resort of sanctions) but to find mechanisms by which norms could translate into practice more efficiently without placing excessive burdens on industrialists at a time when their competitive position was threatened by international pressures. An additional incentive for policy innovation arose from the structural position of the Environment Ministry, since in its early years it could not engage in strong-arm tactics against powerful industrial interests, but needed incremental means to develop its authority.

Lascoumes (1991, 1993) showed how the Directorate for the Prevention of Pollution undertook negotiations with industrialists on a sector-by-sector basis. In a first phase (1972 to 1977), the paper pulp, sugar beet, starch-making, distillery and wood-working industries signed agreements to reduce emissions to air and water, and received subsidies for pollution-abatement investment. The second phase (1977-81) involved the plaster and cement industries, meat renderers, asbestos and aluminium manufacturers; the aim was to reduce toxic wastes but subsidies were not granted. A final phase ran between 1981 and 1985. Lascoumes (1993) noted that the outcomes of these contracts depended on the relative strength or weakness of regulators in relation to specific industrial sectors, with the Environment Ministry enjoying a favourable balance of power against the unpopular and fragmented asbestos industry, but being poorly placed to deal with steel barons in a period of industrial retrenchment.

Although these *contrats de branche* initially succeeded in improving the environmental performance of industry, their wider implications led to criticisms on points of practice and principle. From the late 1970s, the European Commission questioned the distribution of subsidies as leading to market distortions. Further, although a few of these contracts became public, the process was characterised by considerable opacity. Its neo-corporatist orientation was flagrant in that civil society representatives were totally excluded. Following complaints by environmental groups, in 1985 the *Conseil d'Etat* (France's highest administrative court) ruled that contracts with steelmakers such as PUK were invalid because 'during their period of operation, the three agreements effectively prevented the administration from enforcing more stringent requirements on the firms in question . . . The Minister had renounced the prerogatives conferred on him by law'.[9] The adverse ruling was significant not only because it officially identified a case of 'institutional capture' by regulatory targets, but also because it flagged up the declining legitimacy of neo-corporatist policy making. In consequence, the Environment Ministry ended its experiment with the contractualisation of policy, although the practice of negotiation has been maintained in licensing procedures.

The Prevention of Industrial Hazards

The dangers posed by industrial activities have become increasingly stark as a result of major accidents that have occurred

[9] 'au cours de leur période d'application, les trois conventions empêchait en fait l'administration d'imposer aux sociétés des prescriptions plus rigoureuses . . . Le ministre a renoncé à exercer les attributions qui lui sont conférées par la loi'; quoted in Lascoumes (1993: 80).

around the world. Some of the more infamous include Feyzin (France), 1966; Flixborough (England), 1974; Seveso (Italy), 1976; Three Mile Island (USA), 1979; Bhopal (India), 1984; and Chernobyl (Russia), 1986.[10] These events demonstrated that industrial hazards had changed in quantitative and qualitative terms. As stressed by Lagadec (1981: 266), technological risks today can threaten whole cities and spread across borders. Long-term consequences include the possibility of intergenerational transmission through genetic abnormalities caused by exposure to high levels of radioactivity or chemical substances. Irreversible damage to ecosystems can also occur. Terms such as 'risk society' (Beck, 1992) and the 'vulnerable society' (Theys, 1987) have emerged to evoke the scale and novelty of the problems.

Yet legislation and policy have been underpinned by a conception of industrial accidents as a risk to be managed, rather than a danger to be eliminated (Lascoumes, 1994: 136). To develop effective hazard prevention measures and respond efficiently in the event of major accidents, regulatory frameworks have been extended by national and European legislation. In 1982, a think-tank was established within the Environment Ministry to report on major technological hazards, and in the late 1980s specialised appointments were created at junior minister level in this field. The key legislation is the 1976 act on *installations classées* and the 1987 act on major hazards. These have been complemented by the 1982 EC 'Seveso directive' (as modified in 1996) regulating industrial establishments that present the highest levels of hazard.[11] The directive was in any case partly modelled on the 1976 act, providing an example of the 'requisite variety of instruments' available to French policy makers and the scope for 'naturalisation' of European policy (discussed in Chapter 5).

In France in 1998, 427 plants were covered by the 'Seveso directive'. The highest concentrations are in the Bouches du Rhône and Seine-Maritime areas, which have more than thirty each. Lyon

[10] Details of these accidents can be found in Lagadec (1981, 1988) and Gilbert (1990).

[11] Nuclear establishments are excluded from the terms of both the 'Seveso directive' and the 1976 act, being covered by separate regulations, notably the decree of the 11 December 1963, but with no act of parliament to cover them. The technical inspectorate responsible for safety is the *Service central de sûreté des installations nucléaires*. The separate system minimises public access to proceedings. Charbonneau (1992: 117–20) provided analysis of the legal restrictions.

with its *couloir de la chimie* ('chemical industry corridor'), and Bastia (Corsica) have significant numbers of high-risk installations in built-up areas. The directive requires listed firms to identify hazards, develop prevention measures, draw up emergency plans against major accidents, keep the workforce and the local community informed on production processes and emergency plans, and notify the authorities in the event of accidents. This information is collated in an EC database in order to disseminate good practice. A competent authority must be appointed to regulate safety arrangements, carry out rigorous inspections and have powers to shut down operations that threaten a major accident. In France, this role falls to the DRIRE. Because of the hazards posed by 'Seveso' plants, exacting standards of compliance must be maintained and inspection takes several weeks of full-time work (Demarq, 1987: 479). Consequently, a substantial proportion of the time of the *Inspection des installations classées* is devoted to them (Laurent, 1996: 91).

The stress in the 'Seveso' legislation falls on the safety and protection of the population. France had, in any case, progressively developed a range of emergency plans. The oldest are the *plans ORSEC*, dating back to 1952, but updated at several junctures in the 1980s (Prieur, 1987). These are drawn up by the prefect in relation to the individual *département*: they coordinate the fire brigade, medical and other services in the event of major accidents and natural catastrophes. Also contingency plans exist in relation to particular sectors (e.g. petrochemicals, railways). However, company-level plans are now acknowledged as essential. In conformity with the 'Seveso directive', on-site plans called *plans d'opération interne* (POI) are drawn up by company managers to ensure the safety of employees and contain environmental damage within the plant where possible. During an accident, management implements the POI and communicates with the prefect, who coordinates a wider response. To tackle accidents whose effects spread beyond the plant, off-site plans known as *plans particuliers d'intervention* are drawn up and operationalised by the *préfecture* (Zimeray, 1994: 130–34; Ministère de l'environnement et de la prévention des risques technologiques et naturels majeurs, 1991: 31–2).

The 'Seveso directive' gave residents living close to high-risk establishments a right to information regarding industrial dangers and safety plans. In practice, however, the general public in EC countries has not been well informed (Dron, 1995: 72). Impact studies have tended to be optimistic and biased. Emergency plans are organised on a military basis, with residents expected to follow orders. Information provided by public authorities and factory management is usually limited, and distributed in a top-down manner. But, as the fieldwork done by Lalo (1991) showed, the value of passive consumption of information by residents is limited. The 'command and control' stance is questionable, given that major disasters disrupt social organisation and are trauma-inducing. Greater awareness of risk has led to reassessments of urban planning and development, with more attention paid to avoiding increased population density around sensitive sites (Blancher, 1998).

Modes of active involvement, involving public consultation, have started to emerge in France (Lascoumes, 1998). One manifestation has been the establishment of *Secrétariats permanents pour la prévention des pollutions industrielles* (SPPPI) in densely industrialised localities having a large concentration of 'Seveso' establishments and where highly conflictual situations had developed. The first was Fos-Etang de Berre (near Marseille) in 1972, followed by Basse Seine (taking in Le Havre and Rouen), Toulouse, Calais-Dunkirk, Strasbourg, Vallée de Seine (Paris area) and the Loire estuary (Nantes area). In 1991 an analogous structure was set up in Lyon. These organisations provide local channels for discussions between industrialists, politicians, regulators, experts and general public. Each SPPPI comprises a number of commissions, which present studies on industrial pollution of air, water and soil, propose target objectives for pollution abatement and hazard minimisation, as well as provide public information (Andurand, 1996: 43–6; Prieur, 1996: 230). Coordination and coverage of financial costs are undertaken largely by the DRIRE. Assessments of their activities have varied. For Paquiet and Blancher (1997: 43), the SPPPI were successful in defusing tense local situations, whilst Lalo (1996: 56) commented that their collegiate structure made them more credible as an information source to the general public. According to Andurand (1996: 115–19), the older SPPPI could point to tangible achievements, but the results were unsatisfactory in the case of the Vallée de Seine (due to its size and pollution transfers from Paris) and Lyon (due to the ingrained conservatism of the city's industrialists).

Overall, whilst security measures have no doubt tightened, and steps have been taken to widen participation within a budding policy network, the scale of industrial hazards is too large to allow complacency. Yet public attitudes are marked by an ambivalence which oscillates between the desirability of maintaining economic activities and the need to ensure safety. For Charbonneau (1989, 1992), overcoming the 'democratic deficit' would include the public's right to a moratorium on plants generating unacceptably high hazards. That citizen rights are very limited is an indication of the exclusionary ring-fencing applying to hazard prevention.

Environmental Taxation on Firms and the ADEME

Environmental taxation represents a step away from what Mousel (1995: 70) called *'police, contrôle et surveillance'*, but is complementary to – rather than a substitute for – the regulatory framework. The underlying aim is to compensate for 'externalities' – hidden and unpaid environmental costs – rather than to leave them unacknowledged till cumulative damage over time and across media mounts to irreparable levels. In effect, market mechanisms are harnessed to provide a practical implementation of the 'polluter pays' principle.

In France, a number of environmental taxes have been instigated since the 1960s. However, it became apparent that the piecemeal policy required consolidation, leading in 1990 to the establishment of the *Agence de l'environnement et de la maîtrise de l'énergie* (ADEME). The latter's title of the 'Environment and Energy Efficiency Agency' indicated a partial return to the philosophy pertaining in the 1970s when energy-saving measures were essential due to the oil crisis. Since the late 1980s, concerns over the enhanced greenhouse effect caused by the burning of fossil fuels have given a new slant to energy efficiency. The agency's other activities involve the promotion of clean technology, waste management and recycling; the prevention and clean-up of soil contamination; and the reduction of air pollution and noise. It has branches in each of France's regions to allow close cooperation with firms and local authorities. Its research programmes are intended to benefit a wide range of actors, with help to individual firms offered though a *Plan Environnement Entreprise* designed to identify their environmental impacts, take counter-measures and prepare for certification under the environmental standard known as ISO 14000. The ADEME is responsible jointly to the Environment Ministry, the Industry Ministry and the Research Ministry. Although this threefold *tutelle* (reporting relationship) appears cumbersome, Pissaloux (1995: 258–9) argued that the rival claims of the different ministries neutralised each other, effectively increasing the autonomy of the agency.

In financial terms the ADEME is a powerful institution. It receives public funding via each of its three *ministères de tutelle*, in addition to receipts from environmental charges (see Table 7.1). The main examples of the latter relate to landfill waste, used oil, industrial air pollution, and noise from airports. Environmental taxes have been used to complement the regulatory regime, and are operationalised by the same actors and procedures, with the DRIRE identifying firms liable to pay. Charges have never been set so high as to be markedly dissuasive in their effect. Rather, they constitute an example of hypothecated taxation since receipts are returned to firms in the form of research grants, subsidies and loans for environmental protection purposes. Michel Mousel (1995: 67), a former chief executive of the ADEME, defined this approach as 'the French style "polluter pays" principle according to which the sum paid by the polluter is established by reference to clean-up costs'.[12] Because environmental charges serve as the instrument for redistributive policy within the industrial sector, negotiation is part of the policy process, as with the contractual arrangements outlined above. Thus firms can influence the level of taxes and the distribution of state aids. This form of forced investment points to the reliance of French firms on the state to even out competitive pressures caused by environmental liabilities. In addition, the closed circle of exchange relationships provides a further instance of the meso-corporatist arrangements that characterise French environmental policy towards industry.

The ADEME's largest public source of funding is the Industry Ministry, indicating once again the extensive involvement of the latter in environmental issues.[13] But in the period 1992–4, the proportion of public funds to charges almost halved, so increasing the financial autonomy of the agency from ministerial *tutelle*. However, in France such charges are assimilated to a form of taxation. This raises a constitutional issue since the existence of

[12] 'le principe pollueur payeur à la française selon lequel le montant de ce que paie le pollueur est fixé en fonction de ce qui est nécessaire à la réalisation de la dépollution'.

[13] The Industry Ministry had exercised *tutelle* over the constituent agencies of the ADEME before their merger and had not wished to cede 'turf' to the Environment Ministry (Faberon, 1991: 161).

Table 7.1 Revenues of the ADEME

	1992	1993	1994
		millions of francs	
Public funding			
Environment Ministry	56	63	25
Industry Ministry	332	198	150
Research Ministry	181	191	139
Other	66	108	72
Total	635	560	386
Environmental taxes and charges			
Used oil	70	108	19
Air emissions	215	227	173
Waste	–	173	371
Noise	–	24	30
Total	285	532	593
Total revenues	920	1092	979
Public funding as % of total revenues	69%	51%	39%
Taxes and charges as % of total revenues	31%	49%	61%

Source: Pissaloux (1995: 260)

tax-levying authorities other than national and local government is considered to lack democratic legitimacy. In theory, only assemblies elected by universal suffrage are vested with the constitutional right to raise taxes. Although this anomaly persisted for years in relation to charges on both pollution and water (discussed in the next chapter), the Jospin government finally decided to reform environmental taxation. The 1999 Finance Bill proposed a *taxe générale sur les activités polluantes* (TGAP) to bring together various environmental charges, and to return the setting of their levels to the Finance Ministry and parliament. These receipts are to be incorporated into the general budget of the Exchequer, and flow back to the ADEME – via the Environment Ministry. Clearly this would reinforce the Environment Minister's political control over the ADEME, though whether the reform benefits the Environment Ministry or the Finance Ministry remains to be seen. Likewise the logic of the reform, based on the so-called 'double dividend', has yet to be tested. On the one hand, it has been presented as having a dissuasive effect (by encouraging industrialists to reduce emissions). On the other, a wider redistributive outcome is claimed in that the proceeds of environmental taxes are expected to reduce fiscal pressure elsewhere and encourage job creation. Although tension between these objectives cannot be excluded, the TGAP has the makings of an exogenous shock to the entrenched policy community, because it challenges the principle of retention and redistribution of fiscal revenues within sector, and because the Exchequer and parliament may (in theory at least) be willing and able to implement a tougher tax regime to reduce pollution.

Conclusions

The environmental performance of industry has significantly improved, with a halving since 1976 of toxic emissions and waste discharged to water, and sulphur dioxide emissions to air cut by 77 percent between 1980 and 1997; yet industry is still responsible for half of organic wastes and nearly all toxic emissions discharged to water, as well as for 70 percent of sulphur dioxide and 20 percent of nitrogen oxides emitted to air (MATE, 1999a). This mixed level of policy effectiveness has been influenced by the articulations between the public sphere and economic actors, and by the goodness of fit between the policy agenda and the administrative apparatus. Despite appearances of an authoritarian policy style, the 'command and control' orientation in environmental protection has in practice been permeated by a 'logic of negotiation' (Jordan and Richardson, 1982). The policy process was characterised by 'French-style corporatism', based on informal accommodations between regulators and regulated. Consensual elements underpinned both the normative framework per se and its flanking policies, namely contractual arrangements and environmental charges. However 'consensus' was reached within a closed policy community in which regulators stipulated more or less severe norms, but industrialists retained the final word due to 'delegated self-enforcement' (Cawson, 1986: 38). A national tradition of authoritative policy formulation and flexible implementation ensued. In industrial emissions control it largely followed 'a model of repair' (Thelander, 1990). Prevention was exercised more to avert major accidents than to stop cumulative pollution.

Consequently, the French model of environmental protection has displayed a number of deficiencies. These can be highlighted using the criteria proposed by Mazmanian and Sabatier (1989: 29):

> legislation which seeks to significantly change target group behaviour in order to achieve its objectives is most likely to succeed if (a) its objectives are precise and clearly ranked; (b) it incorporates an adequate causal theory; (c) it provides adequate funds to the implementing agencies; (d) there are few veto points in the implementation process and sanctions or inducements are provided to overcome resistance; (e) the decision rules of the implementing agencies are biased toward the achievement of statutory objectives; (f) implementation is assigned to agencies which support the legislation's objectives and will give the program high priority; and (g) participation by outsiders is encouraged through liberalised rules of standing and through provisions for independent evaluation studies.

From the foregoing, it has emerged that the DRIRE inspectors are hampered by a lack of human and financial resources, by a tension between their 'industrial competitiveness' and 'environmental protection' objectives, and by a conflict of loyalties arising from institutional affiliation to both Industry and Environment Ministries. The neo-corporatist policy community has repeatedly allowed the targets of regulation to exercise veto, and incentives to overcome resistance have taken the form of subsidies rather than sanctions. The decision rules of the inspectors are compromised by the influence of the prefect, and the political constraints of *regulation croisée*. Meanwhile current rules of standing largely exclude environmental groups and even marginalise local councillors, whilst independent evaluation studies are rarely seen. In brief, on almost every criterion listed above the French model is found wanting.

Reforms can be envisaged along several dimensions. At the operational level they include more inspectors, greater priority to environmental objectives, and greater scope for sanctions, with more logistical support from lawyers in order to identify promising court actions, present technical proofs and legal arguments to greatest advantage, and more publicity around successful prosecutions to increase the legislation's dissuasive potential. At the political level, the subordination of the environmental inspectorate to the local prefect and the Industry Ministry is questionable; greater independence could lead to greater effectiveness. To offset the centralisation this would imply, the obvious measure of decentralisation is to reinstate the powers of *police générale* of the municipality with regard to environmental damage caused by *installations classées*. The danger of institutional competition between central and local authorities can be minimised by delimiting the powers of the latter to surveillance and 'whistle-blowing' within the framework provided by European and national legislation. At the level of citizens' rights, a review of the scope for third parties to undertake independent evaluations, and of their means to bring court actions against offending firms seems appropriate. Yet the aim cannot be to 'criminalise' firms and managers. The positive component of the 'logic of negotiation' was the development of responsibility, cooperation and partnership. The secular weakness of that style was the skewed membership of the policy community, with economic interests dominant within a meso-corporatist framework.

However, signs of an exit from meso-corporatism have appeared. The recognition that the negotiation of policy within *contrats de branche* led to regulatory capture is one such sign. The forced abandonment of contractual agreements in the mid-1980s as a result of the ruling by the *Conseil d'Etat* provided a fruitful instance of the judiciary being played off against the executive. A further sign is provided by reform of environmental charges. The transfer in 1999 of the setting of tax levels from the ADEME to parliament is significant because it indicates that the location of decision making authority within the polity matters. In both these instances, reform was predicated on shifts in the balance of influence between parliament, judiciary and the executive. Such movement between the tectonic plates of the polity could facilitate policy reform in the future.

8

THE HUMAN ENVIRONMENT:
Widening the Policy Networks

Introduction

This chapter analyses policy related to three media – water, waste and air – where the long-standing tendency has been to prioritise human needs, and particularly health concerns, over broader environmental issues. Policy was to a considerable extent formulated and implemented in terms of an expansion of municipal public services, orchestrated within national frameworks. However, as the construction of environmental problems evolved, as cross-media implications become more apparent and particularly as the challenges increased in scale, so the anthropocentric bias was overlaid with an ecocentric orientation. Further, the need arose to reconcile national preferences with international agreements. These factors changed the character of policy subsystems, with a gradual transition from neocorporatist arrangements to wider policy networks. In order to trace these developments, the chapter devotes a section to each medium. Each case study reviews the legislative framework, surveys substantive developments and assesses their causes, and identifies a distinctively French model for management of the sector. The concluding section indicates how these models are being revised in the face of new pressures.

Water

France is well-resourced in fresh water,[1] though with significant regional variation and recurrent droughts in southern areas. The Environment Ministry estimated that in 1991 water abstraction totalled some 41.4 billion cubic metres, with usage by sector indicated in Table 8.1. Drinking water needs represent a small proportion of total abstraction. Agricultural consumption has increased markedly due to changes in crop production, with a doubling in land irrigated in Midi-Pyrénées and Aquitaine between 1979 and 1988 (Ministère de l'Environnement, 1992: 46). Industrial use remains significant, but water efficiency has improved. However immense quantities of water are required for cooling nuclear reactors, making Electricité de France (EDF) one of the largest water managers in France.

Responding to demand has required the development of political institutions to regulate the sector, as well as economic mechanisms to ensure distribution and treatment of the resource. Comprehensive water planning aims to reconcile (a) individual human requirements with (b) collective economic usages and (c) environmental needs, notably the preservation of ecosystems. However, the development of an integrated system is fraught. Whenever the range of actors broadens, competition between

Table 8.1 Water use in France in 1991

Sector	Abstraction		Consumption	
	quantity (billions of cubic metres)	as percentage	quantity (billions of cubic metres)	as percentage
Electricity production	21.3	51.4	1.5	19.0
Industry	4.9	11.8	0.2	3.0
Agriculture	4.5	10.9	2.9	36.5
Drinking water	5.9	14.3	0.7	8.8
Other (navigation, mines)	4.8	11.6	2.6	32.7
Total	41.4	100.0	7.9	100.0

Source: Sironneau (1992: 209).

[1] For details, see Barraqué et al. (1996).

different types of water usage sharpens. Consequently water policy is an outstanding example of how political, economic and environmental concerns intertwine, and of how natural landscapes need to be explored on the basis of political maps.

The legislative framework

Historically water was one of the first environmental sectors to be regulated. Morand-Deviller (1993: 108–9) noted that the 1829 statute to protect fish, as incorporated into the *Code rural*, remains the most frequently used legal basis for court actions on aquatic pollution. In the 1950s anglers were among the first to notice the deterioration in water quality and lobby for firmer action (Duclos and Smadja, 1985: 136). A major reform of legislation was required, as a result of accelerating industrialisation and urbanisation. The ensuing 1964 Water Act remains the cornerstone for water policy in France, since it overhauled both the institutional framework – by establishing river basin authorities – and the regulatory framework – by revising water charges and introducing water quality objectives. In reality, the setting of the latter was implemented only in the case of a single minor river, the Vire in Brittany. But the act encouraged proactive responses to pollution control by a system of charges, which constituted one of the earliest instances of the 'polluter pays' principle (PPP). From the 1970s to 1990 some twenty-seven items of European Community water legislation contributed to the setting of improved standards (Richardson, 1995: 145). Although their transposition proved a protracted process, the major provisions of the 1964 act were adapted rather than abandoned, indicating the 'absorptive capacity' of the existing French policy frame.

The onset of newer forms of pollution, the recognition that sewerage facilities were inadequate, a lack of winter rainfall, and droughts over 1989–92 led to the new water act of 1992. The 1898 decree had distinguished water usage rights from water ownership,[2] but the new act went further in declaring that water belonged to the nation – *le patrimoine commun de la nation* – and was to be held in public trust. The act aimed to reduce wastage

---

[2] The question of property rights in relation to water is complex but, with exceptions whose importance has diminished over time, water resources per se cannot be privately owned in France. For details, see Sironneau (1992: 140–9) and Prieur (1996: 636–7). Caponera (1992: 65–96) provides cross-national comparison of the legal principles in operation.

and improve quality controls. It introduced a compulsory planning system for integrated water management at the regional level, termed the *schémas directeurs d'aménagement et de gestion des eaux*. It also transposed the 1991 urban waste water directive, making improved provision for sewerage. Finally, the act sketched out an ecocentric approach to water (rather than a solely instrumental one) in establishing a duty to conserve 'aquatic ecosystems'. However, it stopped short of reviewing the institutional framework for water management, leaving in place a highly complex system.

The policy network

In principle, the water policy network coordinates policy formulation at European and national levels with consistent implementation at regional and local levels. Within France the main actors are the Environment Ministry, regional water boards, municipalities (*communes*) and private water companies.

The underlying regime for water is that of a public service run on the principle of democratic accountability. Municipalities are the key actors responsible for water provision and oversight. However, there are over 36,000 *communes* in France, of which the greater number are so tiny as to make independent projects unfeasible. Consequently, various forms of regrouping are practised both in the countryside and in cities. Yet with over 15,000 water distribution services, the system remains enormously fragmented. The local authority is empowered either to provide water services itself (*régie directe*) or to delegate to a private firm. In 1991, about 25 percent of water and sewerage services were provided directly. But the increase in the private sector's role had been rapid, with coverage rising from 13.5 million people in 1956, to 25.5 in 1971 and to 33.5 in 1983 (Barraqué et al., 1992: 21).

Delegation to private companies is one of the most specifically French aspects of the system and one of the oldest, dating to 1808. In principle, rival firms compete for a local authority's custom. Strictly speaking, the system does not involve 'privatisation' of water per se, as elected authorities retain overall responsibility. Different forms of delegation are possible, the main ones being franchises (*concessions*) and lease contract (*affermage*). With franchises, the operator constructs facilities and accepts economic risk, but facilities remain the property of the *communes*. Contracts tend to be long, running for twenty-five or thirty years. Lease contracts usually last twelve years, the operator manages water services, but the local authority constructs facilities. In theory, water prices are controlled by the local authority, but in reality are largely set by the contractor. This system has encouraged the development of giant private firms. Three firms – Générale des Eaux (now called Vivendi), the Lyonnaise des Eaux and SAUR – account for some 75 percent of French household water distribution (Gouverne, 1994: 164; Barraqué et al., 1996: 116–7). Due to this industrialisation, water has been treated as a standardised commodity, a view which obscures ecological considerations.

The 1964 Water Act established the river basin as the central unit of decision making. To this purpose, France was divided into six basins, each having a consultative committee (*comité de bassin*) and an executive board (*agence de l'eau*). The *agences* became the 'government' of the system, whilst the *comités de bassin* are frequently likened to water 'parliaments', bringing together representatives of public and private stakeholders in the interests of equitable compromise. The proportion of seats given over to state representatives stands at 40 per cent, with the chair of each *agence* nominated by ministerial decree. Local and regional authorities have 37 percent of seats; industrialists with 16 percent of seats are the largest single group, consumer groups and environmental groups are among the smallest (each having 2 per cent), whilst other categories make up the balance (CGP, 1997: 198). The basin authorities constitute a unique institution, displaying decentralised structures and a hybrid mode of representation. Though elected politicians have a significant place, representation is not assured by universal suffrage. Neocorporatism is not predominant, but is pronounced. Direct representation of consumers and citizens is nominal. Overall, the regime has mirrored that of *régulation croisée* (see Chapter 4), within which state representatives and local politicians exercised reciprocal influence. Further, it provided a choice of avenues by which economic interests could exercise influence.

This hybrid regime has conditioned the operational modes of the river basin authorities who have sought to promote an efficient and responsible system by the use of economic instruments. The *comités de bassin* determined who paid water charges and agreed on their levels, with decisions implemented by the *agences*. Charges are of two types: abstraction and consumption charges (*redevance pour prélèvement et consommation d'eau*) and pollution charges (*redevance pour pollution*). In principle, users pay not for water itself, but for services and 'externalities' associated with water, namely abstraction, treatment, distribution and collection, and clean-up. For industrial users, pollution charges are based on peak emissions during normal operations, and are proportional to water intake which acts as a proxy for discharge levels.[3] Because norms are calculated with reference to industrial sectors (not on the basis of operating conditions in individual firms), the relationship between emissions and charges is approximate, so the uniform setting of *redevances* means they are a form of tax.[4] As such their levy is contrary to the French constitution, which holds that taxation is the prerogative of assemblies elected by universal suffrage. Despite their unconstitutionality, they have been paid by consumers and industrial users for decades. However, farmers rarely pay for their water,[5] and are mostly exempted from the payment of pollution charges.[6] The proceeds of charges are earmarked as subsidies to private firms and local authorities for capital investment in water treatment facilities. The most original feature of this system of hypothecated taxation is that the *agences* have served as the vehicle for redistributive policy within sector. Consequently Martin (1988: 117) described the *agences* as *mutuelles*, namely organisations based on the principle of a sharing of burdens, rather than on the bearing of individual responsibilities. Overall, the PPP *is* applied in the sense that polluters

---

[3] Levels of effluent discharge from France's 500,000 most polluting industrial firms are set and enforced by the DRIRE (see Chapter 7). As a result of this ring-fencing, local authorities are disempowered from initiating prosecution, despite nominally exercising authority.

[4] In the 1970s and 1980s, the strategy of *contrats de branches* – negotiated agreements between government and industry sector representatives – was applied to ease powerful and potentially recalcitrant economic interests into the new system of water charges (Martin, 1988: 118). Bongaerts and Kraemer (1987: 13–14) found that these contracts did achieve water pollution reductions. The wider implications of *contrats de branches* are discussed in Chapter 7.

[5] It has been estimated that 80 percent of sources of water abstraction by farmers have not been inventoried, whilst most of the remainder have not been fitted with water meters, despite regulatory requirements (CGP, 1997: 117). In these cases, use of water is free.

[6] In 1993, an agreement was reached with livestock farmers over payment of water pollution charges, known as the *programme pour la maîtrise des pollutions d'origine agricole*. Farmers were to receive subsidies for investment in treating animal slurries, and the payment of pollution charges was to be phased in annually. In 1994, the Agriculture and Environment Ministries agreed to simply postpone introduction of charges until 1998 (CGP, 1997: 106).

contribute to water treatment costs, but its application is acknowledged to be too weak to effect major reductions in emissions.[7] The choice of six extremely large river basins had the disadvantages of placing the *agences* at a remove from local concerns and ignoring geographically distinct catchments such as Brittany and Corsica (Fenet, 1973: 386). But their broad geographical base, in conjunction with the ability to raise charges across most categories of user, enabled the boards to fund the very substantial investments necessitated by EC water directives. Between 1964 and 1994, total subsidies distributed by the *agences* amounted to 71 billion francs (Guellec, 1995: 35–8). Spending operates on the basis of five-year plans. The current programme (the seventh) runs from 1997 to 2001 and mobilises some 57 billion francs (MATE, 1999b). To date, all income has remained within the water system, with the *agences* acting as bankers to other actors.[8] However, they have no enforcement function with respect to environmental regulations, they are not a planning authority, nor do they construct or run facilities. These factors inhibit their ability to formulate broad sectoral strategies. But in having their own income and making spending decisions, the *agences* have enjoyed considerable autonomy.

If water services have a regional character because of hydrologic and administrative factors, the system remains under the overall supervision of national government. Over time, the Environment Ministry emerged as the central actor in water planning and regulation. Ministerial reorganisation in 1991 allowed improved coordination of the system, with the creation of a Water Directorate and the establishment of field services. The DIREN have a general remit for water policy implementation at the regional level. The DRIRE have the specific task of monitoring and limiting industrial emissions to water. The central state provides expertise through a number of engineering *corps* (principally *Ponts et Chaussées*, *Mines* and *Génie rural*), who ensure consistency in the application of quality standards throughout France. Other major ministries – Agriculture, Health and *Equipement* – have retained their prerogatives, each having field services with responsibilities

---

[7] See Raack (1987: 358) and Mathieu (1992: 49). Meublat (1998: 79) noted that 'il est plus rentable pour le pollueur de payer sa redevance – et de continuer à polluer'.

[8] As public-sector establishments, the *agences* earn interest on retained revenue, but are debarred from making profits.

for water. Although the state supervises water policy and offers expert support to local authorities, the fragmentation of the system blurs responsiveness and makes reform difficult.

Recent developments

The range of policy requirements and outputs makes generalised assessment of the French system inappropriate.[9] But to provide a measure of evaluation, developments in two subsectors will be considered: sewerage and drinking water.

Repeated criticisms have been made of sewerage facilities. Official statistics suggested that in 1990–1 around 40 percent of domestic wastes were eliminated in water treatment plants (Mathieu, 1992: 48; Tardieu, 1992: 72). The calculation of this 'cleansing rate' is based on the percentage of households connected to the sewerage system multiplied by the average efficiency of treatment plants. The low 'cleansing rate' indicated a need for improvement, particularly as large towns by the sea or on rivers often discharged raw sewage into surrounding waters. Subsequent to the 1991 directive on urban waste water treatment, requiring that agglomerations over 10,000 inhabitants have treatment systems, municipalities invested heavily to bring the proportion of waste water going into sewage plants to 80 percent (Nowak, 1995: 28). The cost has been estimated at some 80 billion francs (Litvan, 1997: 47).

Controversies have arisen, however, over the real scale of the problem and the best solutions to tackle it. Barraqué (1996: 31) maintained that early data were inaccurate, with greater numbers of treatment plants in existence than originally reported. Further, the 'cleansing rate' indicator was argued to be simplistic, since the 20 percent of French people whose dwellings are not connected to mains sewerage (usually rural residents) have septic tanks. The preference for a single system of water elimination – known in French as *tout à l'égout* (everything down the sewer) – is being questioned. Given France's large territory, the cost of connecting the whole population to single systems is prohibitive. In sparsely populated rural areas, pressures on the environment are often low. But single systems collect effluents and concentrate them as semisolids on a large-scale basis, turning a 'water problem' into a 'waste problem'. Although some organic matter can be recycled as

[9] For detailed data on water quality developments, see OECD (1997: 55–62).

agricultural fertiliser, the remainder causes disposal problems. The adverse cross-media consequences of single systems present ongoing challenges.

Concerns over drinking water in France have increased as a result of pollution, high water prices and the connections between the two. In 1997, the *Cour des Comptes* (the public sector auditor) reported that the number of people receiving water that failed to conform to statutory limit values had risen to five million from two million in 1991 (*Le Monde*, 14.11.1997). Diffuse pollution from rainwater run-off on hard surfaces poses a severe problem, as do ammonia from industry and phosphates from domestic and industrial sources (causing eutrophication). In Brittany, the leaching of nitrates spread by farmers results in profuse growths of seaweed on beaches, undermining tourism and making the provision of uncontaminated tap water increasingly difficult (*Le Monde*, 30.6.1998: 13). Gouverne (1994: 72) reported that analyses of drinking water in Finistère indicated levels of 100 milligrams of nitrates per litre, whereas the prescribed limit is 50. Also affected are the cereal growing regions of Brie, Beauce, Champagne, the Garonne valley near Toulouse, and the Rhône valley near Valence.

More stringent standards to protect consumers and the environment necessitated major investments in facilities. The 1992 Water Act, together with government circular M49, placed a requirement on local authorities to charge by volume of water used (rather than a flat rate), and to maintain a balanced budget for water services. In principle, 'water pays for water' (rather than being cross-subsidised). These measures aimed at improving price transparency and discouraging waste of valuable resources. However, they led to increased costs and greater price variations between localities. Household water bills rose on average by 50 percent between 1991 and 1996 (Litvan, 1997: 41), fuelling widespread complaints. INSEE, the national institute for statistics, calculated that the average charge for a cubic metre of water was 14 francs in 1995, but prices varied from 6 to 38 francs (Guellec, 1995: 11; Nowak, 1995: 17–18). Such variation does not reflect the 'market value' of water, since water itself is not sold. Users pay only for services associated with water. Price variations arise from differences in investment and running costs, and the complicated charging system related thereto.[10]

---

[10] Explanations of French water bills can be found in Guellec (1995) and Nowak (1995).

As the financial resources of local authorities were already stretched, meeting the costs of new investments and gaining public acceptance for price rises proved problematic. In 1994, criminal proceedings were brought against several mayors in whose cash-strapped *communes* sewerage facilities fell below standard (Guellec, 1995: 32–3). Solutions to the dilemma included subsidies from the *agences*, whose budgets were doubled over 1992–6. Some mayors previously operating direct services were pushed into the arms of the water companies, since the latter finance immediate investments in construction. However, their costs are recouped via bills over the long term, causing customer disquiet. Possibly as a result of price rises, household consumption of drinking water dropped by 5 percent over 1991–3, having risen by 15 percent between 1983 and 1991 (Guellec, 1995: 10). Recent trends suggest that the dimensions of new installations should be more finely calculated, rather than merely building the largest facilities possible, as had been the time-honoured practice of water engineers. More incentives are needed for 'active prevention' (cutting waste by users, leaking mains etc.). At the same time, water management transcends engineering requirements to embrace a range of sociopolitical dimensions.

Characterisation of the French model of water management

French water management involves a 'mixed implementation incentive system' (Bower, 1983), combining regulatory and economic instruments with infrequent recourse to court actions. The system has demonstrated its flexibility over the long term, bringing together public and private actors in a distinctive 'mixed economy'. As Lorrain (1992: 25–6) pointed out, the 'French model of public services' gives the lie to the received idea that France is solely characterised by a centralised 'Jacobin' state, and hostility between public and private sectors. Indeed, a defining characteristic of the water sector is the continued impact of neocorporatist arrangements. Producer interests shape the organisation and functioning of the sector. Here 'producer interests' refers to three categories of economic actor: private water companies, industrial water users and farmers.

Due to the oligopolistic structure of the French water delivery industry, the market power of the leading private-sector firms – Vivendi and the Lyonnaise des Eaux – is considerable. Their scale and engineering expertise allows them to compete globally, at a time when increasing water shortages are creating major opportunities around the world.[11] However, within France the water companies dwarf the local authorities they serve. Tendering procedures have lacked transparency. Competition is limited by the long-term nature of contracts. Rules meant to protect consumers have favoured entrenched producers: exigent technological and regulatory requirements build high barriers to entry for new competitors. Thus critics have complained that water companies enjoyed quasi-monopolies, that prices were excessive, and that corruption was involved in obtaining contracts.[12] Between 1981 and 1988, the two largest water companies were repeatedly prosecuted for anti-competitive practices, and criticisms were made by the *Cour des Comptes* (Gouverne, 1994: 184). These developments fuelled public unease over the apparent 'privatisation' of a public service.[13] Calls to reinforce competition led to the 1993 *loi Sapin*, requiring that the tendering process be more open, with contracts to be discussed in municipal council meetings. Kickback schemes (*droits d'entrée*) were made illegal and franchises limited to twenty years (Guellec, 1995: 53–5). Moreover, the *grand absent* in the French water landscape is a national regulator. There is no equivalent to the British regulator OFWAT, which oversees pricing and investment decisions in the sector. One obstacle is the fact that the elected local authorities retain control over pricing – but lack the means to implement their prerogatives.

Industrialists and farmers have been favoured by the regime's neocorporatist tendencies. Industrialists are recruited to the *comités de bassin* as sectoral representatives. Within these committees, they defend their interests by their numerical strength, and outside of them by their economic power and access to politicians and administrators. Thus Brénac (1985: 591) noted that the chemicals industry had succeeded in wresting better terms than other sectors. Moreover, the charges system used by the water boards is based on the principle of a *juste retour* (fair return). The ratio of subsidies to charges has been 109 percent (CGP, 1997: 103), meaning that industrial polluters recoup what they pay in. In reality, the

---

[11] The fostering of 'national champions' by providing a domestic springboard from which to conquer international markets constituted a key feature of French industrial policy; see Szarka (1992: 42–76).

[12] For example, Alain Carignon, former Mayor of Grenoble and Junior Minister for the Environment (1986–8), was imprisoned during the period 1994–8 over an illegal contract with the Lyonnaise des Eaux.

[13] See Buller (1996) for discussion.

agences have implemented a complex redistribution of the environmental burden, which the CGP (1997: 97–119) called the *principe pollueur-sociétaire* (polluter cooperative principle). This redistribution has two main components. The first is that the proceeds of charges are recycled as subsidies to promote capital investment in those water treatment facilities which most reduce pollution. Although these subsidies are purportedly allocated to public authorities and private firms on a 'best case' basis, the CGP (1997) concluded the *agences* were not attaining specified water quality objectives at least cost. The second component is that the French public subsidise other users, especially farmers.[14] For the moment, the latter pay few abstraction charges, although their water consumption is the highest of any user group (see Table 8.1 above) and no pollution charges. The explanation stems not from the position of the farming lobby on *comités de bassin* (where it is numerically weak), but from its 'special relationship' with the Agriculture Ministry. In effect, France's most corporatist regime extends to preferential treatment in relation to water.

In summary, the structures of the water policy network have had systemic impacts on the conduct of policy. In the postwar period, the underlying aim was to deliver adequate water, with the need to reduce pollution recognised gradually from the 1950s on. Treating water as an industrialised commodity brought a technocratic orientation to the system. A number of features have survived from this earlier policy community configuration, with its particular forms of political exchange. Relationships between local authorities and private firms were based on reciprocal gains: investment in facilities against company profits, prestigious infrastructures against engineering solutions, democratic representativeness against economic viability. With the invention of the *agences*, the policy community broadened into networks representing a larger number of interests. The new policy tier fostered greater collective responsibility, but still favoured producer interests over the general public. In recent years, newer issues – agricultural pollution, rainwater contamination, eutrophication and drought – have prompted a rethink of policies. In the 1990s,

---

[14] The CGP (1997: 146) noted that 'le système a donc peu de perdants dans son fonctionnement actuel, si ce n'est le consommateur final et la collectivité dans son ensemble (. . .) Les agriculteurs bénéficient de transferts du contribuable et du consommateur d'eau'. The report by the Cour des Comptes (1999: 22) likewise noted that water pollution caused by consumers was a fraction of that from farming, but that pollution charges were in inverse proportions.

French consumers were faced with large water price hikes, and the realisation that the pollution bill was distributed unequally, with inadequate application of both the PPP and the prevention principle. Meanwhile the public remained poorly represented in policy and pricing decisions. European water directives tightened the regulatory framework, but were limited to setting technical standards of water quality. These 'yardsticks' focused attention on shortcomings and empowered citizens' groups to keep firms and public authorities honest. However, given the availability of a 'requisite variety of instruments', they have not catalysed institutional reform in France,[15] nor impacted on network structures and decision making. Moreover, the fragmentation of the system and the distribution of power between categories of actor have meant that no policy broker was able to develop a comprehensive water policy. The challenge for the future is to develop an model of sustainable water management that leaves behind corporatist arrangements, reconciles environmental concerns with divergent social and economic interests, and fosters changes in water usage patterns.

Waste

In contrast to fresh water, a homogenous primary resource, waste is a diverse by-product. This implies a different set of practical challenges, yet French policy solutions have proved fairly similar in both sectors. According to ADEME estimates, total annual waste production rose from some 580 million tonnes in 1990 to 627 in 1996, indicating that France faces increasing disposal problems. In 1996, agriculture produced some 375 million tonnes (often returned directly to the soil), industry produced 94 million tonnes of ordinary waste and at least 9 million tonnes of 'special' (e.g. hazardous) wastes, households producing some 24.5 million tonnes, with other waste streams making up the balance (IFEN, 1998a: 184). Household wastes grew from an average 220 kilograms per person per year in 1960 to 416 in 1993 (Guellec, 1997: 9). In 1996 disposal channels were 52 percent to landfill, 38 percent incinerated and 10 percent recycled, mainly by composting (Vesseron, 1997: 21).

---

[15] Unlike Britain, where the establishment of the Environment Agency arose in part from EU policy implementation requirements.

Landfill has been the cheapest means of waste disposal, at about 60 francs per tonne in 1991, whilst waste-to-energy incineration then cost around 300 francs (Mathieu, 1992). The number of illegal waste tips was estimated to be around 30,000 in the 1980s, indicating the prevalence of fly-tipping. France has three categories of official landfill site. Class 1 sites for hazardous wastes require high standards of substrate impermeability and maintenance; class 2 sites are termed semipermeable, accepting ordinary industrial and household waste; class 3 sites can be permeable, being reserved for inert mining and building waste.[16] The systematic recourse to landfill is now recognised as an inadequate response.

The legislative framework

In the wake of oil and raw material price hikes, the Gruson report (1974) recommended a policy of reducing excessive consumption. This led to the 1975 Waste Act imposing a duty of proper disposal, whose 1977 implementing decree made household waste collection obligatory for local authorities. The major measure with regard to industrial waste was the 1976 act on *installations classées* (discussed in Chapter 7). The National Waste Recovery and Disposal Agency (*Agence nationale pour la récupération et l'élimination des déchets* – ANRED) was set up in 1976 to undertake applied research on waste, offer technical assistance, collect charges and distribute subsidies to third-party projects. It is now incorporated into the ADEME.

In the 1970s these measures were in the vanguard of environmental legislation around Europe, but their limitations become apparent in the next decade. Controls on hazardous wastes were limited, with transborder movements raising concern. Measures for waste recovery and recycling were too limited. Too many landfill sites operated under unsatisfactory conditions, with contamination of water tables by leachates and fermentation of organic matter producing methane (a powerful 'greenhouse gas'). Public outcries were provoked by two scandals. The first was the Seveso affair where, subsequent to an explosion at the Icmesa factory near Milan in 1976, barrels of dioxin – a carcinogenic agent – were imported into France in 1983 and illegally dumped in a landfill

---

[16] The disposal of nuclear wastes constitutes a separate category.

site in Roumazières.[17] The other was the class 1 Montchanin tip, where in the 1980s inadequate safeguards over disposal of hazardous wastes led to environmental and health problems.[18] Clearly, waste policy required upgrading.

Subsequent to the 1990 Lalonde 'green plan', the 1992 Waste Act transposed EC directive 91/156. Emphasising the proximity principle (whereby waste be treated as near to source as possible), it prioritised a reduction in waste and an increase in recovery, recycling and energy conversion. Responding to concern over rubbish dumps, the act stipulated that only 'final' wastes could be consigned to landfill. In principle, there would be a single class 2 site per *département*, meaning the closure of some 6,700 tips by the 2002 deadline.[19] The roles of local authorities were clarified, with the *département* being responsible for planning household waste treatment, and the region for industrial waste. Upper limits on fines for improper disposal were increased from 120,000 to 500,000 francs. A hypothecated tax on household wastes going to landfill of 20 francs per tonne was set, rising to 40 francs in 1998. In 1996, the tax raised 668 million francs (IFEN, 1998a: 198). Proceeds have been used by the ADEME for subsidising waste treatment facilities.

Cross-border movements of waste also came under scrutiny. In 1989, the conventions of Bale and Lomé were signed to limit waste exports to developing countries. In October 1992, the European Council of Ministers imposed restrictions on waste movements in the EC, giving a degree of priority to environmental concerns over the free movement of waste 'goods' (Dron, 1995: 62). In 1988, 1,100,000 tons of waste were imported into France (Bertolini, 1998: 185). By 1994, France imported next to no household waste, whilst imports of industrial wastes stood at 430,000 tonnes and exports at 70,000, a reduction of 30 percent in relation to 1991 (IFEN, 1998a: 189).

Recent developments

In highlighting the problems of the 1992 Waste Act, the Guellec (1997) parliamentary report prompted a revision of policy. It noted

---

[17] See Bouchardeau (1986: 123–6).

[18] For details, see Destot (1993: 99–101) and Meyronneinc (1993: 38–9).

[19] According to Bertolini (1998: 181), some 10,000 were closed between 1978 and 1990.

that by 1996 only forty-seven *départements* (covering a third of the population) had drawn up waste disposal plans. Most of them assumed an increase in waste, and proposed to dispose of some 80 percent of solid waste by incineration, making scant provision for recycling. Incineration was favoured since it allows energy recovery (especially under a co-generation regime producing heating and electricity) and because of the belief that only residues from burning qualified as 'final' waste acceptable for landfill under the terms of the 1992 act. In fact, this interpretation was contrary to its spirit, and had practical drawbacks. Firstly, incineration plants require significant capital investment. With total construction costs estimated at 60 billion francs, local authorities lacked the resources to finance the operation (particularly as the 1991 urban waste water directive had imposed a heavy burden). These investment costs implied that households would have to pay more for waste disposal, as they had done for water and probably with the same discontent. Secondly, large investments and sophisticated technology would make local authorities dependent on specialist firms having the required capital and expertise. The Lyonnaise des Eaux and Vivendi already held around 40 percent of the waste 'market'. A massive switch to incineration raised the prospect of creating new 'toll-pass' businesses: local authorities would have no alternative to channelling public funds for private profits. Moreover, the utilities involved were the same firms whose oligopolistic practices aroused concern in the water sector. Thirdly, incineration plants are economically viable only with large through-puts of waste. They are suitable for big cities, but France's low population density created a conundrum. Each rural *commune* could not reasonably build an incinerator. Grouped facilities were feasible, but required transportation of waste over distance, going against the proximity principle.

These factors militated for a review of policy. Jacques Vernier, then head of the ADEME, called in 1997 for more stress on materials recycling and less on energy recovery by incineration. Operational incidents pointed in the same direction. In January 1998, three incinerators near Lille were shut down by the Environment Ministry after dioxin was found in the milk of cows reared in their vicinity (*Le Monde*, 28.1.1998: 13). Subsequently, a MATE report on dioxin emissions found that of France's seventy-one large incinerators, sixty-five were operating outside of EU norms, prompting further shut-downs (*Le Monde*, 8.5.1998: 10). In April 1998, Environment Minister Voynet instituted a more flexible interpretation of 'final' waste. The revised approach stressed reduction at source, more materials recovery and a target of 50 percent for recycling of household wastes (MATE, 1998). Greater diversity of disposal plans was encouraged to accommodate local conditions. All these measures were calculated to reduce the recourse to both incineration and landfill. The policy was reinforced by economic incentives. Where household collections were made on a separated basis (*collecte sélective*), VAT paid by local authorities fell from 20.6 percent to 5.5 per cent, whilst state subsidies for treatment of separated waste streams were increased.

However, the problems posed by recycling should not be ignored. Meyronneinc (1993: 57) noted that recycling industries are faced with steep price fluctuations in inputs and outputs, and operate in a context of low added value. In the earlier 1990s, a strict policy in Germany of paper recycling, subsided by taxpayers, led to a surplus being exported. Profiting from 'free' imports, French paper producers stopped making domestic purchases, causing national recycling to collapse. Similarly, Courtine (1996: 21) found that compost produced from household waste was difficult to market. To date French householders had not used separate containers, other than in local experiments. The complete separation of organic from non-organic materials at waste treatment centres is impossible. Because the compost contained plastic and glass, agricultural users were wary of the sanitary and safety hazards to their crops. Consequently France dumped a third of home-produced compost in 1991, whilst importing 500,000 tonnes.

On the positive side, partnership between the public authorities and industrialists has allowed progress towards effective recycling. In a context of EC discussions, leading to the 1994 Packaging Directive, the 1992 'Lalonde decree' sought a first-mover advantage by developing a new mode for recovering packaging. Industrialists had either to recover and recycle materials themselves, or pay a third party. The latter alternative has been financed by pro rata payments to a private firm called *Eco-emballages*, set up by participating industrialists as its shareholders. By 1995, around 10,000 firms had contracts with *Eco-emballages*, paying charges of some 550 million francs (IFEN, 1996b: 65). Further, by 1998, some 14,000 *communes* (a population of 29 million people) had recycling agreements with *Eco-emballages* (IFEN, 1998a: 187). The firm redistributes 75 percent of its revenues to local authorities to subsidise recycling operations and makes payments per tonne for materials recovered (Guillon, 1997: 91–2). The scheme has proved to be one of the major drivers in the transition from indiscriminate dumping to selective retrieval procedures. By 1997, 31 percent of all packaging was being recycled, although the target of 15 percent materials reuse set by the 1994 European directive was met only in relation to steel and glass (IFEN, 1998a: 190–1).

Hazardous wastes remain a significant problem. Although each of France's twenty-two regions has a legal responsibility to provide treatment facilities, only twelve class 1 landfill sites exist, just one of which is situated in southern France. Valluy (1996) showed that the repeated failure to open a class 1 site in Rhône-Alpes was due to public distrust of deals done over the heads of local authorities by secretive policy communities. Consequently, 'special' wastes from Lyon and Marseille continue to be transported considerable distances for disposal. Alternative solutions are being developed, notably 'in-house' treatment by 'end of pipe' solutions and trends towards cleaner technology (Bonardi and Delmas, 1996). However, as noted by Lombard (1997: 26), there has been little uptake by French industrialists of environmental audits, such as ISO 14001. Major changes in behaviour have more usually been the result of top-down policies than voluntary initiatives. A prominent example was the French government's ban on asbestos production in December 1996.

Seriously polluted and abandoned sites constitute an associated problem. France has undertaken three inventories of these, with 669 identified in 1994, and 896 in 1996, when eighty-six rehabilitated sites were removed from the list (MATE, 1997a). To finance further rehabilitation, a tax on hazardous wastes treated by third-party operators was created. However, receipts of 83 million francs in 1996 (IFEN, 1998a: 198) are paltry in relation to a problem whose scale has probably been underestimated, given that surveys conducted in Denmark identified 1,500 sites, 25,000 in the Netherlands and 30,000 in the USA.

Characterisation of the French model of waste management

The major actor in terms of policy formulation has been the central state, though European measures have acted as a spur to action. For policy implementation, local authorities have played the main role in conjunction with private firms, notably SITA and

France-Déchets (owned by the Lyonnaise des Eaux), CGEA and SARP Industries (Vivendi) and TREDI (Entreprise minière et chimique). Tightening of the legislative framework meant that by the 1990s all French households benefited from refuse collection, with local authorities directly managing the service in 50 percent of *communes*, private firms in 36 percent and a combined mode operating in the remainder (IFEN, 1998a: 187). Similarly, the framework instituted for *Eco-emballages* is a 'mixed economy' partnership, with the central state as instigator, a private firm and the 'market' as intermediaries, and local authority stewardship. A government agency (originally the ANRED, currently the ADEME) acts as policy coordinator, notably with respect to environmental charges and subsidies. Thus the French model for waste management has many of the components found for water: national standard setting, intermediary agencies providing advice, incentives and sectoral coordination, local authority responsibility, with considerable private sector implementation. Indeed, several of the actors are identical and the danger of a slide towards quasi-monopoly by the private utility firms has entailed policy adjustments in both sectors.

Important differences also emerge. Meso-corporatist arrangements are less marked in waste than in water, though not absent. From its inception, the Environment Ministry sought contractual undertakings with industrial subsectors to improve materials efficiency, encourage 'clean technologies' and reduce wastage (Bertolini, 1998: 173). Negotiated agreements on packaging were signed in 1979 and 1988 (Poquet, 1994: 29). The *Eco-emballages* scheme is another variant of the 'Colbertist' bargain, whereby the state corrects a market failure by setting up a private-sector partner. But, due to structural differences between the sectors, there are no equivalents with waste management to the decentralised *agences de l'eau*. This also means that channels for user representation are limited. Although secular apathy was a contributory factor, the lack of public participation in policy formulation is now problematic. The stress on household waste recycling by separated collection means that individuals become policy implementers, but their enrolment requires communication and shared objectives. Overall, these developments indicate the widening of policy networks, but in an ad hoc and uneven fashion.

Air

Schematically, three levels of atmospheric pollution can be identified: local, regional and global. At the local level, pollution produced by coal combustion has been recognised as a hazard since the industrial revolution. It led to large numbers of deaths in London in the winter of 1952, with similar problems in France in 1954, (Collomb et al., 1993: 182). The early policy aim was pollution abatement from 'fixed' sources, namely the chimneys of factories and houses, with black smoke and sulphur dioxide targeted for major reductions. But with the massive growth in road vehicles, 'mobile' sources today present heightened risks, notably due to nitrogen oxides, fine particles and volatile organic compounds. Among regional-level problems, the most severe has been acid rain, caused by a chemical cocktail (including sulphur dioxide, nitrogen oxides, ammonia and hydrochloric acid) emitted by fossil fuel power stations, factories and vehicles. Prevailing winds can blow emissions several hundred miles before being deposited in the form of acid rain, killing trees and vegetation, and damaging buildings. In Europe, Scandinavia and parts of Germany have been most affected. Two forms of global problems have been much publicised since the 1980s. One is the reduction of stratospheric (high-altitude) ozone over the poles, caused *inter alia* by CFCs and halons; these 'holes' allow greater amounts of ultraviolet light to pass to ground level, with impacts on aquatic ecosystems and greater likelihood of skin cancers. The other relates to increased concentrations of 'greenhouse gases' (such as carbon dioxide and methane) produced by human activities, encouraging climate change. Potential consequences of the latter include alterations in seasons, higher temperatures, increased sea-water levels, modifications in crop regimes and new patterns in the spread of tropical illnesses. Although some air pollutants are primary by-products whose sources can readily be identified (e.g. soot from chimneys), others are secondary compounds resulting from photochemical interactions in the atmosphere. A particular problem is the production of tropospheric (ground-level) ozone from nitrogen oxides, now acknowledged as a health hazard. Episodes of high photochemical pollution have as contributory causes natural phenomena, such as local terrain, absence of wind and thermal inversions. The formation processes are well understood, but the attribution of degrees of responsibility to categories of agent (to simplify, factories versus cars) is problematic because tropospheric ozone is a derived compound, rather than a direct emission. The complexity of atmospheric pollution has posed severe challenges to policy making. Unlike water or waste, air pollution cannot be remedied by treatment (except on a very small scale). Policy must be directed at the reduction and prevention of emissions. But in recent years policy makers have struggled to assign responsibilities, identify the best means for action and develop multisectoral solutions. The transborder and world-wide implications of atmospheric pollution make international coordination of national policies essential, yet practical measures are necessarily local.

The legislative framework

Although in France the 1810 decree recognised the problem of foul smells generated by workshops, the development of a comprehensive framework to combat air-borne pollution was slow. The 1961 act was wide-ranging but ineffective (Huglo, 1993: 4), since it contained no emission standards nor air quality targets, and proposed few sanctions. Neither was a unified regulatory authority set up, with responsibilities being split between several ministries. Lascoumes and Vlassopoulou (1998: 35) argued that this administrative fragmentation prevented the development of a co-ordinated, national policy. On an alternative reading, lack of centralisation was a blessing in disguise since it allowed diversity of response at the local level, where several initiatives met with success. Zoning measures were established in 1963 and extended in 1974, setting up *zones d'alerte* (ZA) and *zones de protection spéciale* (ZPS). In these the use of high sulphur fuels by industry was banned – permanently in ZPS but only during pollution peaks in ZA. The licensing system developed by the 1976 act on *installations classées* (see Chapter 7) also covered industrial sources of air pollution, with the prefect as the key decision maker. During serious air pollution episodes, prefects could impose restrictions on industrial activity, such as compulsory use of low sulphur fuel or curtailment of output, thereby cutting emissions. Zacklad (1996: 12) noted that in the Paris area sulphur dioxide emissions were reduced by a factor of six over a thirty-year period. Knoepfel and Larrue (1985: 52) found that zoning measures imposing use of low sulphur fuels were a key explanation of air quality improvements in several conurbations, although the switch to nuclear generation of electricity was also a remedial factor. Indeed, from their five-country survey of clean air policies, Knoepfel and Weidner (1986: 87) concluded that 'French regional implementation systems turned out to be the most successful'.

A number of international agreements have reinforced national legislation, notably the 1979 UNECE Geneva Convention on Long Range Transboundary Air Pollution, leading in the 1980s to a series of multilateral conventions on sulphur dioxide and nitrogen oxides. In 1987, the Montreal protocol committed its signatories to the phasing out of CFC manufacture. During the same period, the EC developed a 'command and control' approach to air pollution, which involved the permitting of industrial sources, product elimination and substitution. Limit values were set for sulphur dioxide by directive 80/779, for lead by directive 82/884 and for nitrogen oxides by directive 85/203. Emissions from large-scale combustion plants were capped by directives 84/360 and 88/609.[20] The French attitude to the development of EC clean air legislation was neither recalcitrant nor proactive because of three factors: 'the multiplicity of regulatory instruments, the structure of the energy sector, and the under-developed environmental protection equipment industry' (Héritier, Knill and Mingers, 1996: 203). France, lacking the technological lead enjoyed by German firms in pollution abatement equipment, did not have an industrial incentive to champion more demanding air legislation whilst nuclear sourcing of some 75 percent of French electricity production meant that the French did not have the emissions problems associated with fossil fuels found in neighbouring countries. Further, the incorporation of tighter norms into existing regulation posed few difficulties due to the technocratic orientation of ministerial field services, which were largely manned by engineers from the *Corp des mines*.

However, industrial emissions are easier to control than air pollution from 'mobile' sources (Escourrou, 1981:159). In recent decades, atmospheric pollution from industrial sources has fallen but has increased from vehicles.[21] The EC responded in the 1970s with the establishment of vehicle emission limits, including reductions of carbon monoxide, lead and fine particles. These were followed by the 1985 directive promoting unleaded fuel and

---

[20] Further details on EC policy can be found in Aubin (1993).
[21] For detailed data, see OECD (1997: 77–81) and IFEN (1998a: 59–68).

the 1989 directive on catalytic converters. By the 1990s, these technical innovations had improved the environmental performance of new vehicles, with lower emissions of lead, sulphur dioxide and carbon monoxide. However, the total volume of emissions increased because the vehicle pool grew, leading to greater road congestion and reduced fuel efficiency, whilst large numbers of older, high-polluting vehicles remained in use. Despite reductions in the sulphur and lead content of industrial, household and vehicle fuels, air quality was regularly dropping to critical levels in health terms (IFEN, 1998c: 2), and steadily increasing in political salience.

In the mid-1990s, Environment Minister Lepage made new legislation an urgent priority since fresh epidemiological studies stressed the health dangers posed by traffic fumes, particularly to the asthmatic. The Air Quality and Energy Efficiency Act was passed on 30 December 1996, transposing EC directive 96/62. Its major innovation was to stress the reduction of vehicle emissions. It set up a legal requirement for accurate monitoring of air quality, with towns of more than 250,000 inhabitants to set up networks immediately, and a nationwide system to be completed by 2000. The act instituted three levels of air quality warning, with prefects given powers to take exceptional – but temporary – action during the highest level of alert. These included restrictions on heavy goods vehicles, reductions in speed limits by 20 kilometres per hour, and recourse to *circulation alternée* whereby only 50 percent of vehicles for personal use are allowed to use roads during pollution peaks. Regional and departmental plans were to be drawn up to ensure compliance with air quality limit values set by the ADEME in line with European legislation, whilst preventive action in the form of public transport strategies and energy efficiency measures was to be developed. Thus the regulatory framework now covers both abatement of emissions from all sources, and safeguards for ambient air quality.

The 1996 act provoked criticisms for its lack of 'teeth', when several level 2 alerts in Paris and Strasbourg over summer 1997 led to no action. Yet after a level 3 alert on 1 October 1997, Environment Minister Voynet applied the *circulation alternée* measure for the first time in greater Paris, with public transport being made free. Opinion polls showed that over 80 percent of residents agreed with it, and only 5 percent of motorists ignored it. Despite expectations of widespread flouting, the experiment had proved successful – but it has not been repeated to date.

Recent developments

Between 1980 and 1986, sulphur dioxide emissions fell by 60 percent in France, 29 percent in West Germany and 20 percent in the UK, but with little improvement subsequently; carbon dioxide emissions likewise decreased between 1980 and 1986, but increased markedly in the period of strong economic growth at the end of the decade (Ministère de l'Environnement, 1994: 11–12). Increased 'greenhouse gas' emissions provoked worldwide concern, leading in 1992 to the signature in Rio de Janeiro of an international framework convention on climate change, stabilising carbon dioxide emissions at below two tonnes per habitant per year.[22] In France, the level was 1.86 tonnes per habitant (Ministère de l'Environnement, 1994: 12), due to extensive recourse to nuclear power which produces little CO_2. Although at Kyoto in 1997 the USA and China were hostile to emissions cuts (since these might curtail economic growth), the EU pledged to reduce its 'greenhouse gases' by 8 percent below 1990 levels by 2012, with national burdens falling differentially in relation to scale of emissions.[23] Cuts of 12.5 percent and 21 percent were agreed by the UK and Germany respectively. France merely confirmed it would stabilise emissions at 1990 levels till 2010. However, even this target could prove difficult, given that by 1995 emissions had risen by 2 percent (*Le Monde*, 11.1.2000: 10). In January 2000 the Jospin government announced a climate change policy, but it merely offered a sketchy outline whose content is expected to be filled in once decisions at European and international levels are taken.

Characterisation of the French model of air quality control

As with other environmental sectors, early French clean-air policy was based on negotiation between regulators and industrialists.[24] This meso-corporatist orientation imprinted onto the specialised institutions set up to implement policy. The Air Quality Agency was established in 1980 to do research on atmospheric pollution, organise information campaigns, undertake public works, and give loans and subsidies to firms investing in improved air

---

[22] The Rio conference will be discussed in Chapter 9.
[23] For analysis of the proactive role of the EU in international negotiations on climate change, see Sbragia and Damro (1999).
[24] For description of their interactions, see Knoepfel and Larrue (1985: 55–8).

quality. The *'mutuelle de l'air'* was set up in 1985 under Environment Minister Bouchardeau, following the model of the *agences de l'eau* (Bouchardeau, 1986: 96-9).[25] Charges were levied on power stations and industrial plants emitting over 2,500 tonnes of sulphur yearly; proceeds were redistributed to participating companies in the form of subsidies of up to 50 percent of investments in air pollution abatement. The 1985 tax initially covered emissions from 480 large combustion plants; levied at 130 francs per tonne, yearly receipts were around 100 million francs. In 1990, this hypothecated tax was extended to cover nitrogen oxides and hydrochloric acid, increased to 150 francs per tonne and took in some 870 establishments, bringing the yearly receipt to some 190 million francs (Mousel and Herz, 1990: 71). Part of the proceeds went to the financing of air monitoring networks (e.g. AIRPARIF in Paris, COPARLY in Lyon, etc.). Industrialists participate in running such networks, confirming their centrality in both monitoring and implementation. According to Barbier (1995: 327), industrialists accepted these fiscal arrangements as a public demonstration of their commitment to raising environmental standards.

As noted by Knoepfel (1998: 165–6), two characteristics of 'traditional' French air policy stand out: its anthropocentric turn with health concerns paramount, and the tendency to manage air pollution episodes, rather than eliminate their causes. Recent developments have written more starkly the limitations of the meso-corporatist regime and the health protection agenda. Because of the climate change potential of increased concentrations of 'greenhouse gases', the need today is to reduce the total volume of emissions, rather than just dampen short-term fluctuations in ambient air quality. Further, the policy targets have shifted from sulphur to embrace carbon dioxide and nitrogen oxides, and from 'fixed' to 'mobile' sources.

However, the French car industry has repeatedly been uncooperative in gearing up for better environmental performance. In 1985, Jacques Calvet, as head of Peugeot, mounted a rearguard action against the introduction of catalytic converters. Tough measures initially envisaged in the 1996 Air Pollution Act were watered down due to pressure from the car lobby. Reform of

---

[25] In 1990, the functions of *Agence pour la qualité de l'air* and the *Mutuelle de l'air* were incorporated into the ADEME. With the 1996 Air Quality Act, the role of the ADEME was extended to the coordination of air quality surveillance across France.

excise duties was repeatedly ducked. France has one of the highest rates of tax on unleaded fuel in Europe but below-average rates on diesel (Radanne, Bonduelle and Bossoken, 1997: 10). This has stimulated the sale of diesel vehicles, accounting for nearly half of new car registrations in France in the mid-1990s. Having taken a lead in diesel engine technology, French car manufacturers were unreceptive to medical reports published in 1997–8 indicating the health risks posed by the fine particles emitted by diesel fuels, notably aggravated asthma and lung cancer. This resistance may now be waning. The French car industry has made some (limited) progress towards marketing electric cars. In 1999, a compromise was finally accepted to increase excise on diesel to petrol levels, but phased in over a seven-year period.

Yet simply stigmatising cars, their manufacturers or their drivers, is an inadequate response. The motor car is only one aspect of a lifestyle which is partly chosen by but partly imposed on Western populations. Broad-based strategies to encompass attendant problems are required. These include technical measures (low-emissions vehicles, greater energy efficiency, recourse to renewable energy) and economic measures (revised tax structures, more public transport). But the need for social measures, such as greater security on public transport and reduced necessity to commute, tend to be neglected. Moreover, the emerging policy frame involves the very opposite of the corporatist relations which had characterised the French model: it implies a major widening of policy networks through integration between environmental, transport and social policies, and a much bigger role for the general public.

In summary, the policy model which in the 1970s and 1980s successfully combated local health hazards due to sulphur dioxide emissions from 'fixed' sources, only partially translated in the 1990s into effective measures to limit the 'greenhouse gases' from 'mobile' and other sources which catalyse global climate change. For the twenty-first century, completing the cognitive switch from the anthropocentric focus of the former issue to the ecocentric implications of the latter constitutes an invisible barrier to policy reformulation.

Conclusions

The French models for water and waste management have converged. In principle each is a public service run by democratically accountable bodies, yet at the operational level policy has favoured the development of 'high-tech' private companies enjoying quasi-monopolies. The stress is on a technocratic mode of environmental problem solving, bringing together prestigious public organisations (the *grands corps*) and private expertise. European legislation has influenced the rate of change, but not its direction: the 'naturalisation' process (see Chapter 5) was eased by the technical orientation of European directives, which were readily assimilated into existing policy arrangements. Although the considerable capital expenditure involved in regulatory upgrades was financed from the public purse, the French have rarely been consulted over policy options. Even in areas where public involvement is essential, such as the sorting of household waste, moves towards greater participation have been limited. Indeed, the French public often feels as if it has no input, but that the state must find solutions. On the other hand, the governance of water, waste and air has been marked by meso-corporatist bargaining between state officials and industrialists over the implementation of regulatory frameworks and fiscal policies. Redistribution of environmental tax revenues within the industrial sector to subsidise cleaner technology has been the distinctive feature of the French model.

Because of the suspicion that arrangements with industrialists were too cosy, the effectiveness of institutions managing fiscal redistribution came under scrutiny in the 1990s. At the start of the decade, the agencies for wastes, air and energy were merged into the ADEME, a reform which, according to its former director Mousel (1995: 70), enabled the attainment of greater policy coherence across media. At the end of the decade, the *agences de l'eau* also encountered criticisms of ineffectiveness, notably in the CGP report (1997), but to date no structural changes have been implemented. Thus France has no cross-media 'Environmental Agency' on the British model. Rather, changes in conduct have been sought by the use of economic instruments. The meso-corporatist bargain has been challenged by a fiscal reform which partly abandons the principle of hypothecated taxes. The 1999 Finance Bill established the *taxe générale sur les activités polluantes* (TGAP), which incorporated the pollution charges levied by the ADEME as of 1999, and is set to extend its coverage to water charges in 2000, and energy consumption in 2001. However, the TGAP is a double-edged blade. On the one hand, it represents a political coup for Environment Minister Voynet since it reinforces her ministry's *tutelle* over subordinate institutions whose superior resources had transformed them into rivals.[26] On the other, the TGAP is statist in character since it recentralises environmental charges under the aegis of France's most powerful institution, the Finance Ministry. Fiscal reform extends to institutional reform, since the autonomy of decentralised agents in relation to central government is reduced. This has provoked controversy because of its reversal of the trend to local political control, and because the role of the *agences de l'eau* seemed threatened.[27] Although charges are set to rise in order to augment their dissuasive effect on pollution, the Finance Ministry will return only part of the proceeds of the TGAP to the *agences* and the ADEME. The planned diversion of monies undermines the long-standing principle of the hypothecation of environmental tax revenues. Already by 1997 unused tax receipts on waste – in principle earmarked for upgrading treatment facilities – totalled some three billion francs (IFEN, 1998a: 198). Future usage of environmental tax receipts will be subject to negotiation between Finance and Environment Ministries, with the latter being historically the weaker partner. In effect, Environment Minister Voynet accepted a deal whereby environmental charges would subsidise the short-term costs of the change-over to a 35-hour week – a measure which her party, the *Verts,* has vigorously supported. Ironically, the extension of French ecologism's social agenda could be at the cost of reduced environmental spending.

In summary, policy change in relation to water, waste and air has run along three dimensions. Firstly, policy content was reformed, with a tightening of the regulatory framework, generally through technical prescriptions bearing on emissions and ambient media quality. The 1990s were marked by a rapid succession of new laws and a 'ratcheting-up' of environmental standards. Secondly, the structures and operation of the relevant policy subsystems were exposed. The legitimacy and scale of influence of neocorporatist organisation were called into question. Ironically, this may undermine the most distinctive, and perhaps most effective, component of the 'old' policy regime, namely hypothecated taxation. Although the reinforcement of democratic procedures has been hesitant and limited, nevertheless over time the French model evolved by an opening-out of policy networks.

---

[26] See Chapter 4 for discussion.

[27] The debate organised by the French senate brought together the various arguments: see François-Poncet and Oudin (1998).

Finally, at the cognitive level, the beginnings of a shift occurred from a short-term anthropocentric view towards a long-range ecocentric perspective. This in turn raises the question of how committed policy makers are to achieving sustainable development.

9

TOWARDS SUSTAINABLE DEVELOPMENT?

Introduction

As previous chapters have indicated, environmental policy in its 'classic' forms – namely a sectoral approach which focused on conserving the natural environment, reducing the dysfunctions of industrial activities and meeting human needs – inevitably spilt over into wider economic issues and required broad social bargains to function, yet lacked a coherent cognitive basis for integrating its economic and social dimensions. Further, because of its compartmentalisation, 'classic' environmental policy no longer fully responds to changing realities. New challenges facing humanity such as global climate change, as well as persisting ones such as Third World destitution, have encouraged reconceptualisation of the remit of environmental policy. Of these the most salient has been the notion of sustainable development. Accordingly this chapter first reviews the development of the concept of sustainability, and considers elements of practice associated with it. Secondly, it traces their particular inflexions in the French context. Measures at the national level are discussed, leading on to appraisal of local and regional initiatives. Whilst the ambitious scale of the concept of sustainable development makes rapid attainment of 'targets' improbable, the question for the immediate future is whether policies can be turned around to at least face in the direction of sustainability.

The International Dimensions of Sustainable Development

The road to Rio: the development of a concept

Held in Stockholm in 1972, the first major international conference on the environment produced two major outcomes: one was
to accelerate the building of institutional capacity (with a number
of national Environment Ministries set up at this time), and the
other was to stimulate expansion of legislation. However, the tension between visions stressing environmental protection (largely
promoted by industrialised countries of the northern hemisphere)
and preferences for economic development (which preoccupied
the struggling south) made it difficult to find policies suited to
widely differing geographical, social and economic contexts. An
embryonic accommodation between North and South emerged
around the notion of the 'pollution of poverty', which pointed
both to the environmental problems faced by the poor – such as
lack of clean water or sanitation – and to the cycle of environmental degradation caused by poverty (Elliott, 1994: 9).

The 1987 report by the Brundtland Commission, put together
under the auspices of the World Conference on Environment and
Development (WCED), systematically linked environmental problems and development issues. Though not the inventor of the term
'sustainable development', the Brundtland Commission was
instrumental in disseminating its usage. It offered the now canon-
ical definition of the concept as 'development that meets the needs
of the present without compromising the ability of future generations to meet their own needs' (WCED, 1987: 43). The report
stressed the interrelationship between the elimination of poverty
and the attainment of intergenerational equity, and reiterated a
view that had gained momentum over the 1980s that environmental protection and socioeconomic development were not contradictory but complementary goals. It also called for an
international conference on the environment to explore and
propagate this vision.

Held in Rio de Janeiro in June 1992, the United Nations
Conference on Environment and Development – also known as
the 'Earth Summit I' – was the largest world forum to date, with
182 countries and around 30,000 people participating. Its aims
were ambiguous from the start, with disagreements between
countries of the northern and southern hemispheres over the main

focus. Whereas developed countries were preoccupied with environmental degradation, southern nations continued to emphasise economic development. Nevertheless the conference debated a vast range of international relations themes, including world trade, economic growth and sustainable development, demographic change, health, education and poverty, changing patterns of production and consumption, land use, soil quality and food production, energy and resource management, drinking water and sanitation, biodiversity, the atmosphere and climate change, as well as addressing the risks related to wastes and hazardous materials.

At Rio the sustainable development concept was stabilised by the call for 'the progressive integration of economic, social and environmental issues in the pursuit of development that is economically efficient, socially equitable and responsible, and environmentally sound' (UN, 1993: 96). 'Earth Summit I' produced a number of international conventions: the Statement of Forest Principles, the Convention on Biodiversity and the Convention on Climate Change, with the Convention on Desertification completed subsequently. The Declaration on Environment and Development enumerated a set of non-legally binding principles to achieve sustainable development and promote social justice within and between nations, whilst respecting the needs of future generations. Principle 1 read 'human beings are at the centre of concern for sustainable development. They are entitled to a healthy and productive life in harmony with nature', whilst principle 3 maintained that 'the right to development must be fulfilled so as to equitably meet developmental and environmental needs of present and future generations' (UN, 1993: 3–4). In proclaiming that 'states should reduce and eliminate unsustainable patterns of production and consumption and promote appropriate demographic policies', principle 8 contained a call for radical change to the economic systems of the developed nations, as well as hinting at birth control measures for populous regions. The Rio perspective emphasises that the planet's 'sources and sinks' – whether crops and fish stock, energy supplies or the capacity to absorb increased volumes of 'greenhouse gases' – are limited. A framework for progress towards the goals of the Rio Declaration was outlined in Agenda 21, which stressed the need for participatory democracy, a theme already present in the Brundtland report (WCED, 1987: 8). At the same time, successful implementation of Agenda 21 was considered 'first and foremost the responsibility of governments' (UN, 1993: 12).

The road from Rio: the beginnings of a practice

Earth Summit II took place in New York in June 1997 to review progress on Agenda 21. The UN Secretary-General's briefing report summarised developments as follows:

> Since 1992, sustainable development has been more widely accepted as an integrating concept that seeks to unify and bring together economic, social and environmental issues in a participatory process of decision making. . . . real progress has been made in establishing a conceptual framework within which planning for sustainable development can take place. . . . it is clear that the policy process is far more advanced in some areas than others. Some are still at the stage of defining problems and agreeing on necessary responses. Others have moved to the stage of target-setting and deployment of new policy instruments to achieve change. In a few cases, intervention has already brought measurable results.[1]

The report stressed that governments alone could not achieve sustainable development. A major role must be assumed by civil society through innovative, bottom-up initiatives at local and regional levels, whilst the private sector needs to embrace sustainable production. The year 2005 was set by the OECD as the deadline for adoption of national sustainable development strategies.

In the European context, the second article of the 1992 Maastricht Treaty stated the aim of attaining 'sustainable and non-inflationary growth respecting the environment'. This ambiguous wording was amended in the 1997 Amsterdam Treaty, whose article 2 refers to the promotion of 'a harmonious, balanced and sustainable development of economic activities', along with the objective of 'sustainable and non-inflationary growth'. The Fifth Action Programme entitled *Towards Sustainability* (Commission of the EC, 1993) committed the EU to achieving policy integration in five key sectors: tourism, industry, energy, transport and agriculture. Yet three years later the Commission of the EC (1996b: 3) acknowledged that assessment of progress was problematic since 'the Fifth Programme targets and actions are not all well defined in operational terms'. An underlying problem noted by Weale and Williams (1992) was that policy makers failed to clarify what is involved in integration and how it is to be achieved in practice.

---

[1] Referenced E/CN.17/1997/Z 31 January 1997, reproduced in Osborn and Bigg (1998: 91).

Similarly, the observation that the operationalisation of the sustainable development concept has been plagued by its inherent ambiguity is a constant theme in the literature. Baker et al. (1997: 32) went so far as to claim: 'one of the legacies of the Brundtland formulation . . . is that the concept is analytically contentless'. Yet considerable intellectual efforts have been expended to identify content for the term.

A core idea is that we should leave to the next generation a stock of assets no smaller than that which we have inherited. Authors such as Pearce, Markandya and Barbier (1989) and Barde (1990) developed this theme by specifying that this stock divides into artificial capital, namely artefacts, machinery etc., and natural capital, such as water, air, the ecosystems found in seas, forests etc. Different forms of artificial capital can be interchanged, but the scope for substitution of natural with artificial capital is limited. This implies the need for an equitable and parsimonious use of the former. Thus Meadows, Meadows and Randers (1992: 209) specified that the usage rates of renewable resources should not exceed regeneration rates, that the usage rates of non-renewable resources should not exceed the rate at which sustainable substitutes are developed, and that levels of polluting emissions should not exceed the assimilative capacity of the environment.

However, the ability to assess threshold limits and regeneration rates remains immature. The means to distinguish between sustainable and unsustainable production have yet to be properly developed. A system of resource accounting is required which is capable of measuring consumption rates with due regard to renewability (or exhaustion) of capital stocks. Economic indicators such as GDP are incomplete and even misleading. An often cited example is that pollution clean-up expenditure is currently tabled as an increase in wealth, rather than as a debilitating cost or a decrease in amenity. Various organisations have embarked on the identification of sustainable development indicators to allow reliable measurement of past and potential practice. Barde (1990: 35) listed three types: 'flow indicators', measuring the quantity of pollutants released into air, water or soil; 'quality indicators', measuring the concentration of pollutants in media; and 'resource indicators', measuring *inter alia* forests, fresh water resources and biodiversity. More radical proposals, from organisations such as the New Economic Foundation and Friends of the Earth, have included a well-being index, social inequality indicators and the notion of 'ecological footprints'.

Yet if some practices are clearly unsustainable (such as the overirrigation which led to the exhaustion of the Aral sea, or overfishing in many coastal waters), sustainable development does not imply the prescription of a single way forward. In order to gain better purchase on its implications, commentators have developed 'grids' or 'ladders' of sustainability, where the concept is characterised in terms of degrees of intensity.[2] Thus 'weak' sustainability has been characterised as commitment to economic growth in a context of regulatory and fiscal controls to limit environmental damage, a technological perspective aimed at the replacement of natural capital with artificial capital, but with limited attention to equity or participatory democracy. Conversely, 'strong' sustainability would involve local economic self-sufficiency, a tendency to replace capital-intensive with labour-intensive systems, the limitation of production and consumption within replenishment limits as revealed by new indicators, and a polity founded on extensive citizen decision making directed at attaining equity within and between generations. A chronological gradation can also be envisaged in which, over the long term, modest initiatives towards sustainability snowball into new societal forms (although such developments by no means follow automatically).

The challenges posed by sustainability are commonly acknowledged. Even advocates such as O'Riordan (1996: 140–1) have made reservations: 'The sustainability transition is an illusion . . . What we tend to talk about in practice is a society that is less unsustainable'. Further, outright critics such as Beckerman (1995: 126) have argued against sustainable development since 'it mixes up together the technical characteristics of a particular development path with a moral injunction to pursue it', implementation is tortuous and perhaps impossible, and alternative programmes – such as welfare maximisation – may be preferable. However, a social aim such as welfare maximisation suffers from comparable conceptual and practical problems, whilst omitting the environmental dimensions which form an integral part of 'quality of life' debates. But whatever the practical difficulties posed by the concept, two factors make its pursuit inescapable: firstly, the reliance on *unsustainable* activities is ultimately a dead-end, and secondly, following Rio and the EU's Fifth Action Programme, countries

[2] For examples, see Baker et al. (1997: 8–18).
[3] 'le premier texte transversal en matière d'environnement'.

such as France are now committed to some – as yet unclear – form of sustainable development.

Sustainable Development in France: a Faltering Start

Although the French had rarely heard of sustainable development (CFDD, 1996a: 56), over the 1990s initiatives at political and institutional levels increased in momentum, although operationalisation of the concept remained elusive.

Legislative renewal: the 1995 loi Barnier

French political traditions make a legislative response a necessary part of new policy initiatives. The *loi Barnier* forms the cornerstone of France's commitment to sustainable development. A large and ambitious bill, it went on the statute books in 1995 after a difficult passage through parliament lasting eighteen months and involving over 1,000 amendments. Environment Minister Barnier (1996: 200) described it as 'the first transversal bill in the environmental domain'.[3] Whilst including an array of specific environmental measures, it was notable for its incorporation of general principles, including the 'polluter pays' principle, prevention at source, the precautionary principle and the public's right to information and participation. Agreements and treaties at European and international levels meant that France already subscribed to most of these principles, notably by the 1987 Single European Act and the 1992 Maastricht Treaty. However, their transposition into domestic legislation was incomplete; parliamentary debate aimed to establish how legal force was to be given to them.

French environmental legislation had suffered from severe limitations, being an accrual of piecemeal measures. Often enacted by government decrees rather than by parliamentary bills, it regulated specific media (water, air, soil) or sectors (nature conservation, industrial pollution etc.). The resulting fragmentation was compounded by the legislation being consigned under various pre-existing categories of law (town-planning, countryside law etc.). Environmental legislation contained few overarching statements of aims to guide the courts in their application of particular,

---

[4] 'les lois et règlements qui organisent le droit de chacun à un environnement sain'.

usually highly technical, measures. It remained largely a sub-branch of administrative law governing the actions of public bodies, rather than giving citizens rights to defend environmental objectives. A number of negative consequences ensued. Bringing cases of environmental damage before the courts was arduous or even impossible. Not only was legal action costly and time-consuming, but serious difficulties arose in identifying both a culprit and a victim. Because the verdicts of the courts were difficult to predict, the legislation tended to dissuade victims of damage from taking legal action, rather than deter polluters and destroyers of the environment. Moreover, recourse to the courts usually presupposed that harm had been done, and implied the possibility of redress. Yet when natural resources are polluted, marshlands are drained or species annihilated, the loss can be irreversible. To begin to remedy these shortcomings, the 1995 act proposed two new orientations. Firstly, a clear need had emerged to supplement the logic of repair enshrined in the 'polluter pays' principle with the logic of conservation implied in the prevention and precaution principles. This meant taking prudent action before the event rather than remedial action thereafter. Secondly, the act incorporated the notion of environmental rights, an innovation which had repeatedly been broached. The first principle of the 1972 Stockholm declaration outlined environmental rights, which were incorporated into the constitution of states such as Portugal and Greece. Barnier had envisaged a similar constitutional amendment, but abandoned it as too ambitious. After lengthy debate, the final drafting of his bill made reference to 'the laws and regulations which organise every person's right to a healthy environment',[4] a wording which stressed the legal context of the right rather than its substantive content.

Overall, the Barnier bill constituted an ambitious but lop-sided reform. Points of legal principle were clarified, and environmental law was strengthened, though not rationalised.[5] Institutional

[5] The scattered nature of the environmental legislation is clear from comparison with other domains. Branches of French legislation such as labour law, rural law, etc. have been compiled in the form of a 'code' – a single volume which systematically presents relevant legislation. This makes application of the law more predictable and 'safe'. A call to draw up a *code de l'environnement* was already present in Lalonde's 'green plan'. The *loi Barnier* paved the way for parliamentary debate and it fell to Environment Minister Lepage to present a bill in 1996. The early dissolution of parliament in April 1997 interrupted its passage. Only in Zool did a new *code* materialise.

[6] See République française (1994).

reforms were few and limited, brokering little decentralisation of environmental policy (despite Barnier's earlier intentions), nor were mechanisms for the integration of environmental concerns into core policy sectors outlined. Despite these limitations, the *loi Barnier* proposed a shift from a technical and normative environmental regime to a framework of rights and principles. In this transition from a coercive to an emancipatory ideology, the bill paved the way for the more participatory policy modes that sustainable development implies. However, the translation of legal provisions into an articulated system of policy preferences has proved problematic.

National initiatives: the Commission française du développement durable

Subsequent to Rio, France took four-and-a-half years to present a national strategy on sustainable development (Laville, 1997: 9). Early initiatives to set up specialised committees to promote sustainable development quickly stalled. In 1993, President Mitterrand set up the *Conseil pour les droits des générations futures* (Council for the Rights of Future Generations), with Jacques Cousteau as chair. However, in 1995 Cousteau resigned in protest over President Chirac's decision to restart nuclear testing. The Council has not been resuscitated. The French Commission for Sustainable Development (*Commission française du développement durable* – CFDD) was also set up in 1993. Its brief made explicit reference to the Rio principles, stressing the interrelations between social, economic and environmental spheres (CFDD, 1996b: 228). After hesitation over institutional affiliation, it was decided that the commission report to the Environment Minister, with its chair nominated by the Prime Minister. The CFDD is not a committee formed of ministers, nor an instrument for interministerial coordination (as are cognate institutions in some other countries), but is a quasi-independent body. Because it has no operational remit within government and lacks powers to implement its proposals, it works largely as a 'think tank'.

In an initial phase under the chairmanship of Bernard Esambert, the Commission's output was modest. Its first report (CFDD, 1994) was a discussion document, which sought to

---

[7] The report by Comité 21 (1996) is largely in this mould.

disseminate the sustainable development concept in the French context, as outlined in the Rio documents. During this phase, the French government reported on progress to implementation of Agenda 21 at the second meeting of the UN Commission of Sustainable Development, held in New York in 1994.[6] The report mainly reiterated policy measures already in train at the time of Rio. The revisiting of past practice to discover instances of Agenda 21 initiatives *avant la lettre* set a tendency to 'rebadge' previous policy measures, rather than develop new ones specifically aimed at sustainable development.[7] In 1995, J.-P. Souviron was appointed to the chair of the CFDD, with a brief to focus on sustainable development indicators and on the quality of urban life. However, little progress was made as Souviron resigned after the presidential elections of mid-1995, creating a hiatus in the work of the commission.

In a second phase of activity, greater continuity and direction emerged once Christian Brodhag, formerly a spokesperson for the *Verts*, was appointed to the CFDD chair during the period 1996 to 1998. The 1996 CFDD report was an ambitious text which explored the principles of sustainable development, evaluated progress achieved in France and outlined priorities for the future. The right to a safe environment, as set out in the Rio principles, was reiterated (CFDD, 1996a: 3).The aims of sustainable development were defined as the satisfaction of human needs, the attainment of social equity, economic effectiveness, the improvement of environmental quality and the preservation of resources for the long term (CFDD, 1996a: 11). Problems in the implementation of sustainability policies were highlighted. The report acknowledged that slow uptake in France of the concept was due in part to the 'not invented here' syndrome.[8] France's institutional landscape was characterised as being too compartmentalised and rigid to accommodate the integrated approach involved in sustainable development (CFDD, 1996a: 158). In the face of these obstacles, the report set a number of 'action priorities', making thirty-five proposals to promote sustainable development, clustered into eight

---

[8] The CFDD (1996a: 71–2) commented: 'La France, pays jacobin que la régionalisation a bousculé, a toujours eu de grosses difficultés à intégrer des concepts de développement venus d'ailleurs'. The strategy document prepared by the Juppé government in early 1996 outlining reform of the state made no mention of the concept of sustainable development.

[9] See for example Benko (1987), DATAR (1990) or Wackermann et al. (1996).

themes: the role of public authorities, citizen participation, transparency and evaluation, education, mobilising economic actors, reinforcement of civil society, regional planning and clean technology.

The 1997 CFDD report reviewed progress towards government implementation of the earlier thirty-five proposals, together with assessments by environmental groups. Although most of the proposals had been incorporated into official strategy, few had been translated into concrete measures. In international environmental negotiations, France still kept a low profile (CFDD, 1997a: 14). In core sectors, such as agriculture, transport, energy and education, not only was no progress reported, but interaction with existing policy subsystems was not discernible. The major interlocutors of the CFDD were environmental groups – who, ironically enough, complained of their inability to respond to the demands of improved public consultation procedures because of a lack of resources (see Chapter 2).

By the end of the 1990s, the limits of the CFDD were patent. The need had emerged for a higher-profile institution, bringing together prominent politicians and with the capacity for influencing policy in core sectors. Yet overall, the CFDD proved instrumental in clarifying a sustainability agenda. It set out four main tools to achieve sound governance: the development of local Agenda 21s, the use of sustainable development indicators, the identification and dissemination of good practice and the promotion of citizen participation (CFDD, 1997a: 39). Under Brodhag, the attainment of greater participation was implemented by consultation with environmental groups. This strategy accorded with the spirit of Rio and with the lineage of 'green' thought. The culmination of this tendency was the CFDD's 1998 report, which provided a compendium of actors and publications – but no policy evaluation. Whilst the latter omission suggests that there was little progress to report, the insistence on the dissemination of ideas and the encouragement of networking between a wide range of organisations accorded with the need to go beyond top-down measures and generate momentum towards sustainable development at regional and local levels.

Local Agenda 21

The impetus for producing 'local Agenda 21s' (LA21s) came from the Rio conference, whose final report stated:

Because so many of the problems and solutions being addressed by Agenda 21 have their roots in local activities, the participation and cooperation of local authorities will be a determining factor in fulfilling its objectives. Local authorities construct, operate and maintain economic, social and environmental infrastructure, oversee planning processes, establish local environmental policies and regulations, and assist in implementing national and subnational environmental policies. As the level of governance closest to the people, they play a vital role in educating, mobilising and responding to the public to promote sustainable development. (UN, 1993: 393)

The target set was that by 1996 most local authorities in each country should have undertaken consultations with their populations and 'achieved a consensus on a "local Agenda 21" for the community' (UN, 1993: 393). However, the time-frame proved unrealistic. In addition, the content and form of LA21s were not specified. Lafferty and Eckerberg (1998: 2) claimed that this indicated recognition of the variations in central government-local authority relations around the world. Nevertheless, the lack of specification introduced yet another puzzle for policy makers to solve, coming on top of the ambiguities surrounding the sustainable development concept itself. Further, the reference to local authorities holding the 'solutions' to progress to sustainable development was overstated. National and international political and economic systems shape the contexts in which local authorities operate. In countries such as the UK, the powers and resources of local government had been cut back in the 1980s and 1990s, whilst in countries such as France they were late in developing.

Prior to Rio France did, however, have experience in promoting local environmental policies. In 1982–3, Environment Minister Crépeau had organised a major consultation with local citizens' groups called the *états régionaux de l'environnement*. The exercise produced an inventory of the state of the environment in the regions and led to initiatives such as the *Conseil permanent régional des associations de l'environnement* in Midi-Pyrénées (Prieur, 1985: 182–3). However, the initial project of a national 'Environmental Charter' to be adopted by parliament was abandoned, since the results of the exercise could not be translated into a legislative format (Prieur, 1983: 112). Nevertheless, local experiments continued. In 1983 eight towns signed 'urban environmental protocols' (Ministère de l'Environnement, 1997). Over 1990–1, Environment

Minister Lalonde promoted municipal and departmental environmental plans, of which around a hundred were drawn up (Rocaboy, 1993: 34).

In the wake of Rio, these initiatives were developed and formalised by Environment Minister Barnier under the name of *chartes pour l'environnement* (environmental charters). In the manual prepared for local authority usage by Barnier (1994), references to Earth Summit I abound, sustainable development is presented as the main aim and the Rio declaration is reproduced in full. Of the manual's three sections, one is devoted to discussion of the integration of environmental issues into social and economic policies, another to local environmental policy per se and a third discusses the means, including the need for wide consultation and preparation. Around 150 environmental charters were completed by 1997 (Ministère de l'Environnement, 1997).Yet the *chartes pour l'environnement* are not LA21s either in name or content. Whilst the theme of sustainable development was aired, it was not developed. The stress fell on 'classic' environmental concerns – air, water, waste, noise etc. – with little attention to social equity. The policy process was envisaged as a process of top-down planning and implementation, with the government manual stressing the objectives of the Environment Ministry. Local authority environmental charters were contractual documents that gave eligibility for state subsidies, being vetted and agreed by the departmental prefect as the representative of central government. Often environmental charters were viewed as 'quality badges' awarded to the most deserving local authorities, rather than as forward-looking documents (CFDD, 1997b: 40).

Ironically, the relative success of the *chartes de l'environnement* opened up an implementation gap in relation to actual LA21s. The ICLEI (1997) survey reported that fifteen French local authorities had drawn up or were drafting LA21s, compared to 415 in Norway, 285 in Britain and thirty in Germany. Holec and Coméliau (1999) calculated that if a wider range of criteria were used, such as being a signatory to the Aalborg charter or recipient of a European Prize for Sustainable Cities, then around fifty French towns could be reckoned to be making progress towards sustainable development. Several explanations for this limited uptake can be identified. The ICLEI (1997) survey made three main recommendations for the successful development of LA21s: national campaigns endorsed by central government but managed by local authority associations; the availability of national (and international) funds; and the provision of a supportive national policy and fiscal framework. Gaps in all three of these areas account for slow progress in France. Firstly, unlike in the UK, where the local authorities associations and the Local Government Management Board played the major role in promoting LA21s, in France the equivalent organisation (the *Association des maires de France*) did not take a leading role. Secondly, very limited national resources were made available. A series of conferences was held in 1996, and in December 1997 the Environment Ministry put out calls for pilot projects to local authorities willing to experiment with LA21s, offering subsidies of up to 100,000 francs to successful authorities. Only fifty-one authorities applied, of whom sixteeen were selected (MATE, 1997b: 8). Whilst these initiatives demonstrated the willingness to relaunch LA21s, few lessons were drawn from the *Chartes de l'environnement* which, despite their limitations, proposed a clear implementation methodology. Thirdly, at the level of national policy and fiscal framework, government support can be described as emergent at best.

Although the limits on progress to LA21s are clear, rather than simply pointing the finger at French local authorities as being slow, it is more revealing to investigate the effects of contextual factors and of structural features of the polity. Firstly, the resources of French local authorities were overstretched in the 1990s, given fiscal stringency and increased social needs, notably due to high unemployment. Competition for political attention between diverse policy streams encouraged the 'not invented here' syndrome: politicians tend to prioritise local demands over distant nostrums. Secondly, although the decentralisation process of the 1980s and 1990s replaced a local politico-administrative system with genuine local government (discussed in Chapter 4), it also placed new stresses on politicians. A survey commissioned by the *Association des maires de France* revealed widespread unease among French mayors due to the greater complexity of statutory requirements and increased expectations of citizens, leading to a climate of litigation; some 45 percent of them did not wish to renew their mandates (*Le Monde*, 11.11.1998: 13). Thirdly, the complex division of responsibilities between the three tiers of subnational government in France – comprising over 36,000 *communes*, 100 *départements* and 26 regions – raised perennial questions over the fragmentation of local government. Consequently, the appropriate territorial unit for developing sustainable development strategies remains to be established. Arguably, LA21s constitute a suitable policy vehicle for small or medium-sized towns, but offer poor 'goodness of fit' for sprawling mega-cities or sparsely populated rural enclaves. The limitations of the most local form of government – the *commune* – have long been recognised. Yet it is an open question whether *départements* and regions can be reckoned 'local' enough to constitute appropriate units for LA21s. In addition, modes of policy coordination between national government and local/regional levels are themselves under review.

Regional planning and sustainable development

France has been marked by a long history of centralisation around Paris. Concerns about territorial inequity led to the tier of regional policies known as *aménagement du territoire,* which date from 1964 and the establishment of the DATAR. As the history of regional policy is well covered in the literature,[9] only the developments most pertinent to sustainability will be covered here. Over 1993–4, the Balladur government reopened the regional planning question with 'un grand débat national pour l'aménagement du territoire', leading to new legislation sponsored by Interior Minister Pasqua. Known as the *loi d'orientation pour l'aménagement et le développement du territoire,*[10] and voted on 4 February 1995, the act promoted sustainable regional development and sought to provide a comprehensive planning framework to last until 2015. Because it called for a national system to integrate the planning documents of each of France's regions in relation to higher education and research, cultural facilities, transport, telecommunications and health, the bill was interpreted as a 'recentralisation' of Paris-periphery relations (Balligand 1995; Cascales, 1995: 25). Curiously, it made no attempt to integrate the European dimension into regional planning, despite the increased importance of EU structural funds. The bill's execution proved disappointing. Its implementation required a series of reports and follow-on statutes, which were not drawn up. Local tax reform to finance new initiatives was not attempted. Moreover, the bill failed to provide substantive content for sustainable development in the French regional planning context (Lacaze, 1995: 73). Subsequently

[10] A *loi d'orientation* outlines major policy directions, without indicating detailed measures.
[11] The connection between environmental policy and *aménagement du territoire* was present from the origin of the Environment Ministry; see Chapter 4 for details.

the Juppé government, in a context of budgetary rigour, quietly dropped the bill's proposals (Cascales, 1996: 188).

On nomination to the Jospin government in 1997, Dominique Voynet (de facto leader of the *Verts*) was given a joint portfolio which brought together environmental and regional policy within the *Ministère de l'aménagement du territoire et de l'environnement* (MATE).[11] The widened brief sat well with her policy programme. Devolution of decision making to regional levels had been a long-standing feature of political ecology. Implementing this philosophy in France rekindled, however, the latent tension between centralising and decentralising, 'Jacobin' and 'Girondin' leanings. Voynet set about overturning the centralising provisions of the 1995 Pasqua act by putting forward a new bill, the *loi d'orientation pour l'aménagement et le développement durable du territoire* (LOADDT), which aimed to promote sustainability by harnessing the state-region planning process.[12] Voynet (1998, 1999) contrasted the traditional top-down approach to regional planning, which pushed resources from the Paris to the 'underdeveloped' periphery, with a bottom-up approach, whereby subnational authorities adopted an entrepreneurial attitude and fielded a development 'project' that national government would aid financially, rather than impose unilaterally.[13] Following in the Brundtland and Rio vein, considerable stress was placed on sustainable development, conceptualised as a process combining economic effectiveness, social justice and environmental quality. The bill sought to improve on the 1995 act by responding to local needs to improve the quality of life, redressing the balance between rural and urban patterns of development, reinforcing decentralisation, and integrating French and EU regional policy. The LOADDT bill retained the planning documents indicated by the 1995 act (for higher education and research, cultural facilities, transport, telecommunications, health) and added two new ones (natural and rural spaces, and energy), whilst stressing the bottom-up development of their content. The transport scheme was split into two – one for

---

[12] For discussions of *contrats de plan Etat-régions*, see Cascales (1994) and Chain (1995).

[13] The act built on the notion of *pays* – which was already present in the Pasqua bill – as a potential territorial unit for local projects. In this context, *pays* refers to 'small territorial areas which share a common identity but which do not . . . coincide with existing administrative limits' (Négrier, 1999: 129).

people, another for goods – and the accent shifted from road to rail. The energy scheme aimed at encouraging greater efficiency and use of renewable sources. During parliamentary debate in early 1999, the bill encountered substantial opposition with some 1,500 amendments tabled, and was extensively modified by the Senate (where the right still enjoyed a majority). Measures favouring rail over road, incentives to new partnerships between *communes*, and extra financial resources for nature conservation and rural renewal were downgraded. With the bill only voted in June 1999, it remains uncertain how sustainability issues will be addressed in practical terms. Nevertheless the ambitions of the LOADDT bill bear witness to Voynet's intention to modify the 'rules of interaction' which had prevailed in French environmental policy making by seeking to integrate environmental, social and economic dimensions within a single framework.

Conclusions

The French case illustrates the iterative nature of progress towards sustainable development. In an initial stage during the mid-1990s, the conceptual framework had to be mastered and communicated, and new institutions and coordinating mechanisms established. In a second phase corresponding to the late 1990s, national and local actors sought to identify problems and means of addressing them, by central government initiatives, notably the 1999 LOADDT bill, and with some limited recourse to LA21s. In principle, the new century will bring a third phase of implementing practical change.

However, given the ambiguities surrounding the concept, sustainable development offers not so much a set of 'solutions' as a hermeneutic which, through its interlinking of social, economic and environmental concerns, shapes the understanding of a set of problems. The transition even to a species of 'weak' sustainability raises major challenges. The process requires the integration of environmental and social aims into core sectors, notably agriculture, transport and energy, whereas in the past the attainment of economic growth objectives was paramount. Yet in France traditional policy subsystems have remained untouched by the sustainable development debate. When Environment Minister Voynet attempted to rectify this in 1998–9, her proposals met with outright hostility. Although at a remove from EU negotiations over reform of the Common Agricultural

Policy, Voynet's ministerial offices were ransacked by farmers in February 1999. Her proposals to increase tax on diesel to unleaded petrol levels met the hostility of the transport lobby and were shelved for two years. France remains wedded to nuclear energy, with little diversification into renewable energy sources. Even on the issue of storing nuclear waste, Voynet's proposals resulted in defeat and she publicly distanced herself from government decisions on deep-site burial. As a sponsor of sustainable development, Voynet appears a lonely figure within government ranks, despite official lip service to the concept. Given her left-wing political ecology background, her policy orientation seems to be considered as an exogenous and unwelcome source of change, prompting resistance from entrenched policy communities.

Under these circumstances, significant progress towards sustainable development is improbable until the concept is fully accepted within mainstream French political culture. As argued by Sachs (1997: 75): 'statements of 'sustainable development' implicitly or explicitly position themselves in terms of the crisis of justice and the crisis of nature'. In the French case, the positioning of sustainable development in official discourse has implicitly been in terms of the crisis of nature (conceived in terms of resource allocation, depletion and disposal), rather than in terms of a crisis of justice. This is not because France has been impervious to discourses of justice: the very opposite is true. From the French revolution and the development of republicanism, and across much of the current political spectrum, the leitmotif of social justice has been constant. To date, French initiatives to combat poverty and its effects (such as the social security system, minimum income benefit, or universal health cover) have had no direct links with sustainable development perspectives. However, the long tradition of political discourse on justice offers scope for the irrigation of social policy by sustainability perspectives. Bringing together the 'crisis of justice' with 'the crisis of nature' offers the means to broaden the appeal and communicate the urgency of the sustainability transition. The transformation of the concept of sustainable development into an endogenous culture, rather than an exogenous graft, is probably the precondition for its taking root.

10

GENERAL CONCLUSIONS

In investigating the shaping of French environmental policy, this study first sought to establish the cognitive dimensions of policy making by attention to various constructions of the environment. From the perspective of a political disaggregation of the environment into discrete policy domains, it identified the major policy actors by environmental sector, the ways in which they negotiated policy, and the manners in which policy was implemented. The case studies revealed the prevalence of exchange relationships between political authorities and special interests. More specifically, the 'traditional' French approach to the natural environment, the industrial environment and the human environment was largely shaped by meso-corporatist bargains between central state officials and sectoral representatives. Special-interest groups such as hunters, farmers and industrialists imposed their preferences at key junctures in terms of both policy formulation (as regards its content and omissions) and implementation (since their cooperation was essential). In exchange for guarantees of social order and incremental improvements in environmental performance, the authorities offered a legitimisation of producer interest group representation as well as financial incentives.

The central state – *l'Etat régalien* in the telling French phrase – preserved the *appearance* of its top-down prerogatives, imposing a corset of strictures on the behaviour of producer groups by using regulatory frameworks. But in its orchestration of a complex array of 'constituent', 'distributive' and 'redistributive' policy modes, the *reality* of policy implementation was consensual rather than authoritarian. Legislation played a central role in setting out

French policy, but it left considerable space for negotiation, through procedures such as the *contrats de branche*. The regulatory framework from the 1960s to the 1980s largely omitted precise requirements (such as emissions limits and ambient quality measures) or, where they were specified in a negotiated licence, regulators gave generous time allowances for compliance. The recourse to hypothecated taxation was particularly distinctive since it guaranteed a redistribution of fiscal revenues within sector. Contributors could expect to recoup what they paid in by bidding for public subsidies. In sweetening the pill, this recourse contributed to policy success by winning over regulatory targets. For industrialists, it amounted to a system of forced investment using state aids which buttressed their competitive positions.

Whilst these arrangements allowed the more obvious forms of pollution and environmental degradation to be addressed, it favoured special interests, excluded the public and a range of third-party organisations, as well as imposing hidden costs. The penalties for environmental deterioration – so called 'externalities' – were spread across society. But the reality of a sharing of burdens was often invisible, being veiled by the complexities inherent in the accounting of economic transfers and public subsidies, in the scientific measurement of damage to the environment and human health, and in the unquantifiable notion of reduced 'quality of life'. Yet as knowledge advanced, a range of social groups gradually become more aware of these costs and organised themselves to force rectification. In more pluralist societies, such as the USA or the UK, the inclusion of NGOs in policy subsystems progressed fairly quickly (if unevenly). In France, however, the ideology of *intérêt général* (public interest), which animates central state action, slowed down the inclusion of environmental associations which, due to the confrontational nature of the green social movement and particularly of its early anti-nuclear component, could be portrayed as unrepresentative, extremist and illegitimate. This apparently high-minded exclusion preserved bias within the polity, by shielding entrenched producer groups, organised within a system of *corporatisme à la française*. At the practical level, this meant that environmental groups often found themselves in an unequal conflict with established public institutions and powerful private actors.

The resistance to change created an unconstructive tension which social pressures – whether exercised by active association or the passive medium of opinion polls – could not surmount.

This made inevitable the recourse of the environmental movement to a politicisation of its agenda, taking the institutional forms of party organisation and electoral contests in order to participate in the executive caucuses that directed policy. Once greens entered into political executives, it became clear that the characterisation of the French polity as 'closed' to new views – which used to prevail among political ecologists – turned out to be overstated. At one level, this entry was a generic development, common to a number of European polities. However, the specifically French inflection is the political polarisation of a range of green parties, who found that early attempts to maintain non-alignment failed, leaving a stark choice between a refusal of the left-right divide and disappearance, or an acceptance of it and survival. Thus in the late 1990s the left-leaning *Verts* entered into coalition with the Socialists, and tried to pursue a radical policy with the 'plural left' government; whilst *Chasse, Pêche, Nature, Tradition* sought to influence the right-wing RPR in a conservative direction.

At the analytical level, these developments invite a review of the applicability of Sabatier's concept of 'advocacy coalition framework' to the French case. In the Sabatier model, a dominant advocacy coalition can, in principle, be replaced by a previously minority one. But power reversal within a neocorporatist policy community implies not just a shift in allegiances, but also a reallocation of economic and/or political resources, as well as new 'rules for interaction'. In practice, 'advocacy coalitions' in France have displayed a markedly political character and institutional focus, leading to contests for control over the levers of central and local government. Having gained access to political power, previously excluded groups, environmental or otherwise, can act as forces of change. This suggests that both politics and institutions matter in achieving policy change in France.

The contention made by Mazmanian and Sabatier (1989: 307) that 'major alterations in the policy core will normally be the product of changes external to the subsystem – particularly large-scale socio-economic perturbations or changes in the systemwide governing coalition' is partially proved, but calls for recalibration. In Chapter 3 we saw that the modification in the 'systemwide governing coalition', instanced by the inclusion of political ecologists in government, did not radically alter core features of the polity or of policy making. For this to occur, the 'rules of interaction' needed to be changed. Such change was indeed an aim of leading political ecologists. However, at the political level, the specific change in the 'rules' initially sought by ecologists was a realignment of the party system. When realignment failed to materialise, short-term constraints required that ecology parties accept the status quo and attempt to influence policy through the usual incremental channels, with all of the limitations involved. Notwithstanding this defeat, their strategy has been to review both the construction of environmental issues and the 'rules of interaction' in order to accommodate a greater diversity of interests within policy negotiation, and thereby achieve new ends. The ability of environmental groups and political ecology parties to attain bold aims has been restricted by their minority position in society and among the electorate. Further, access to political executives has not presented a rapid solution, since the functioning of existing institutions is subject to constraints defined by their development paths.

Studies of policy making in France have often stressed the prerogatives of the unitary state, benefiting from considerable financial, administrative and human resources, with a marked penchant for centralisation of decision making and which historically proved capable of ambitious entrepreneurship. The French state's traditional leitmotifs – interventionism, 'Colbertism' and *dirigisme* – combined to form a 'heroic' policy style, incorporating a belief in a rationalist, forward-looking approach. However, the development of environmental policy did not conform to type. Even in the 1970s, when national policies were still marked by *dirigisme*, the Environment Ministry was unable to operate in that mode. An unmanageably large range of environmental problems, combined with miserly resources, restricted its initiatives. The irony is that environment ministers were expected to follow the 'heroic' French policy style – which went into decline just as the Environment Ministry was born. In the 1980s and 1990s, the gap widened between the reputation of the 'strong state' and the reality of an enfeebled one due to ongoing developments at levels below and above the nation. Environmental policy in particular was characterised by a mismatch between ambitions and means. Thus it was assumed that legislators could decree whilst central and local administration would mobilise material resources and information flows in a top-down fashion, thereby enabling functionaries to implement policy. Yet adequate resources were not mobilised and information needed to flow bottom-up. In practice state officials found that their role was not to implement policy but to negotiate compliance with regulatory targets in a regime of 'delegated self-enforcement' (Cawson: 1986: 38). These outcomes cracked the veneer of a unitary and powerful French state.

In consequence, the attainment of environmentalist aims meant exploiting the statist paradigm but also transcending it, by acting in concert with broader forces pushing for change in society and the economy. In tandem with domestic alliances, this meant adopting a transnational orientation wherever possible, so opening up new spheres for 'advocacy coalitions'. To this end, two major arenas presented themselves: the institutions for European integration and international fora promoting sustainable development.

The European influence on French environmental policy cannot be reduced to the stereotype of an imposition from Brussels of a 'command and control' regime based on technical, normative directives. This is not to deny this orientation in EC environmental policy, only to reiterate that the diversity and flexibility of existing French policy instruments made the 'naturalisation' of most European measures a relatively painless, if sometimes expensive, process. Viewed in a long-term perspective, European environmental policy has been significant for France not just because of its substantive content, but also because of its *procedural* and *communicative dimensions*. By the *procedural dimension* is understood the development of wide policy networks, embracing many countries and many categories of agent. When the European Commission practises an 'open door' policy to all parties in 'Franco-French' discussions contesting the legitimacy of environmental groups on the grounds of *intérêt général* is no longer such a winning tactic. A revolution in the status of environmental associations and ecology parties in France has not occurred, but a gradual accretion of respectability is evident. By the *communicative dimension* is understood the accumulation of scientific knowledge related to the environment, its dissemination to wider publics, and especially the institutionalisation of these processes by the establishment of specialist agencies – the European Environmental Agency with its national counterparts – dedicated to making cross-national comparisons of environmental performance which can then inform European and national decision making. This has led to expectations of ever-greater openness in environmental matters, exposing and undermining the culture of secrecy and exclusion which permeated neocorporatist policy making in France. Here, too, it may be premature to speak of a transformation in attitudes, but the pressure in favour of more open environmental policy has certainly increased.

Fora for sustainable development constitute the second major arena for expansion of the environmental remit. The limitations on the transition to sustainability continue to loom large, namely vague conceptualisation, genuine difficulties of implementation, lip service by policy actors and major economic players. Yet the debate has highlighted a crucial and inescapable factor: on a time horizon of 50 to 100 years, many current practices are simply unsustainable. Conventional energy supply presents an acute dilemma: either pessimistic estimates are correct and fossil fuels will rapidly be depleted, or the burning of vast reserves will accelerate climate change. Intensive agriculture is impoverishing the soil and polluting water. Shortages of fresh water supplies already occur in different parts of the planet. Vehicle emissions are poisoning the air of such major cities as Los Angeles, Mexico City, Bangkok, Athens and, indeed, Paris. At the start of the twentieth-first century, policy makers have to decide whether predictions about global climate change made in the 1980s are coming true, and to act accordingly. These developments have already led to new constructions of environmental challenges. Rather than conceptualising environmental damage only in relation to specific media and public health, the changed orientation involves an eco-centric approach stressing the continued integrity of habitats occupied by human and non-human life-forms. Further, sustainability involves renewed attention to the reconciliation of environmental needs, economic processes and social justice. For their attainment, these aims require innovative and proactive policy modes, the invention of new patterns of social interaction (involving *inter alia* less travel and commuting) and the reconfiguration of a range of economic activities (notably to decrease their material requirements).

The combination of these inputs – domestic, European and international – signals the beginnings of paradigm change in policy. The process that Richardson (1996: 32) called 'the gradual shift in emphasis from a world of policy making characterised by tightly knit policy communities to a more loosely organised and therefore less predictable policy process' was underway in the USA and the EC by the 1970s but took longer to develop momentum in France. However, by the 1990s clear signs had emerged in the key domains of water, waste and air of an exit from neocorporatism. As a greater range of organised interests made their influence felt, so the policy networks progressively widened. At the same time, the policy stress moved away from bargaining with special-interest groups to environmental problem solving. For the long term, it is essential that the incipient transition to more effective representation gathers pace: the widening of policy networks will be a part of this process.

The paradigm of sustainability requires a coordination of policy sectors and an articulated 'network of policy networks'. Achieving that coordination represents a massive challenge. The institutions of representative democracy and the market economy have framed and directed the formulation and implementation of environmental policy. However, these institutions are often incomplete in their coverage and enter into contradiction with each other. Various 'democratic deficits', losses of control and direction, and 'organisational bias' have opened up in each, leading to gaps in the development of public policies in general, and environmental policy in particular. The recourse to regulatory policy has proved too limited. The recent embrace of economic instruments, notably via tax reform, is a logical development. But for the long term, an environmental 'new deal' is essential, involving wider societal bargains. To achieve this, broader based policies, bringing in stabilising, distributive and redistributive modes, are required. At the least, the success of such a 'new deal' will require an equitable spread of burdens. But rather than return to the arid opposition between economic growth and environmental protection, it will ideally be based on a 'win-win' outlook, providing quality of life gains for all.

BIBLIOGRAPHY

Aguilar Fernández, S. (1994) 'Convergence in environmental policy? The resilience of national institutional designs in Spain and Germany', *Journal of Public Policy*, 14:1, 39–56.

Alphandéry, P., Bitoun, P. and Dupont, Y. (eds) (1991) 'La Sensibilité écologique en France', Paris, Documentation française, *Problèmes politiques et sociaux*, no. 651.

——— (1992) *L'Equivoque écologique*, Paris, Editions La Découverte.

Andurand, R. (1996) *Saga des Secrétariats Permanents de Prévention des Problèmes Industriels*, Bordeaux, Editions Préventique.

Ashford, S. and Halman, L. (1994) 'Changing attitudes in the European Community', in Rootes, C. and Davis, H. (eds) *Social Change and Political Transformation*, pp. 72–85, London, UCL Press.

Assemblée Nationale (1996a) *Les Gouvernements et les assemblées parlementaires sous la Ve Republique, 1958–1974*, Paris, Assemblée Nationale.

——— (1996b) *Les Gouvernements et les assemblées parlementaires sous la Ve Republique, 1974–1995*, Paris, Assemblée Nationale.

Aubin, A. (1993) *La Communauté européenne face à la pollution atmosphérique*, Rennes, Apogées.

Autexier, C. and Heppenheimer, M. (1971) 'Essai de définition de l'administration de mission', *Bulletin IAAP*, 18: 89–129.

Baker, S. et al. (1997) 'Introduction: the theory and practice of sustainable development in EU perspective' in Baker, S. et al. (eds) *The Politics of Sustainable Development. Theory, Policy and Practice within the European Union*, pp. 1–40, London, Routledge.

Baldock, D., Holzner, J. and Bennett, G. (1987) *The Organisation of Nature Conservation in Selected Countries*, London, Institute for European Environmental Policy.

Balligand, J.-P. (1995) 'Le retour de l'Etat', *Revue politique et parlementaire*, 975 (janvier–février), 13–16.

Balme, R. (1995) 'French regionalisation and European integration: territorial adaptation and change in a unitary state', in Jones, B. and Keating, M. (eds) *The European Union and the Regions*, pp. 166–88, Oxford, Clarendon Press.

Barbier, M. (1995) 'Gestion locale de la qualité de l'air et légimité industrielle: la "vallée de la chimie" lyonnaise', *Nature, sciences, politiques*, 3:4, 319–335.

Barde, J.-P. (1990) 'The path to sustainable development', *OECD Observer*, 164 (June–July), 33–7.

Barnier, M. (1994) *Chartes pour l'environnement: livret de présentation*, Paris, Ministère de l'Environnement.

—— (1996) 'L'apport du loi', *Revue française de droit administratif*, 12:2 (mars–avril), 200–2.

Barraqué, B. (1994) 'Risque d'inondation: urbanisme réglementaire ou servitude négociée?', *Espaces et sociétés*, 77: 133–52.

—— (1996) 'Regard européen sur la gestion des services d'eau à la française', *Pouvoirs locaux*, 29 (juin), 25–33.

—— et al. (1992) *La Gestion de l'eau*, Paris, Documentation française, *Problèmes politiques et sociaux*, no. 686.

—— et al. (1996) *Les Politiques de l'eau en Europe*, Paris, La Découverte.

—— and Theys, J. (eds) (1998) *Les Politiques d'environnement. Evaluation de la première génération: 1971–1995*, Paris, Editions Recherches.

Barthélémy, M. (1994) 'Les associations dans la société française: un état des lieux', *Les Cahiers du CEVIPOF*, nos. 10 and 10A.

Barthod, C. (1998) 'La forêt et le bois en France: atouts et défis', *Revue politique et parlementaire*, 992 (janvier–février), 109–118.

Beck, U. (1992) *Risk Society: Towards a New Modernity*, London, Sage.

Beckerman, W. (1995) *Small is Stupid: Blowing the Whistle on the Greens*, London, Duckworth.

Benko, G. (1987) 'French regional policy in the early 1980s' *International Social Science Journal*, 112 (May), 233–54.

Bennahmias, J.-L. and Roche, A. (1992) *Des Verts de toutes les couleurs. Histoire et sociologie du mouvement écolo*, Paris, Albin Michel.

Beraud, R.-C. (1979) 'Fondements juridiques du droit de l'environnement dans le traité de Rome', *Revue du Marché Commun*, 35–8.

Bergeron, H., Surel, Y and Valluy, J. (1998) 'L'advocacy coalition framework: une contribution au renouvellement des études de politiques publiques?', *Politix*, 41: 195–223.

Bertolini, G. (1998) 'La politique française des déchets', in Barraqué, B. and Theys, J. (eds) *Les Politiques d'environnement. Evaluation de la première génération: 1971–1995*, pp. 171–88, Paris, Editions Recherches.

Bidou, D. (1985) 'Ecologistes: le malentendu', *Revue politique et parlementaire*, 914: 72–79.

Billaudot, F. (1991) 'Les mutations administratives de l'environnement. Aspects de l'application du plan national pour l'environnement', *Revue juridique de l'environnement*, 3: 333–53.

Blancher, P. (1998) 'Scénarios de risque industriel et prévention par l'aménagement', in Decrop, G. and Galland, J.-P. (eds) *Prévenir les risques: de quoi les experts sont-ils responsables?*, pp. 127–48, La Tour d'Aigues, Editions de L'Aube.

Blatrix, C. (1997) 'La loi Barnier et débat public: quelle place pour les associations?', *Ecologie et politique*, 21(février), 77–92.

Bodiguel, M. and Buller, H. (1995) 'Environmental policy and the regions in France', in Loughlin, J. and Mazey, S. (eds) *The End of the French Unitary State? Ten Years of Regionalisation in France (1982–1992)*, pp. 92–109, London, Frank Cass.

Bomberg, E. (1998) 'Issue networks and the environment: explaining EU environmental policy', in Marsh, D. (ed.) *Comparing Policy Networks*, pp. 167–84, Buckingham, Open University Press.

Bonardi, J.-P. and Delmas, M. (1996) 'Incertitude réglementaire et stratégies de traitement des déchets spéciaux', *Gérer et comprendre*, 46 (décembre), 4–15.

Bongaerts, J.C. and Kraemer, R.A. (1987) 'Water pollution charges in three countries', *European Environment Review*, 1:4 (September), 12–19.

Booth, P. (1998) 'Decentralisation and land-use planning in France: a 15 year review', *Policy and Politics*, 26:1, 89–105.

Bornstein, S.E. (1988) 'The Greenpeace affair and the peculiarities of French politics', in Markovits, A.S. and Silverstein, M. (eds) *The Politics of Scandal: Power and Process in Liberal Democracies*, pp. 91–121, London and New York, Holmes and Meier.

Bouchardeau, H. (1986) *Le Ministère du possible*, Paris, Editions Alain Moreau.

Bourdieu, P. (1993) *Sociology in Question*, London, Sage.

Bower, B.T. (1983) 'Mixed implementation systems for water quality management in France, the Ruhr, and the United States', in Downing, P.B. and Hanf, K. (eds) *International Comparisons in Implementing Pollution Laws*, pp. 212–27, Boston, Kluwer-Nijhoff Publishing.

Boy, D. (1981) 'Le vote écologiste en 1978', *Revue française de science politique*, 31:2 (avril), 394–416.

—— (1992) 'Les écologistes en France', *French Politics and Society*, 10:3 (Summer), 1–25.

—— et al. (1995) *L'Ecologie au pouvoir*, Paris, Presses de la Fondation nationale des sciences politiques.

—— and Roche, A. (1995) 'Du Nord au Sud: l'écologie dans tous ses états', in Perrineau, P. and Ysmal, C. (eds) (1995) *Le Vote des douze. Les élections européennes de juin 1994*, pp. 75–110, Paris, Presses de Sciences Po.

——, Roche, A. and Le Seigneur, J.V. (1992) 'L'écologie à deux visages', *Le Monde*, 13 novembre, 8.

Bréchon, P. (1992) 'Les écologistes aux urnes', *Regards sur l'actualité*, 178 (février), 3–16.

Brénac, E. (1985) 'Les rapports entre l'Etat et les entreprises et la politique d'environnement industriel', *Cahiers du GERMES*, 10: 585–98.

—— (1988) 'Corporatismes et politique intersectorielle: la politique de l'environnement', in Colas, D. (ed.) *L'Etat et les corporatismes*, pp. 127–46, Paris, PUF.

Brenton, T. (1994) *The Greening of Machiavelli. The Evolution of International Environmental Politics*, London, Earthscan.

Bridgford, J. (1978) 'The ecological movement and the French general election of 1978', *Parliamentary Affairs*, 31:3 (Summer), 314–323.

Buffotot, P. and Hanley, D. (1995) 'Les élections européennes de 1994: élection européenne ou élection nationale?' *Modern and Contemporary France*, NS3: 1, 1–17.

Buller, H. (1996) 'Privatisation and Europeanisation: the changing context of water supply in Britain and France', *Journal of Environmental Planning and Management*, 39:4, 461–82.

——— (1998) 'Reflections across the Channel: Britain, France and the Europeanisation of national environmental policy', in Lowe, P. and Ward, S. (eds) *British Environmental Policy and Europe*, pp. 67–83, London, Routledge.

———, Lowe, P.D. and Flynn, A. (1993) 'National responses to the Europeanisation of environmental policy: a selective review of comparative research', in Liefferink, J.D., Lowe, P.D. and Mol, A.P.J. (eds) *European Integration and Environmental Policy*, pp. 175–95, London, Belhaven Press.

Calderon, N. (1994) 'Droit et littoral en Europe', *Etudes rurales*, 133–34, 59–75.

Cameron, D.R. (1996) 'National interest, the dilemmas of European integration and malaise', in Keeler, J.T.S. and Schain, M.A. (eds) *Chirac's Challenge: Liberalization, Europeanization and Malaise in France*, pp. 325–82, Basingstoke, Macmillan.

Cans, R. (1994) 'Le partenariat commercial du WWF', *Le Monde*, 24 novembre, VI.

Caponera, D.A. (1992) *Principles of Water Law and Administration* Rotterdam, A.A. Balkema.

Carnelutti, A. (1988) 'L'administration française face à la règle communautaire', *Revue française d'administration publique*, 48 (octobre), 523–39.

Cascales, M. (1994) 'Le contrat de plan Etat-région: outil partenarial d'une stratégie de développement territorialisé', *Revue d'économie régionale et urbaine*, 4, 705–9.

——— (1995) 'Aménagement du territoire, le débat', *Revue politique et parlementaire*, 975 (janvier–février), 17–26.

——— (1996) 'La loi d'orientation pour l'aménagement et le développement du territoire', in Institut de la décentralisation (eds) *La Décentralisation en France*, pp. 187–201, Paris, La Découverte.

Cawson, A. (1986) *Corporatism and Political Theory*, Oxford, Basil Blackwell.

Cerny, P.G. (ed.) (1982) *Social Movements and Protests in France*, New York, St Martin's Press.

CFDD (1994) *Les Conditions et les moyens du développement durable: un guide pour l'action*, Paris, CFDD.

——— (1996a) *Rapport 1996. Eléments de bilan*, Paris, CFDD.

——— (1996b) *Rapport 1996. 8 Thèmes, 35 propositions*, Paris, CFDD.

——— (1997a) *Rapport 1997. De la prise de conscience vers la mobilisation*, Paris, CFDD.

—— (1997b) *Dossier de presse de la CFDD sur les enjeux de la 19e session extraordinaire de l'Assemblée générale des Nations-Unies, le 10 juin 1997*, Paris, CFDD.

—— (1998) *Rapport 1998. Répertoire*, Paris, CFDD.

CGP (Commissariat général du plan) (1997) *Evaluation du dispositif des Agences de l'eau*, Paris, Documentation française.

Chafer, T. (1984) 'Ecologists and the bomb', in Howorth, J. and Chilton, P. (eds) *Defence and Dissent in Contemporary France*, pp. 217–32, London, Croom Helm.

—— (1985) 'Politics and the perception of risk: a study of the antinuclear movements in Britain and France', *West European Politics*, 8:1, 5–23.

Chain, P. (1995) 'Les contrats de plan Etat-régions', *Regards sur l'actualité*, 215 (novembre), 32–46.

Charbonneau, S. (1989) 'L'acceptabilité du risque d'accident technique majeur', *Revue juridique de l'environnement*, 3: 269–284.

—— (1992) *La Gestion de l'impossible. La protection contre les risques technologiques majeurs*, Paris, Economica.

—— (1994) 'Administration du travail et administration de l'environnement', in Société française pour le droit de l'environnement (eds) *Droit du travail et droit de l'environnement*, pp. 127–32, Paris, Litec.

—— (1996) 'Natura 2000: mauvaise méthode', *Revue du droit rural*, 248 (décembre), 449–51.

Chartier, D. (1997) 'Les ONG d'environnement oublient l'écologie politique', *Ecologie et politique*, 20 (printemps), 15–30.

Chibret, R.-P. (1991) 'Les associations écologiques en France et en Allemagne. Une analyse culturelle de la mobilisation collective', Paris, Université Paris I Panthéon-Sorbonne, doctoral thesis.

Clausade, J. de (1991) *L'Adaptation de l'administration française à l'Europe*, Paris, Documentation française.

CNVA (1992) *Bilan de la vie associative en 1990–1*, Paris, La Documentation française.

Cohen, J.L. (1984) 'Rethinking social movements', *Berkeley Journal of Sociology*, 28 (Autumn), 97–113.

—— (1985) 'Strategy or identity: new theoretical paradigms and contemporary social movements', *Social Research*, 52:4 (Winter), 663–716.

Cole, A. (1995) '*La France pour tous?* – The French presidential elections of 23 April and 7 May', *Government and Opposition*, 30:3 (Summer), 326–46.

Collier, U. and Golub, J. (1997) 'Environmental policy and politics', in Rhodes, M., Heywood, P. and Wright, V. (eds.) *Developments in West European Politics*, pp. 226–243, Basingstoke, Macmillan.

Collins, K. and Earnshaw, D. (1992) 'The implementation and enforcement of EC environment legislation', *Environmental Politics*, 1:4, 213–49.

Colliot, J. and Font-Reaulx, B. de (1979) 'La prise en charge de l'inspection des installations classées par les services de l'Industrie et des Mines', *Annales des Mines* (juillet–août), 41–6.

Collomb, B. et al. (1993) *Croissance et environnement. Les conditions de la qualité de la vie. Rapport de la commission environnement, qualité de vie, croissance,* Paris, Documentation française.

Comité 21 (1996) *Le Développement durable? 21 entrées, soixante-quinze initiatives concrètes en France,* Paris, Comité français pour l'environnement et le développement durable.

Commission of the EC (1984; 2nd ed.) *The European Community's Environmental Policy,* Luxembourg, Office for Offical Publications of the EC.

——— (1993) *Towards Sustainability: a European Community Programme of Policy and Action in Relation to the Environment and Sustainable Development,* Luxembourg, Office for official publications of the EC.

——— (1996a) *Thirteenth Annual Report on Monitoring the Application of Community Law,* Luxembourg, Office for Offical Publications of the EC, COM (96) 600 Final.

——— (1996b) *Towards Sustainability - Progress Report from the Commission on the Implementation of the European Community Programme of Policy and Action in relation to the Environment and Sustainable Development,* Luxembourg, Office for Offical Publications of the EC, COM (95) 624 Final.

——— (1997) *Fourteenth Annual Report on Monitoring the Application of Community Law,* Luxembourg, Office for Offical Publications of the EC, COM (97) 299 Final.

——— (1998) *Fifteenth Annual Report on Monitoring the Application of Community Law,* Luxembourg, Office for Offical Publications of the EC, COM (98) 317 Final.

Cottereau, G. (1982) 'Les délégations parlementaires pour les Communautés européennes', *Revue du droit public et de la science politique,* 1: 35–63.

Coulombie, H. (1992) 'Aménagement et protection du littoral', *Etudes foncières,* 54 (mars) 4–14.

Cour des comptes (1999) *Le Rapport public 1998,* Paris, Les Editions des Journaux Officiels.

Courtine, D. (1996) *Décharge proscrite,* Paris, Economica.

Cox, A. and Hayward, J. (1983) 'The inapplicability of the corporatist model in Britain and France: the case of labour', *International Political Science Review,* 4:2, 217–40.

Crozier, M. and Thoenig, J.-C. (1975) 'La régulation des systèmes organisés complexes. Le cas du système de décision politico-administratif en France', *Revue française de sociologie,* 16:1, 3–32.

Cunningham, W.P. et al. (1998) *Environmental Encyclopedia,* London, Gale.

Dalal-Clayton, B. et al. (1996) *Getting to Grips with Green Plans. National-Level Experience in Industrial Countries,* London, Earthscan.

Dalton, R.J. (1993) 'The environmental movement in Western Europe', in Kamieniecki, S. (ed.) *Environmental Politics in the International Arena.*

Movements, Parties, Organisations and Policy, pp. 41–68, New York, State University of New York.

—— and Kuechler, M. (eds) (1990) *Challenging the Political Order. New Social and Political Movements in Western Democracies*, Cambridge, Polity Press.

Darbon, D. (1997) *La Crise de la chasse en France*, Paris, L'Harmattan.

DATAR (1990) *Une nouvelle étape pour l'aménagement du territoire*, Paris, La Documentation française.

Debièvre, A. (1993) 'Les associations au tournant', *L'Environnement Magazine*, 1522 (novembre), 14–15.

Decrop, G. (1991) 'Les risques majeurs naturels et technologiques, objet de politique publique?' *Cahiers de la sécurité intérieure*, 6 (août-décembre), 17–29.

Délégation de l'Assemblée nationale pour les Communautés européennes (1994) 'La Délégation de l'Assemblée nationale pour les CE – compétences et activités', Paris, Assemblée Nationale.

Demarq, F. (1987) 'La prévention des risques industriels majeurs en France: le rôle de l'évaluation dans la décision publique', in Fabiani, J.-L and Theys, J. (eds) *La Société vulnérable. Evaluer et maîtriser les risques*, pp. 475–82, Paris, Presses de l'Ecole Normale Supérieure.

Denis-Lempereur, J. (1983) 'Les déchets de Seveso sont-ils en France?', *Science et Vie*, 787 (avril), 16–23.

Department of the Environment (1992) *The UK Environment*, London, HMSO.

Dequéant, J. (1995) 'Une ligne de conduite pour la prévention', *Le Moniteur*, 3 février, 46–9.

Derville, G. (1997) 'Le combat singulier Greenpeace - SIRPA. La compétition pour l'acces aux médias lors de la reprise des essais nucléaires français', *Revue française de science politique*, 47:5 (octobre), 589–629.

Destot, M. (1993) *Déchets industriels*, Paris, Economica.

Deveze, J. and Sanson, C. (1993) 'La répartition des compétences entre l'Etat et les collectivités territoriales: le point de vue des DIREN', *Aménagement et nature*, 110: 2–4.

Diederichs, O. and Luben, I. (1995) *La Déconcentration*, Paris, PUF.

Dobré, M. (1995) *L'Opinion publique et l'environnement*, Paris, IFEN.

Doherty, B. (1992) 'The fundi-realo controversy: an analysis of four European Green parties', *Environmental Politics*, 1:1 (Spring), 95–120.

Downs, A. (1972) 'Up and down with ecology – the "issue attention cycle"', *Public Interest*, 28: 38–50.

Drake, H. and Milner, S. (1999) 'Change and resistance to change: the political management of Europeanisation in France' *Modern and Contemporary France*, 7:2 (May), 165–78.

DRIRE-Ile de France (1997) *Industrie et protection de l'environnement en Ile de France*, Paris, Ministère de l'aménagement du territoire et de l'environnement.

Dron, D. (1995) *Environnement et choix politiques*, Paris, Flammarion.

Ducasset, P. (1997) 'Les installations classées', *Après-demain*, 394 (mai), 30–2.

Duchêne, F. (1996) 'French motives for European integration', in Bideleux, R. and Taylor, R. (eds) *European Integration and Disintegration*, pp. 22–35, London, Routledge.

Duclos, D. and Smadja, J.J. (1985) 'Culture and the environment in France', *Environmental Management*, 9:2, 135–40.

Dunlap, R.E. and Van Liere, K.D. (1977) 'The new environmental paradigm', *Journal of Environmental Education*, 9, 10–19.

——, Gallup, G.H. and Gallup, A.M. (1993) 'Of global concern. Results of the Health of the Planet Survey', *Environment*, 35:9, 7–39.

Dupuy, F. and Thoenig, J.-C. (1983) *Sociologie de l'administration française*, Paris, Armand Colin.

Duran, P. and Thoenig, J.-C. (1996) 'L'Etat et la gestion publique territoriale', *Revue française de science politique*, 46:4, 580–623.

Duyvendak, J.W. (1994) *Le Poids du politique. Nouveaux mouvements sociaux en France*, Paris, L'Harmattan.

Economist Intelligence Unit (1990) *French Policy on the Environment. Unsung Achievements, Emerging Anxieties and Possible New Directions*, London, Economist Intelligence Unit, EIU Special Report no. 2063.

Eder, K. (1985) 'The "new social movements": moral crusades, political pressure groups or social movements?', *Social Research*, 52:4 (Winter), 869–90.

Elliott, J.A. (1994) *An Introduction to Sustainable Development. The Developing World*, London, Routledge.

Elliot, L. (1997) 'French nuclear testing in the Pacific: a retrospective', *Environmental Politics*, 6:2 (Summer), 144–9.

Escourrou, G. (1981) 'La pollution atmosphérique en France' *Revue géographique de l'est*, 3, 153–62.

Ester, P, Halman, L. and Seuren, B. (1993) 'Environmental concern and offering willingness in Europe and North America', in Ester, P., Halman, L. and Moor, R. de (eds) *The Individualizing Society. Value Change in Europe and North America*, pp. 163–81, Tilburg, Tilburg University Press.

European Environment Agency (1999) *Environment in the European Union at the Turn of the Century*, http://www.eea.eu.int/frnew.htm.

Faberon, J.-Y. (1991) 'L'Agence de l'environnment et de la maîtrise de l'énergie', *Revue juridique de l'environnement*, 2, 153–70.

Fabiani, J.-L. (1982) 'Quand la chasse devient un sport. La redéfinition sociale d'un loisir traditionnel', *Etudes rurales*, 87–88, 309–23.

—— (1985) 'La crise de légitimité de la chasse et l'affrontement des représentations de la nature', *Cahiers du GERMES*, 11, 137–46.

Fabre, G. et al. (1989) 'Nîmes: les leçons d'une catastrophe', *Aménagement et nature*, 95 (automne), 1–21.

Faucon, A. (1992) 'L'action du conservatoire de l'espace littoral', *Revue de droit rural*, 204 (juin-juillet), 271–3.

Favret, J.-M. (1996) *Droit et pratique de l'Union Européenne*, Paris, Gualino.

Fenet, A. (1973) 'L'administration de l'eau en France', *Revue administrative*, 26, 384–96.

FNE (1998) 'Etude sur les acteurs du développement durable. Les associations d'environnement', Paris, Ministère de l'Environnement.

Foing, D. (ed.) (1994) Le Livre des Verts. Dictionnaire de l'écologie politique, Paris, Editions du Felin.

François, P. (1996) Une Ecotaxe communautaire: quels effets environnementaux, économiques et institutionnels?, Paris, Rapports du Sénat, no. 210.

François-Poncet, J. and Oudin, J. (eds) (1998) La Taxe générale sur les activités polluantes: une remise en cause radicale de la politique de l'eau?, Paris, Imprimerie nationale, Les rapports du Sénat no. 112.

From, J. and Stava, P. (1993) 'Implementation of Community law: the last stronghold of national control?', in Andersen, S.S. and Eliassen, K.A. (eds) Making Policy in Europe. The Europeification of National Policymaking, pp. 55–67, London, Sage.

Fromageau, J. and Guttinger, P. (1993) Droit de l'environnement, Paris, Eyrolles.

Fuchs, D. and Rucht, D. (1994) 'Support for new social movements in five western European countries', in Rootes, C. and Davis, H. (eds) Social Change and Political Transformation, pp. 86–111, London, UCL Press.

Garraud, P. (1979) 'Politique électro-nucléaire et mobilisation: la tentative de constitution d'un enjeu', Revue française de science politique, 29:3 (juin), 448–74.

Gerbaux, F. (1988) 'Les politiques publiques peuvent-elles se passer du corporatisme? L'exemple de la montagne', in Colas, D. (ed.) L'Etat et les Corporatismes, pp. 147–59, Paris, PUF.

Gerbet, P. (1969) 'La préparation de la décision communautaire au niveau national français', in Gerbet, P. and Pepy, D. (eds) La Décision dans les Communautés européennes, pp. 195–208, Bruxelles, Presses Universitaires de Bruxelles.

Gilbert, C. (ed.) (1990) La Catastrophe, l'élu et le préfet, Grenoble, Presses Universitaires de Grenoble.

Glim, C.M.S. (1990) European Environmental Legislation. What Does It Really Mean?, Delft, Eburon.

Goetschy, J. (1987) 'The neo-corporatist issue in France' in Scholten, I. (ed.), Political Stability and Neo-Corporatism. Corporatist Integration and Societal Cleavages in Western Europe, pp. 177–94, London, Sage.

Golub, J. (1996a) 'Sovereignty and subsidiarity in EU environmental policy', Florence, European University Institute, EUI Working Paper RSC 96/2.

——— (1996b) 'Why did they sign? Explaining EC environmental policy bargaining', Florence, European University Institute, EUI Working Paper RSC 96/52.

Gorgeu, Y. (1992) 'L'exemple des parcs naturels régionaux', Revue de droit rural, 204 (juin–juillet), 268–70.

Gouverne, L. (1994) Histoires d'eau. Enquête sur la France des rivières et des robinets, Paris, Calmann-Lévy.

Greenaway, J., Smith, S. and Street, J. (1992) Deciding Factors in British Politics. A Case-studies Approach, London, Routledge.

Grémion, P. (1976) *Le Pouvoir périphérique. Bureaucrates et notables dans le système politique français*, Paris, Editions du Seuil.

Grunberg, G. and Schweisguth, E. (1990) 'Libéralisme culturel et libéralisme économique', in Boy, D. and Mayer, N. (eds) *L'Electeur français en questions*, pp. 45–69, Paris, Presses de la Fondation nationale des sciences politiques.

Gruson, C. et al. (1974) *La Lutte contre le gaspillage*, Paris, La Documentation française et le Ministère de la Qualité de la Vie.

Guellec, A. (1995) 'Le prix de l'eau: de l'explosion à la maîtrise? Rapport d'information sur l'eau', Paris, Assemblée Nationale, Commission de la production, no. 2342.

—— (1997) 'Déchets ménagers: pour un retour à la raison. Rapport d'information sur les déchets ménagers', Paris, Assemblée Nationale, Commission de la production, no. 3380.

Guillaume, M. (1992) 'Déficit démocratique et déficit juridique: quoi de neuf en France?', *Revue française d'administration publique*, 63 (juillet–septembre), 435–46.

Guillon, E. (1997) 'Eco-Emballages: emballage jeté n'est pas perdu', *Réalités industrielles. Annales des Mines* (novembre), 90–4.

Gurin, D. (1979) 'France: making ecology political and politics ecological', *Contemporary Crises*, 3, 149–69.

Guyomarch, A., Machin, H. and Ella, R. (1998) *France in the European Union*, Basingstoke, Macmillan.

Habermas, J. (1981) 'New social movements', *Telos*, 49, 33–37.

Haigh, N. (1992) 'The European Community and international environmental policy', in Hurrell, A. and Kingsbury, D. (eds) *The International Politics of the Environment*, pp. 228–49, Oxford, Clarendon Press.

Hainsworth, P. (1990) 'Breaking the mould: the Greens in the French party system' in Cole, A. (ed.) *French Political Parties in Transition*, pp. 91–105, Aldershot, Dartmouth.

—— (1999) 'The right: divisions and cleavages in *fin de siècle* France', *West European Politics*, 22:4 (October 1999), 38–56.

Hassenteufel, P. (1995) 'Do policy networks matter? Lifting descriptif et analyse de l'Etat en action', in Le Galès, P. and Thatcher, M. (eds) *Les Réseaux de politique publique. Débat autour des policy networks*, pp. 91–107, Paris, L'Harmattan.

Hastings, M. (1994) 'Le discours écologiste: un exemple d'hermaphrodisme idéologique', in Bréchon, P. (ed.) *Le Discours politique en France: évolution des idées partisanes*, pp. 115–36, Paris, Documentation française.

Hatem, F. (1991) 'A propos du plan vert français', *Futuribles*, 152 (mars), 69–73.

Hayward, J. (1982) 'Mobilising private interests in the service of public ambitions: the salient element in the dual French policy style?', in Richardson, J. (ed.) *Policy Styles in Western Europe*, pp. 111–140, London, George Allen and Unwin.

———— (1984) 'Pressure groups and pressured groups in Franco-British perspective', in Kavanagh, D. and Peele, G. (eds) *Comparative Government and Politics*, 92–116, London, Heinemann.

———— (1996) 'Has European unification by stealth a future?', in Hayward, J. (ed.) *Elitism, Populism, and European Politics*, pp. 252–7, Oxford, Clarendon Press.

Hecht, G. (1998) *The Radiance of France: Nuclear Power and National Identity after World War II*, Cambridge, Mass, MIT Press.

Heijden, H.-A. van der (1997) 'Political opportunity structure and the institutionalisation of the environmental movement', *Environmental Politics*, 6:4 (Winter), 25–50.

Heijden, H.-A. van der; Koopmans, R. and Guigni, M. (1992) 'The west European environmental movement', in Finger, M. (ed.) *Research in Social Movements, Conflicts and Change. The Green Movement Worldwide*, pp. 1–41, Greenwich, Connecticut, JAI Press.

Hémain, J.-C (1989) 'Nîmes: l'événement du 3 octobre 1988', *La Houille blanche*, 6, 423–28.

Héritier, A. (1996) 'The accommodation of diversity in European policymaking', *Journal of European Public Policy*, 3:2 (June), 149–67.

Héritier, A., Knill, C. and Mingers, S. (1996) *Ringing the Changes in Europe. Regulatory Competition and Redefinition of the State: Britain, France, Germany*, Berlin, Walter de Gruyter.

Hofferbert, R.I. (1974) *The Study of Public Policy*, Indianapolis, The Bobbs-Merrill Company.

Hoffmann-Martinot, V. (1991) 'Grünen and Verts: two faces of European ecologism', *Western European Politics*, 14:4 (October), 70–95.

Hofrichter, J. and Reif, K. (1990) 'Evolution of environmental attitudes in the European Community', *Scandinavian Political Studies*, 13:2, 119–46.

Holec, N. and Coméliau, N. (1999) 'Les Agendas 21 locaux en France: état des lieux', http//www.globenet.org/horizon-local/4d/9905a21.html.

Holliday, I. (1993) '*Une présidente Verte* in Nord-Pas de Calais: the first year's experience', *Environmental Politics*, 2:3 (Autumn), 486–94.

———— (1994) 'Dealing in green votes: France, 1993', *Government and Opposition*, 29:1, 64–79.

Hostiou, R. (1990) 'Les installations classées et la décentralisation', in Jeannot, G., Renard, V. and Theys, J. (eds) *L'Environnement entre le maire et l'Etat*, pp. 43–8, Paris, ADEF.

House of Lords Select Committee on the EC (1992) *Implementation and Enforcement of Environmental Legislation*, London, HMSO, House of Lords Session 1991–2, 9th report.

Howorth, J. (1984) *France: The Politics of Peace*, London, Merlin Press.

Huglo, C. (1992) 'Les contraintes du droit européen de l'environnement sur le droit interne de l'environnement', *Petites affiches*, 2 (3 janvier), 10–14.

———— (1993) 'L'apport du droit européen au droit interne de la pollution atmosphèrique', *Les Petites affiches*, 154 (24 décembre), 4–10.

——— and Mafoua Badinga, A.T.G. (1993) 'Contraintes du droit européen sur le droit interne de l'environnement', *Les Cahiers du CNFPT*, 38 (avril), 83–97.

ICLEI (1997) 'Local Agenda 21 survey. A study of responses by local authorities and their national and international associations to Agenda 21', http//www.iclei.org/la21rep.htm.

IFEN (1994) *L'Environnement en France 1994–5*, Paris, Dunod

——— (1996a) 'La pollution de l'air préoccupe de plus en plus les Français', *Les Données de l'environnement*, 24 (septembre).

——— (1996b) *L'Environnement en France. Approche Régionale. Edition 1996-7*, Paris, IFEN / La Découverte.

——— (1996c) 'La diversité des espaces protégés en France', *Les Données de l'environnement*, 21 (avril–mai).

——— (1998a) *L'Environnement en France. Edition 1999*, Paris, La Découverte.

——— (1998b) 'Les Français sont pour le respect des limitations des périodes de chasse', http://www.ifen.fr/chasse/chasse5.htm.

——— (1998c) *Chiffres-clés de l'environnement*, Orléans, IFEN.

INSEE (1995) *Tableaux de l'économie française 1995-6*, Paris, INSEE.

Jacob, J. (ed.) (1995) *Les Sources de l'écologie politique*, Paris, Arléa-Corlet.

Jaffeux, H. (1990) 'Protection de la nature', in ENGREF (ed.) *La Politique européenne de l'environnement*, pp. 140–149, Paris, Editions Romillat.

Janin, P. (1991) 'Chasse', *Revue juridique de l'environnement*, 1, 49–64.

Jänicke, M. and Jörgens, H. (1998) 'National environmental policy planning in OECD countries: preliminary lessons from cross-national comparisons', *Environmental Politics*, 7.2 (Summer), 27–54

Jasper, J.M. (1990) *Nuclear Politics. Energy and the State in the United States, Sweden and France*, Princeton, N.J., Princeton University Press.

Jégouzo, Y. (1995) 'La gestion de l'environnement en France: l'annonce d'une décentralisation', in Institut international d'administration publique (eds) *Dossiers et débats. Délocalisations administratives. Politiques européennes d'environnement*, pp. 49–54, Paris, Documentation française.

Jenkins, J.C. and Klandermans, B. (eds) (1995) *The Politics of Social Protest: Comparative Perspectives on States and Social Movements*, London, UCL Press.

Jenson, J. (1989) 'From *baba cool* to a *vote utile*: the trajectory of the French Verts', *French Politics and Society*, 7:4, 1–15.

Jez, P. (1989) 'Nîmes: indemnisation des sinistrés', *Aménagement et nature*, 95 (Automne), 20.

Jobert, B. (1988) 'La version française du corporatisme', in Colas, D. (ed.) *L'Etat et les Corporatismes*, pp. 3–18, Paris, PUF.

Jordan, G. (1990) 'Policy community realism versus 'new' institutionalist ambiguity', *Political Studies*, 38:3 (September), 470–84.

——— and Richardson, J. (1982) 'The British policy style or the logic of negotiation', in Richardson, J. (ed.) *Policy Styles in Western Europe*, pp. 80–110, London, George Allen and Unwin.

—— and Richardson, J. (1983) 'Policy communities: the British and European style', *Policy Studies Journal*, 11 (June), 603–15.

Josselin, C. and Commissariat général du plan (1983) *Rapport du groupe de travail Environnement. Préparation du IXe plan 1984–1988*, Paris, Documentation française.

Journès, C. (1979) 'Les idées politiques du mouvement écologique', *Revue française de science politique*, 2 (avril), 230–54.

—— (1982) 'Les écologistes, l'Etat et les partis', in Bacot, P. and Journès, C. (eds.) *Les Nouvelles idéologies*, pp. 45–72, Lyon, Presses Universitaires de Lyon.

Jullien, B. (1998) 'Analyse économique du système cat-nat', *Risques*, 34 (avril–juin), 63–68.

Kassim, H. (1997) 'French autonomy and the European Union', *Modern and Contemporary France*, 5:2 (May), 167–80.

Keeler, J.T.S. (1981) 'Corporatism and official union hegemony: the case of French agricultural syndicalism' in Berger, S. (ed.) *Organizing Interests in Western Europe. Pluralism, Corporatism and the Transformation of Politics*, pp. 185–208, Cambridge, Cambridge University Press.

Kempf, H. (1994) *La Baleine qui cache la forêt. Enquêtes sur les pièges de l'écologie*, Paris, Editions La Découverte.

Kitschelt, H. (1990) 'La gauche libertaire et les écologistes français', *Revue française de science politique*, 40:3 (June), 339–65.

—— (1993) 'The Green phenomenon in Western party systems', in Kamieniecki, S. (ed.) *Environmental Politics in the International Arena. Movements, Parties, Organisations and Policy*, 93–112, New York, State University of New York.

Knill, C. (1998) 'European policies: the impact of national administrative traditions', *Journal of Public Policy*, 18:1, 1–28.

Knoepfel, P. (1998) 'Remarques d'un observateur étranger sur la lutte contre la pollution atmosphérique en France', in Barraqué, B. and Theys, J. (eds) *Les Politiques d'environnement. Evaluation de la première génération: 1971–1995*, pp. 153–70, Paris, Editions Recherches.

—— and Larrue, C. (1985) 'Distribution spatiale et mise en oeuvre d'une politique publique: le cas de la pollution atmosphérique', *Politiques et management public*, 3:2, 43–69.

—— and Weidner, H. (1986) 'Explaining differences in the performance of clean air policies', *Policy and Politics*, 14:1, 71–91.

Kramer, S. (1994) *Does France Still Count? The French Role in the New Europe*, Westport, Connecticut, Praeger.

Krämer, L. (1988) 'Du contrôle de l'application des directives communautaires en matière d'environnement', *Revue du marché commun*, 313, 22–28.

—— (1991) 'The implementation of Community environmental directives within member states: some implications of the direct effect doctrine', *Journal of Environmental Law*, 3:1, 39–56.

———— and Kromarek, P. (1994) 'Droit communautaire de l'environnement. 1er octobre 1991–31 décembre 1993', *Revue juridique de l'environnement,* 2–3, 209–248.

Kriesi, H. et al. (1995) *New Social Movements in Western Europe,* London, UCL Press.

Kunzlik, P. (1994) *Environmental Policy,* London, Longman, European Union Policy Briefings.

Lacaze, J.-P. (1995) 'L'aménagement du territoire: faux débats et vrais enjeux', *Futuribles,* 199 (juin), 61–73.

Lafferty, L.M. and Eckerberg, K. (1998) 'The nature and purpose of Local Agenda 21', in Lafferty, L.M. and Eckerberg, K. (eds) *From the Earth Summit to Local Agenda 21. Working towards Sustainable Development,* pp. 1–16, London, Earthscan.

Lagadec, P. (1981) *Le Risque technologique majeur,* Paris, Pergamon Press.

———— (ed.) (1988) *Etats d'urgence: défaillances technologiques et déstabilisation sociale,* Paris, Seuil.

Lalo, A. (1991) 'De la loi à l'action. Bilan d'une campagne d'information du public sur les risques technologiques majeurs', *Les Cahiers de la sécurité intérieure,* 6 (août–octobre), 31–57.

———— (1996) 'Intérêt public et intérêts du public. Limites des politiques de prévention face à la demande sociale en matière d'environnement', Paper given at the conference on 'Quel environnement au XXIème siècle?', Abbaye de Fontevraud, France.

Lanneaux, M.-A. and Chapuis, R. (1995) 'Les parcs régionaux français', *Annales de géographie,* 573, 519–33.

Larrue, C. and Chabason, L. (1990) 'Truciao fragmented policy and consensual implementation', in Hanf, K. and Jansen, A.-I. (eds.) *Governance and Environment in Western Europe.* pp. 60–81, Harlow, Longman.

Lascoumes, P. (1989) 'La formalisation juridique du risque industiel en matière de protection de l'environnement', *Sociologie du travail,* 31:3, 315–33.

———— (1991) 'Les contrats de branche et d'entreprise en matière de protection de l'environnement en France', in Morand, C.-A. (ed.) *L'Etat propulsif,* pp. 221–35, Paris, Editions Publisud.

———— (1993) 'Négocier le droit, formes et conditions d'une activité gouvernementale conventionnelle', *Politiques et management public,* 11:4, 48–83.

———— (1994) *L'Eco-pouvoir. Environnements et politiques,* Paris, La Découverte.

———— (1995) 'Les arbitrages publics des intérêts légitimes en matière d'environnement. L'exemple des lois Montagne et Littoral', *Revue française de science politique,* 1995, 3 (juin), 396–419.

———— (1998) 'La scène publique, nouveau passage obligé des décisions?', *Annales des Mines. Responsabilité et Environnement* (avril), 51–62.

—— and Le Bourhis, J.-P. (1997) *L'Environnement ou l'administration des possibles. La création des Directions Régionales de l'Environnement*, Paris, L'Harmattan.

—— and Vlassopoulou, C.A. (1998) 'Protéger l'air ou réguler les sources de pollution atmosphérique?', *Regards sur l'actualité* (mars), 31–40.

Laurens, L. (1995) 'Les parcs naturels, du concept à la pratique d'une agriculture environnementale', *Annales de géographie*, 584, 339–359.

Laurent, J.-L. (1996) 'Administration et environnement en France', in Université de droit d'Aix-en-Provence (eds.) *Annuaire européen d'administration publique*, Vol. XIX, pp. 79–94, Aix-en-Provence, Presses universitaires d'Aix-Marseille.

Laville, B. (1997) 'Rio + 5 – 1', *Responsabilité et environnement*, 5 (janvier), 5–10.

Le Galès, P. (1992) 'New directions in decentralisation and urban policy in France: the search for a post-decentralisation state', *Environment and Planning C: Government and Policy*, 10, 19–36.

—— and Thatcher, M. (eds) (1995) *Les Réseaux de politique publique. Débat autour des policy networks*, Paris, L'Harmattan.

Le Grand, J.-F. (1994) 'La protection de l'environnement rural', Paris, Ministère de l'Environnement.

Le Prestre, P. (1981) 'France's administration of its environment', *Revue internationale des sciences administratives*, XLVII:1, 42–50.

Ledoux, B (1995) *Les Catastrophes naturelles en France*, Paris, Payot.

Legrand, H. (1996) 'La loi du 2 février 1995 et la prévention des risques naturels', *Revue française de droit administratif*, 12:2 (mars–avril), 228–35.

Lepage, C. (1998) *"On ne peut rien faire Madame le ministre . . ."*, Paris, Albin Michel.

Lequesne, C. (1987) 'L'adaptation des administrations nationales à l'existence des communautés européennes: le cas des ministères français', *Revue française d'administration publique* (avril–juin), 275–92.

—— (1993) *Paris-Bruxelles. Comment se fait la politique européenne de la France*, Paris, Presses de la Fondation Nationale des Sciences Politiques.

—— (1995) 'L'administration centrale de la France et le système politique européen', in Mény, Y., Muller, P. and Quermonne, J. (eds.) (1995) *Politiques Publiques en Europe*, pp. 143–53, Paris, L'Harmattan.

Liberatore, A. (1995) 'The social construction of environmental problems', in Glasbergen, P. and Blowers, A. (eds) *Perspectives on Environmental Problems*, pp. 59–83, London, Arnold.

Liefferink, D. and Andersen, M.S. (1998) 'Strategies of the "green" member states in EU environmental policy-making', *Journal of European Public Policy*, 5:2 (June), 254–70.

Ligot, M. (1991) 'La transposition des directives communautaires en droit interne', Paris, Imprimerie nationale, Assemblée Nationale, Délégation nationale pour les CE, rapport d'information no. 2292.

Littmann-Martin, M.-J. (1987) 'Le nouveau régime répressif des installations classées', *Revue juridique de l'environnement*, 1, 26–58.

Litvan, D. (1997) 'Les coûts de la réglementation environnementale', *Regards sur l'actualité* (mai), 41–53.

Lombard, D. (1997) 'De la réglementation vers une approche contractuelle', *Annales des Mines. Réalités industrielles* (novembre), 22–7.

Lorrain, D. (1992) 'L'eau en France. Le modèle français', in Barraqué, B. et al. *La Gestion de l'eau*, Paris, Documentation française, *Problèmes politiques et sociaux*, no. 686.

Loughlin, J. and Mazey, S. (eds) (1995) *The End of the French Unitary State? Ten Years of Regionalisation in France (1982–1992)*, London, Frank Cass.

Lovelock, J. (1988) *The Ages of Gaia. A Biography of Our Living Earth*, Oxford, Oxford University Press.

Lowe, P. and Ward, S. (1998) 'Britain in Europe: themes and issues in national environmental policy', in Lowe, P. and Ward, S. (eds) *British Environmental Policy and Europe*, pp. 3–30, London, Routledge.

Lowi, T. (1972) 'Four systems of policy, politics and choice,' *Public Administration Review*, 32 (July–August), 298–310.

Macrory, R. (1992) 'The enforcement of Community environmental laws: some critical issues', *Common Market Law Review*, 29, 347–69.

Majone, G. (1996) 'A European regulatory state?', in Richardson, J.J. (ed.) *European Union: Power and Policy-making*, pp. 263–77, London, Routledge.

Malafosse, J. de (1981) 'Chasse et nature, Europe et décentralisation', *Revue juridique de l'environnement*, 4, 305–13.

Maloney, W.A., Jordan, G. and McLaughlin, A.M. (1994) 'Interest groups and public policy: the insider / outsider model revisited', *Journal of Public Policy*, 14:1, 17–38.

Marks, G. and McAdam, D. (1996) 'Social movements and the changing structure of political opportunity in the European Union', in Marks, G. et al. (eds) *Governance in the European Union*, pp. 95–120, London, Sage.

Marsh, D. (1995) 'Théorie de l'Etat et modèle de réseaux d'action publique', in Le Galès, P. and Thatcher, M. (eds) *Les Réseaux de politique publique. Débat autour des policy networks*, pp. 141–63, Paris, L'Harmattan.

Martin, Y. (1988) 'Quelques réflexions sur l'évolution des agences de bassin', *Annales des mines*, 7–8 (juillet–août), 117–19.

MATE (1997a) 'Présentation de l'inventaire 1996 des sites et sols pollués', http://www.environnement.gouv.fr/actua/cominfos/Com1997/comnov97/solpol.htm.

——— (1997b) *Dossier de présentation des lauréats: 'Les outils et démarches en vue de la réalisation d'Agenda 21 locaux'*, Paris, MATE.

——— (1998) 'Circulaire Plans déchets', http://www.environnement. gouv.fr/actua/cominfos/dosdir/DIRPPR/cpla5.htm.

——— (1999a) 'Journée de l'Inspection des installations classées, le 11 mai 1999', http://www.environnement.gouv.fr/actua/cominfos/commai99/instaclassee.htm.

——— (1999b) 'Les agences de l'eau et le VIIème programme',

http://www.environnement.gouv.fr/actua/cominfos/dosdir/DIR EAU/ag-o-7.htm.

Mather, A.S., Fairbairn, J. and Needle, C.L. (1999) 'The course and drivers of forest transition: the case of France', *Journal of Rural Studies*, 15:1, 65–90.

Mathieu, J.-L. (1992) *La Défense de l'environnement en France*, Paris, PUF.

Mathieu, R. (1987) *La Chasse à la française*, La Charce: Quelle est belle Company.

Mazey, S. and Richardson, J. (1993) 'EC policy-making: an emerging European policy style?', in Liefferink, J.D., Lowe, P.D. and Mol, A.P.J. (eds) *European Integration and Environmental Policy*, pp. 114–25, London, Belhaven Press.

Mazmanian, D.A. and Sabatier, P.A. (1989) *Implementation and Public Policy*, New York, Lanham.

Meadows, D.H., Meadows, D.L., Randers, J. and Behrens, W.W. (1972) *The Limits to Growth. A Report for the Club of Rome's Project on the Predicament of Mankind*, London, Pan.

———, Meadows, D.L. and Randers, J. (1992) *Beyond the Limits. Global Collapse or a Sustainable Future?*, London, Earthscan.

Melucci, A. (1991) 'Qu'y a-t-il de nouveau dans les "nouveaux mouvements sociaux"?', in Maheu, L. and Sales, A. (eds.) *La Recomposition du politique*, pp. 129–62, Paris, L'Harmattan.

Mennessier, M. (1992) 'Vaison: un torrent de négligences', *Sciences et vie*, 902, 96–103.

Mény, Y. (1985) 'Variations sur un thème donné: l'application des directives par les Etats membres', *Revue française d'administration publique*, 34 (juin), 179–89.

——— (1986) 'La légitimation des groupes d'intérêt par l'administration française', *Revue française d'administration publique*, 39, 483–94.

——— (1987) 'France: the construction and reconstruction of the centre, 1945–86', *West European Politics*, 10:4, 52–69.

——— (1989a) 'The national and international context of French policy communities', *Political Studies*, 37:3 (September), 387–99.

——— (1989b) 'Interest groups and politics in the Fifth Republic' in Godt, P. (ed.) *Policy Making in France: From De Gaulle to Mitterrand*, pp. 91–101, London, Pinter.

——— (1995) 'Politiques publiques en Europe: une nouvelle division du travail', in Mény, Y., Muller, P. and Quermonne, J. (eds.) *Politiques Publiques en Europe*, pp. 335–42, Paris, L'Harmattan.

——— and Chérel, M.-P. (1988) 'France: la mise en oeuvre des directives communautaires', in Siedentopf, H. and Ziller, J. (eds) *Making European Policies Work. The Implementation of Community Legislation in the Member States*, Vol. 2, pp. 277–321, London, Sage.

Meublat, G. (1998) 'La politique de lutte contre la pollution des eaux', in Barraqué, B. and Theys, J. (eds) *Les Politiques d'environnement. Evaluation de la première génération: 1971–1995*, pp. 67–90, Paris, Editions Recherches.

Meyronneinc, J.-P. (1993) *Plaidoyer pour les déchets*, Paris, Editions Apogée.

Michel, H. (1998) 'Government or governance? The case of the French local political system', *West European Politics*, 21:3 (July), 146–69.

Ministère de l'Environnement (1997) *Cahiers méthodologiques pour l'élaboration des plans et chartes pour l'environnement*, Paris, Ministère de l'Environnement.

—— (1992) *Pour que l'eau vive*, Paris, Documentation francaise.

—— (1994) *Données économiques de l'environnement*. Edition 1992–1993, Paris, Documentation française.

Ministère de l'environnement et de la prévention des risques technologiques et naturels majeurs (1991) *Eléments d'information sur les risques technologiques et naturels majeurs*, Paris, Documentation française.

Mol, A.P.J. (1997) 'Ecological modernisation: industrial transformations and environmental reform', in Redclift, M. and Woodgate, G. (eds) *The International Handbook of Environmental Sociology*, pp. 138–49, Cheltenham, Edward Elgar.

Morand-Deviller, J. (1993) *Le Droit de l'environnement*, Paris, PUF.

Moreau Defarges, P. (1996) 'La France, province de l'Union Européenne?', *Politique Etrangère* (printemps), 37–48.

Morin, G. and Caracostea, M. (1988) 'Cinq ans et demi de loi cat-nat', *L'Assurance française* (1–15 janvier), 1–28.

Mosse, F. (1996) *A la découverte des réserves naturelles de France*, Paris, Nathan.

Mousel, M. (1995) 'L'administration de l'environnement: agences et services déconcentrés de l'Etat en France' in Institut international d'administration publique (eds) *Dossiers et débats. Délocalisations administratives. Politiques européennes d'environnement*, pp. 65–70, Paris, Documentation française.

—— and Herz, O. (1990) 'La politique française de prévention de la pollution atmosphérique', *Annales des Mines* (novembre), 69–73.

Muller, P. (1990) 'Les politiques publiques entre secteurs et territoires', *Politiques et management public*, 8:3 (septembre), 19–33.

—— (1992) 'Entre le local et l'Europe: la crise du modèle français des politiques publiques', *Revue française de science politique*, 42:2 (avril), 275–97.

—— and Saez, G. (1985) 'Néo-corporatisme et crise de la représentation', in Arcy, F. de (ed.) *La Répresentation*, pp. 121–40, Paris, Economica.

Négrier, E. (1999) 'The changing role of French local government', *West European Politics*, 22:4 (October), 120–40.

Niang, A. (1992) 'L'application du droit communautaire à rude épreuve', *Enjeux*, 128 (octobre), 16–18.

Nicolino, F. (1990) 'Seveso l'aveu', *Politis* (12 avril), 22–35.

Norris, P. (1997) 'Are we all green now? Public opinion on environmentalism in Britain', *Government and Opposition*, 32:3 (Summer), 320–39.

Nowak, F. (1995) *Le Prix de l'eau*, Paris, Economica.

O'Neill, M. (1997) *Green Parties and Political Change in Contemporary Europe: New Politics, Old Predicaments*, Aldershot, Ashgate.

O'Riordan, T. (1996) 'Democracy and the sustainability transition', in Lafferty, W.M. and Meadowcroft, J. (eds) *Democracy and the Environment. Problems and Prospects*, pp. 140–156, Cheltenham, Edward Elgar.

OECD (1997) *Environmental Performance Reviews: France*, Paris, OECD.

Osborn, D. and Bigg, T. (1998) *Earth Summit II. Outcomes and Analysis*, London, Earthscan.

Palard, J. (1981) 'Le mouvement associatif et le système politique local en France', *Sociologia internationales*, 19, 213–32.

Paquiet, P. and Blancher, P. (1997) 'Les SPPPI: pour un environnement industriel collectivement maîtrisé', *Economie et Humanisme*, 342 (octobre), 42–4.

Parkin, S. (1989) *Green Parties. An International Guide*, London, Heretic Books.

Pearce, D., Markandya, A. and Barbier, E.B. (1989) *Blueprint for a Green Economy*, London, Earthscan.

Peixoto, O. (1993) *Les Français et l'environnement*, Paris; Editions de l'Environnement.

Peyret, L. (1986) 'Les risques majeurs: les plans d'exposition aux risques', *Revue générale de sécurité*, 57 (octobre), 32–9.

Pezet, M. (1992) 'Rapport d'information déposé par la Délégation de l'Assemblée nationale pour les Communautés européennes sur la transposition des directives communautaires en droit interne', Paris, Assemblée Nationale, 9ème législature, no. 2902.

Picaper, J.-P. and Dornier, T. (1995) *Greenpeace: l'écologie à l'an vert*, Paris, Editions Odilon Media.

Pierré-Caps, S. (1991) 'L'adaptation du Parlement français au système communautaire', *Revue française de droit constitutionnel*, 6, 233–73.

Piétrasanta, Y. (1993) *L'Echarpe verte. Combats pour une nouvelle écologie*, Paris, Albin Michel.

Pisani, E. (1956) 'Administration de gestion, administration de mission', *Revue française de science politique* (avril), 315–30.

Pissaloux, J.-L. (1995) 'L'Agence de l'environnement et de la maîtrise de l'énergie: un établissement public de type nouveau', *La Revue du Trésor*, 5 (mai), 251–61.

Poquet, G. (1994) 'La poubelle des Français: perspectives d'évolution et modes de consommation', *Revue française de marketing*, 147, 23–33.

Portelli, H. (1994) 'L'élection européenne des 9 et 12 juin 1994', *Regards sur l'actualité*, 203 (juillet–août), 3–13.

Poujade, R. (1975) *Le Ministère de l'impossible*, Paris, Calmann-Lévy.

Prendiville, B. (1992) 'French ecologists at the cross-roads', *Environmental Politics*, 1:3, 448–57.

——— (1994) *Environmental Politics in France*, Boulder, Colorado, Westview Press.

——— (1997) 'Ecologism', in Flood, C. and Bell, L. (eds) (1997) *Political*

Ideologies in Contemporary France, pp. 140–161, London, Cassell Academic.

——— and Chafer, T. (1990) 'Activists and ideas in the Green movement in France', in Rüdig, W. (ed.) *Green Politics One*, pp. 177–209, Edinburgh, Edinburgh University Press.

Prieur, M. (1983) 'Administration de l'environnement', *Revue juridique de l'environnement*, 2, 105–17.

——— (1985) 'Les compétences locales en matière d'environnement', in Moderne, F. (ed.) *Les Nouvelles compétences locales*, pp. 172–85, Paris, Economica.

——— (1987) 'Les plans ORSEC', in Fabiani, J.-L and Theys, J. (eds) *La Société vulnérable. Evaluer et maîtriser les risques*, pp. 511–38, Paris, Presses de l'Ecole Normale Supérieure.

——— (1988) 'La répartition des compétences entre la CEE, les Etats et les collectivités régionales et locales en matière d'environnement: le cas de la France', in Charpentier, J. (ed.) *La Protection de l'environnement par les communautés européennes*, pp. 87–97, Paris, Editions A. Pedone.

——— (1994) 'Le laboratoire français du rattachement environnement-gouvernement', *Studi parlamentari e di politica constituzionale*, 104 (2e trimestre), 55–92.

——— (1996) *Droit de l'environnement*, Paris, Dalloz.

Raack, M. (1987) 'L'eau et l'industrie', in Loriferne, H. (ed.) *40 ans de politique de l'eau en France*, pp. 351–72, Paris, Economica.

Radanne, P., Bonduelle, A. and Bossoken, E. (1997) 'La pollution urbaine', *Après demain*, 391 (mai), 0 11.

Raveneau, A. (1986) 'Quelques mythes fondateurs', in Grillet, T. and Le Conte des Floris, C. (eds) *Les Natures du vert*, pp. 148–61, Paris, Autrement.

République française (1994) *Rapport de la France à la Commission du Développement Durable des Nations-Unies*, Paris, Imprimerie nationale.

——— (1996) *Projet de loi de finances pour 1997 – Environnement. Etat récapitulatif de l'effort financier consenti en 1996 et prévu en 1997 au titre de l'environnement*, Paris, Imprimerie nationale.

——— (1997) *Projet de loi de finances pour 1998 – Environnement. Etat récapitulatif de l'effort financier consenti en 1997 et prévu en 1998 au titre de l'environnement*, Paris, Imprimerie nationale.

Rhodes, R.A.W. (1990) 'Policy networks: a British perspective', *Journal Of Theoretical Politics*, 2:3, 293–317.

——— and Marsh, D. (1995) 'Les réseaux d'action publique en Grande-Bretagne', in Le Galès, P. and Thatcher, M. (eds) *Les Réseaux de politique publique. Débat autour des policy networks*, pp. 31–68, Paris, L'Harmattan.

Ribes, J.-P. (1978) *Pourquoi les écologistes font-ils de la politique? Entretiens avec Brice Lalonde, Serge Moscovici et René Dumont*, Paris, Seuil.

Richardson, J. (1995) 'EU water policy: uncertain agendas, shifting networks and complex coalitions', in Bressers, H., O'Toole, L.J. and Richardson, J. (eds) *Networks for Water Policy, A Comparative Perspective*, pp. 139–67, London, Frank Cass.

—— (1996) 'Actor-based models of national and EU policy-making', in Kassim, H.H. and Menon, A. (eds) *European Union and National Industrial Policy*, pp. 20–51, London, Routledge.

Rigaud, J. and Delcros, X. (1984) *Les Institutions administratives françaises: les structures*, Paris, Paris, Presses de la Fondation Nationale des Sciences Politiques.

Rivasi, M. and Crié, H. (1998) *Ce Nucléaire qu'on nous cache*, Paris, Albin Michel.

Rocaboy, A. (1993) 'L'expérience des plans d'environnement en France', *Pouvoirs locaux*, 17 (juin), 34–40.

Roche, A. (1993) 'Mars 1993: un révélateur des faiblesses des écologistes', *Revue politique et parlementaire*, 964 (mars–avril), 34–41.

—— (1995) 'Les candidats écologistes: la chasse aux signatures', in Perrineau, P. and Ysmal, C. (eds) *Le Vote de crise. L'élection présidentielle de 1995*, pp. 81–94, Paris, Presses de Sciences Po.

Rohrschneider, R. (1991) 'Public opinion toward environmental groups in Western Europe: one movement or two?', *Social Science Quarterly*, 72:2 (June), 251–66.

Romi, R, (1989) 'Droit de la chasse', *Revue juridique de l'environnement*, 2, 173–85.

—— (1990a) *L'Administration de l'environnement*, Paris, Editions de l'Espace Européen.

—— (1990b) 'La place du département en matière de protection de l'environnement: vers une revalorisation?', *Les Petites affiches*, 75 (22 juin), 9–13.

—— (1990c) '1989: le droit de la chasse entre l'Europe et le nationalisme', *Revue juridique de l'environnement*, 3, 367–94.

—— (1992) 'L'administration de l'environnement entre décentralisation et déconcentration', *Revue du droit public*, 6, 1771–92.

—— (1993a) 'La répartition des compétences d'environnement: une décentralisation très retenue et trop orientée', *Les Cahiers du CNFPT*, 38 (avril), 50–61.

—— (1993b) *L'Europe et la protection juridique de l'environnement*, Paris, Victoires Editions.

—— (1993c) 'Risque et droit: quelle problématique?', in Bernard, I. et al. *La Prévention des risques naturels. Echec ou réussite des plans d'exposition aux risques?*, pp. 19–37, Nice, Université de Nice, Centre de recherche en droit économique.

—— (1997) *Droit et administration de l'environnement*, Paris, Montchrestien.

Roseren, P. (1992) 'Review by French courts of the conformity of national provisions with Community law', in Curtin, D. and O'Keeffe, D. *Constitutional Adjudication in European Community and National Law*, pp. 257–69, Dublin, Butterworth.

Rouban, L. (1990) 'La modernisation de l'Etat et la fin de la spécificité française', *Revue française de science politique*, 40:4 (août), 521–45.

Rouyère, A. (1996) 'La répartition des pouvoirs locaux. Les approches nationales: la France', *Droit et ville*, 42, 65–109.

Royal, S. (1994) 'Discours', in Prieur, M. and Doumbé-Billé, S. (eds) *Droit de l'Environnement et développement durable*, pp. 15–18, Limoges, PULIM.

Rucht, D. (1989) 'Environmental movement organisations in West Germany and France: structure and interorganisational relations', in Klandermans, B. (ed.) *Organising for Change. Social Movement Organisations in Europe and the United States*, pp. 61–94, Greenwhich, Connecticut, JAI Press.

―――― (1994) 'The anti-nuclear movement and the State in France', in Flam, H. (ed.) *States and Anti-nuclear Movements*, pp. 129–62, Edinburgh, Edinburgh University Press.

Rüdig, W. (1996) ''Green parties and the European Union', in Gaffney, J. (ed.) *Political Parties and the European Union*, pp. 254–72, London, Routledge.

―――― (ed.) (1990) *Anti-nuclear Movements*, London, Longman.

―――― and Franklin, M.N. (1992) 'Green prospects: the future of Green parties in Britain, France and Germany', in Rüdig, W. (ed.) *Green Politics Two*, pp. 37–58, Edinburgh, Edinburgh University Press.

Sabatier, P. (1986) 'Top-down and bottom-up approaches to implementation research: a critical analysis and suggested synthesis', *Journal of Public Policy*, 6.1 (January), 21–40.

―――― (1992) 'Political science and public policy: an assessment' in Dunn, W.N. and Kelly, R.M. (eds) *Advances in Policy Studies since 1950*, pp. 27–57, New Brunswick, Transaction Publishers.

―――― (1993) 'Policy change over a decade or more' in Sabatier, P. and Jenkins-Smith, H.C. (eds) *Policy Change and Learning. An Advocacy Coalition Approach*, pp. 13–39, Boulder, Colorado, Westview Press.

―――― and Jenkins-Smith, H.C. (1993) 'The advocacy coalition framework: assessment, revisions and implications for scholars and practitioners' in Sabatier, P. and Jenkins-Smith, H.C. (eds) *Policy Change and Learning. An Advocacy Coalition Approach*, pp. 211–234, Boulder, Colorado, Westview Press.

Sachs, W. (1997) 'Sustainable development', in Redclift, M. and Woodgate, G. (eds) *The International Handbook of Environmental Sociology*, pp. 71–82, Cheltenham, Edward Elgar.

Sainteny, G. (1987) 'Le vote écologiste aux élections régionales', *Revue politique et parlementaire*, 927 (janvier–février), 38–46.

―――― (1992) *Les Verts*, Paris, Presses Universitaires de France.

―――― (1993) 'Les deux familles de l'écologie', in Duhamel, O. and Jaffré, J. (eds) *L'Etat de l'opinion: 1993*, pp. 49–62, Paris, Editions du Seuil.

―――― (1998a) 'Génération Ecologie: ascension et déclin d'une machine électorale', *Pouvoirs*, 85, 135–149.

——— (1998b) 'L'émergence d'un nouvel enjeu de politique publique: le pouvoir face à l'environnement', *Politiques et management public,* 16:2, 129–58.

——— (1999) 'Une politique du paysage', *Regards sur l'actualité,* 250 (avril), 19–32.

Sauron, J.-L. (1995) *L'Application du droit de l'Union Européenne en France,* Paris, Documentation française.

Sbragia, A. (1992) 'Environmental policy in the EC: the problem of implementation in comparative perspective', in European Institute (eds) (1992) *Towards a Transatlantic Environmental Policy,* pp. 47–95, Washington DC, European Institute.

——— (1996) 'Environmental policy: the "push-pull" of policy-making', in Wallace, J. and Wallace, W. (eds.) *Policy-making in the European Union,* pp. 235–55, Oxford, Oxford University Press.

——— and Damro, C. (1999) 'The changing role of the EU in international environmental politics: institution building and the politics of climate change', *Environment and Planning C: Government and Policy,* 17:1, 53–68.

Scheuch, E.K. (1994) 'The puzzle of the "quality of life"', in D'Antonio, W.V., Sasaki, M. and Yonebayashi, Y. (eds) *Ecology, Society and the Quality of Social Life,* pp. 81–111, London, Transaction Publishers.

Schmitter, P.C. (1970) 'Still the century of corporatism?', *Review of Politics,* 36, 85–131.

Shull, T. (1996) 'Green politics and political mobilisation: contradictions of direct democracy', in Daley, A. (ed.) *The Mitterrand Era: Policy Alternatives and Political Mobilization in France,* pp. 225–40, London, Macmillan.

Siedentopf, H. and Hauschild, C. (1988) 'L'application des directives communautaires par les administrations publiques (étude comparative)', *Revue française d'administration publique,* 48 (octobre–décembre), 547–55.

Simon, D. and Rigaux, A. (1991) 'Les contraintes de la transcription en droit français des directives communautaires: le secteur de l'environnement', *Revue juridique de l'environnement,* 3, 270–332.

Simonnet, D. (1994) *L'Ecologisme,* Paris; PUF.

Sironneau, J. (1992) 'La loi sur l'eau ou la recherche d'une gestion équilibrée', *Revue juridique de l'environnement,* 2, 137–223.

Smith, A. (1999) 'Public policy analysis in contemporary France: academic approaches, questions and debates', *Public Administration,* 77:1, 111–31.

Spaargaren, G. and Mol, A.P.J. (1992) 'Sociology, environment and modernity: ecological modernisation as a theory of social change', *Society and Natural Resources,* 5, 323–44.

Spanou, C. (1991) *Fonctionnaires et militants. L'administration et les nouveaux mouvements sociaux,* Paris, L'Harmattan.

Stokes, D.E. (1992) 'Valence politics', in Kavanagh, D. (ed.) *Electoral Politics,* pp. 141–64, Oxford, Clarendon Press.

Szarka, J. (1992) *Business in France*, London, Pitman.

—— (1997) 'Campaign strategies in the 1995 French presidential elections: a candidate interaction analysis', *Political Science*, 48:2 (January), 135–61.

—— (1999) 'The parties of the French "plural left": an uneasy complementarity', *West European Politics*, 22:4 (October), 20–37.

Tardieu, J.-P. (1992) 'L'eau: les enjeux d'une reconquête', *Géopolitique*, 40 (hiver) 72–4.

Ténière-Buchot, P.-F. (1985) 'L'opinion publique et l'environnement', *Futuribles*, 89 (juin), 83–9.

Thelander, J. (1990) 'The obscure problems: rationalisation, power and the discovery of environmental problems', in Brimblecombe, P. (ed.) *The Silent Countdown*, pp. 248–61, Berlin, Springer-Verlag.

Theys, J. (1987) 'La Société vulnérable' in Fabiani, J.-L. and Theys, J. (eds) *La Société vulnérable. Evaluer et maîtriser les risques*, pp. 3–35, Paris, Presses de l'Ecole Normale Supérieure.

—— and Chabason, L. (1991) 'Le Plan national pour l'environnement', *Futuribles*, 152 (mars), 45–68.

Thiebaut, L. (1988) 'Pouvoir politique et protection de la nature', in Cadoret, A. (ed.) *"Chasser le naturel . . ."*, pp. 81–9, Paris, Editions de l'Ecole des Hautes Etudes en Sciences Sociales.

Thoenig, J.-C. (1978) 'State bureaucracies and local government in France', in Hanf, K. and Scharpf, F.W. (eds.) *Interorganisational Policymaking*, pp. 167–97, London, Sage.

Touraine, A. (1985) 'An introduction to the study of social movements', *Social Research*, 52.1 (Winter), 749–87.

—— et al. (1983) *Anti-Nuclear Protest: The Opposition to Nuclear Energy in France*, Cambridge, Cambridge University Press.

Trilling, J. (1981) 'French environmental politics', *International Journal of Urban and Regional Research*, 5, 67–82.

UN (1993) *Report on the UN Conference on Environment and Development. Volume 1: Resolutions Adopted by the Conference*, New York, UN.

Untermaier, J. (1988) 'Des petits oiseaux aux grands principes', *Revue juridique de l'environnement*, 4, 455–78.

Vadrot, C.-M. (1978) *L'Ecologie, histoire d'une subversion*, Paris, Syros.

—— (1986) 'Les chasseurs ne sont pas aux abois', in Grillet, T. and Le Conte des Floris, C. (eds) *Les Natures du vert*, pp. 100–18, Paris, Autrement.

Vallet, O. (1975) *L'Administration de l'environnement*, Paris, Editions Berger-Levrault.

Valluy, J. (1996) 'Coalition de projet et délibération politique', *Politiques et management public*, 14:4 (décembre), 101–31.

Vermont, O. (1997) *La Face cachée de Greenpeace. Infiltration au sein de l'internationale écologiste*, Paris, Albin Michel.

Vesseron, P. (1981) 'Conjoncture économique et prévention des nuisances', *Futuribles*, 44 (mai) 63–9.

—— (1988) 'Les fûts de Seveso', in Lagadec, P. (ed.) *Etats d'urgence:*

défaillances technologiques et déstabilisation sociale, pp. 135–59, Paris, Seuil.

—— (1997) 'L'évolution de l'action de l'Etat', *Annales des Mines. Réalités industrielles* (novembre), 18–21.

Viard, J. (1990) *Le Tiers espace: essai sur la nature*, Paris, Méridiens Klincksieck.

Vignier, J. (1995) 'Chasse aux gibiers d'eau et oiseaux de passage et droit communautaire', *Revue juridique de l'environnement*, 2, 299–311.

Vigouroux, C. (1996) 'La hiéarchie de normes en montagne (loi montagne, loi Bosson, loi relative à l'aménagement du territoire)', *Petites affiches*, 23 (21 février), 4–9.

Villalba, B. (1996a) 'Le clair-obscur électoral des Verts 1989–1995', *Ecologie et politique*, 16 (printemps), 75–88.

—— (1996b) 'La chaotique formation des Verts, 1984–1994', *Politix*, 35, 149–170.

—— (1997) 'L'ordalie parlementaire des écologistes', *Ecologie et politique*, 21 automne–hiver), 127–37.

Vogel, D. (1986) *National Styles of Regulation. Environmental Policy in Great Britain and the United States*, Ithaca, Cornell University Press.

Voynet, D. (1994) 'Chez les Verts, on n'a jamais affronté de face les problèmes du pouvoir', *Politis*, 20 octobre, 8–10.

—— (1995) 'Travailler moins, une constitution pour l'Europe et parité femme/homme', *Revue politique et parlementaire*, 976 (mars–avril), 39–44.

—— (1998) 'Dominique Voynet présente en Conseil des Ministres le projet de loi d'orientation pour l'aménagement et le développement durable du territoire', http://www.environnement.gouv.fr/actua/cominfos/Com1998/comjuill98/LOADT.htm#s.

—— (1999) 'Présentation du projet de loi d'orientation pour l'aménagement et le développement durable du territoire, Assemblée nationale, mardi 19 janvier 1999', http://www.environnement.gouv.fr/actua/cominfos/comjan99/loaddtdicours.htm#s.

Wackermann, G. et al. (1996) *L'Aménagement du territoire français: hier et demain*, Paris, SEDES.

Waechter, A. (1990) *Dessine-moi une planète. L'écologie, maintenant ou jamais*, Paris, Albin Michel.

Wägenbaur, R. (1991) 'The European Community's policy on implementation of environmental directives', *Fordham International Law Journal*, 14, 455–77.

Waters, S. (1998) 'New social movement politics in France: the rise of civic forms of mobilisation', *West European Politics*, 21:3 (July), 170–86.

WCED / Brundtland, G. (1987) *Our Common Future*, Oxford, Oxford University Press.

Weale, A. (1992) *The New Politics of Pollution*, Manchester, Manchester University Press.

——— (1996) 'Environmental rules and rule-making in the European Union', *Journal of European Public Policy*, 3:4 (December), 594–611.

——— and Williams, A. (1992) 'Between economy and ecology? The Single Market and the integration of environmental policy', *Environmental Politics*, 1:4, 45–64.

Whiteside, K.H. (1995) 'The resurgence of ecological political thought in France', *French Politics and Society*, 13:3 (Summer), 45–58.

Wiarda, H. J. (1997) *Corporatism and Comparative Politics*, New York, M.E. Sharpe.

Williamson, P. (1985) *Varieties of Corporatism*, Cambridge, Cambridge University Press.

Witherspoon, S. (1994) 'The greening of Britain: romance and rationality', in Jowell, R. et al. (eds) *British Social Attitudes Survey. The Eleventh Report*, pp. 107–39, Aldershot, Gower.

——— (1996) 'Democracy, the environment and public opinion in Western Europe', in Lafferty, W.M. and Meadowcroft, J. (eds) *Democracy and the Environment. Problems and Prospects*, pp. 39–70, Cheltenham, Edward Elgar.

Yearley, S. (1991) *The Green Case. A Sociology of Environmental Issues, Arguments and Politics*, London, Harper Collins.

Zacklad, G. (1996) 'Pollution de l'air: l'état des incertitudes', *Problèmes économiques*, 2474 (29 mai), 10–13.

Zimeray, F. (1994) *Le Maire et la protection juridique de l'environnement*, Paris, Litec.

INDEX